THE
WATCHMAKER'S
AND
MODEL ENGINEER'S
LATHE

By the same author

PRACTICAL WATCH REPAIRING
PRACTICAL CLOCK REPAIRING
WITH THE WATCHMAKER AT THE BENCH
BRITISH TIME
WATCH AND CLOCK ENCYCLOPEDIA
COMPLICATED WATCHES AND THEIR REPAIR
HOROLOGY
CLOCK AND WATCH REPAIRING
PRACTICAL WATCH ADJUSTING AND SPRINGING
CLOCKS AND THEIR VALUE
WATCHES AND THEIR VALUE

THE
WATCHMAKER'S
AND
MODEL ENGINEER'S
LATHE

A User's Manual

DONALD DE CARLE, F.B.H.I.

Medallist British Horological Institute
Liveryman Worshipful Company of Clockmakers

Illustrations by
E.A. AYRES

Revised by Eric Restall

ROBERT HALE

First published in 1952

Sixth edition published in 2010 by Robert Hale,
an imprint of The Crowood Press Ltd,
Ramsbury, Marlborough, Wiltshire SN8 2HR

enquiries@crowood.com

www.crowood.com

This impression 2024

British Library Cataloguing-in-Publication Data
A catalogue record for this book is available from the
British Library.

ISBN 978 0 7090 9003 8

Printed and bound in India by Parksons Graphics Pvt Ltd

PREFACE TO THE SIXTH EDITION

The most important development since the publication of the last edition is unquestionably the introduction of the Internet, which provides instant access to a range of websites enabling one to determine the availability of new and secondhand lathes, spares, instruction booklets and accessories from around the world. There are specialist forums devoted to a single lathe and a whole range of mini lathe sites of special interest to the model engineer. The archive database www.lathes.co.uk is essential viewing. We are seeing a growth in e-commerce businesses who deal exclusively online. Most manufacturers and their stockist agents now have illustrated and informative websites, some offering instructional video programmes.

There are hopeful signs that the era of cheap and nasty lathes from the Far East is finally coming to an end. But, the practise of misleading descriptions as to country of origin still prevails.

De Carle described some forty watchmaker's lathes, made by twenty-one manufacturers; today just a handful of makers remain. One of the reasons for the enduring appeal of de Carle's original text, with its superb technical illustrations of long obsolete machines, is simply that this book is now the only source of information for many owners of secondhand lathes.

My special thanks to Tony Griffiths who unstintingly gave of his time in dealing with my numerous queries, created the Myford comparison table for me, and allowed the use of material from his website. Thanks also to the manufacturers and their agents who co-operated in the complete revision of Chapter 14, 'Lathes Today'. Once again Andy Lofquist of Metal Lathe Accessories helped with sources on the American scene, which was further added to through the pages of *The Home Shop Machinist*. To www.littlemachineshop.com for permission to quote from their mini lathe comparison site. To the German and Swiss Embassies in London for help in the location of lathe manufacturers in their countries. Finally, to Bryan Tate of Pro Machine Tools Ltd, for his constructive advice.

ERIC RESTALL

Chawton, 2010

PREFACE TO THE FIFTH EDITION

Donald de Carle, who sadly died in 1989, supervised the preparation of the last edition of this book, for which I was responsible. Precisely the same principles have been applied to this new edition which has required considerably more research this time to maintain the book's reputation as the most comprehensive guide to the small precision lathe past and present.

The bulk of de Carle's original text, most of which is concerned with matters of basic construction, selection, care of and accessories for the lathe and its uses, has been retained. Likewise the chapter entitled 'Lathes of the World' has also been kept in its entirety for it represents an unparalleled source of information to the purchaser of secondhand lathes and lathe accessories, the manufacture of which ceased many years ago.

The current scene is dealt with at length in the final chapter, 'Lathes Today' and is the result of extensive world-wide research prepared with the full co-operation of manufacturers or their agents. Lathes of particular interest to the model engineer, which were introduced for the first time in the previous edition, make up the hulk of this section.

Grateful thanks are due to the many manufacturers who generously assisted in the preparation of this edition. Also to the editors, and their readers, of *Model Engineer, Model Engineering Workshop, Clocks* and *Engineering in Miniature* who responded so freely to my queries. Information on the American market came via *The Home Shop Machinist* and was added to by Andy Lofquist of Metal Lathe Accessories. For constructive advice my thanks to Stan Warburton, Adrian Hill of Henri Picard Frere Ltd and J. M. Wild who also put me on track of the BTM lathe. Dr Alan Shenton and J. L. Hammond for information on the BTM lathe, also the latter for the loan of an original brochure, and Ian Fowler for German translation. The Danish, German and American embassies were most helpful with the location of lathe manufacturers in their countries.

ERIC RESTALL

Hindhead, 1997

PREFACE TO THE FOURTH EDITION

This book was first published some thirty years ago and has become, to quote one reviewer, " a standard work on the subject ". In preparing this new edition I make no apology for retaining the bulk of the original text, most of which is concerned with matters of basic construction, selection, care of and accessories for the small precision lathe and its uses. The original section entitled " Lathes of the World " has also been kept in its entirety, for I know from long experience that most of it represents the only source of information for the purchaser of secondhand equipment. Where necessary the text has been annotated to mark the demise of a particular model and/or manufacturer.

The completely new section " Lathes Today " at the end of the book is the result of extensive world-wide research and contains information and illustrations of small precision lathes and accessories currently available. For the first time, and reflecting the change of title, lathes of particular interest to the model engineer are included. The details have been prepared in full co-operation with the manufacturers or their agents.

Once again I am indebted to all the manufacturers who so generously co-operated in the compilation of this revised edition. I am especially grateful to the following for constructive advice, particularly with regard to locating successors of several firms that had ceased trading but whose products are still being manufactured under licence or under another name: S. Warburton of A. Shoot & Sons Ltd., V. J. Marston of Crawford Collets Ltd., L. I. Loch of Adam Machine Equipment Ltd., J. L. Pearton of Eric H. Bernfield, my old friend Henry B. Fried for information on the American scene, C. Worner of E. M. E. Ltd., J. P. Carter of H. S. Walsh & Sons Ltd., Paul Turnell, Cecil H. Smith, and lastly Eric Restall of my publishers who bore the brunt of the research work.

D. DE CARLE

Highcliffe, Dorset, 1985

PREFACE TO THE SECOND EDITION

THE FIRST edition of this work has been out of print for some years and is generally unobtainable. There is however a persistent demand for copies and I have therefore been requested to prepare a second edition.

I have taken this opportunity to add an appendix summarising new developments and a number of photographs have been incorporated. This new material does, I believe, bring the work fully up-to-date.

Details and illustrations of lathes (Chapter 10) no longer produced have been retained for the benefit of those who already own or might purchase second-hand equipment.

It is with great regret that I must report the deaths of Professor D. S. Torrens and Mr. E. A. Ayres both of whom played a valuable part in the original production of this book.

Professor Torrens, formerly Dean of the Medical Fraternity at Trinity College, Dublin, was a tower of strength in the field of horology and was always most generous with his knowledge. Mr. Ayres' draughtsmanship was superb as readers of this book will observe and his skills never surpassed at least in modern times. The death of these two men is indeed a sad loss to horology.

D. DE CARLE

Pinner, 1971.

PREFACE TO THE THIRD EDITION

IN THIS edition I have taken the opportunity of expanding the Appendix by giving details and illustrations of several additional lathes.

D. DE CARLE

Highcliffe, Dorset, 1980

PREFACE TO FIRST EDITION

WITHOUT THE lathe there would probably be no engineering or metal work and certainly the world would be without machines, much of its transport, and without the benefits of mass-production. We should still be in the dark ages as far as material comforts are concerned. The lathe is really the fundamental tool of industry and from it have developed many other machines, which in turn manufacture the major portion of the commodities in daily use.

In this book we are mainly concerned with the lathe as a watchmaker's tool on which are performed repairing operations or the making of new parts for repair jobs.

The age-old argument of whether it is better to use the turns where the workpiece is revolved between fixed centres, or to use the lathe where the workpiece is held in a split chuck, will possibly never be settled because both the lathe and the turns are so much instruments of a craftsman's individual skill ; indeed the work done with either expresses his individuality.

At first glance it may appear to be unnecessary to illustrate and describe so many lathes when they all appear to spring from the same prototype and all to have very similar, in many cases identical, characteristics of design and usefulness. Moreover, many of the tools would appear to be mere duplications, but to the user and particularly to the enthusiast every lathe will have its individuality, every tool its precise purpose and every fitting its exact place for the work it is intended to do.

The work done on a watchmakers' lathe is so small and particular that the lathe must be made with extreme care and accuracy. It must also be made in such a way that accessories can be fitted to it repeatedly without any doubt that they will always fit easily and accurately and operate as the maker intended and the user desires.

No other book on the watchmakers' lathe has been published since the beginning of this century and the one then issued dealt only with lathes made in the United States of America. This book attempts to deal with every lathe available on the market to-day, many of them of European manufacture and one from as far away as Australia. Some of the makers have a series of models, so that although there are 65 illustrations of manufacturers' lathes, there are actually specifications of many more and tools, fittings and accessories may well run to thousands, as the reader will see.

Special efforts have been made to induce each manufacturer to provide the latest information on his models and photographs from which

ix

accurate drawings could be made. The task of illustrating has been heavy but this method of reproduction has been followed in order to emphasise design and construction rather than polish and finish. As these lathes are such precise mechanical instruments their makers have, naturally, applied satisfactory finishes. Nickel-plating predominates and it is apparent that care and attention will be lavished on a tool which has a good appearance.

His lathe is the watch repairer-craftsman's pride and joy and this book is intended to assist him to select the lathe and accessories most suited to the conditions of his work and the type of work he has to do.

The grateful thanks of both the author and the publisher are extended to all the manufacturers who took so much trouble to send photographs, drawings and particulars of their products. The author extends his thanks to Professor D. S. Torrens for advice and assistance, to Mr. Maurice Aimer who has read through the manuscript and to Mr. Eric M. Bruton who has been particularly helpful with constructive criticism and has corrected the manuscript and seen the book through the press, and also to Mr. E. A. Ayres who has devoted care and skill to the execution of the drawings.

D. DE CARLE.

Pinner, 1951.

CONTENTS

PREFACE TO THE SIXTH EDITION v

PREFACE TO THE FIFTH EDITION. vi

PREFACE TO THE FOURTH EDITION vii

PREFACE TO THE SECOND AND THIRD EDITIONS viii

PREFACE TO THE FIRST EDITION ix

DIRECTORY OF LATHE MANUFACTURERS xiii

INTRODUCTION 1

CHAPTER 1. THE LATHE AND ITS COMPONENTS. Basic design and construction of the watchmaker's and model engineer's lathe considered, described and illustrated. Principal components and assemblies listed and described. Foot, bed, headstock, mandrel, pulleys, tailstock, runner. T-rest, tool holder, etc. Functions of the parts ; main dimensions 3

CHAPTER 2. WHERE AND HOW TO MOUNT THE LATHE. The best position for light and work ; firm fixation ; left and right hand lathes ; belting ; protective cover 5

CHAPTER 3. SELECTING A LATHE. Importance of accessories and standardisation of equipment ; views of noted maker ; " W.W." standards and dimensions ; the heart of the lathe ; construction of spindle (mandrel) ; thin and thick walled spindles compared ; cone-bearing spindle ; double cone bearing ; adjustment ; V-pulley grooves ; correct and incorrect angles for round belting ; ball bearings and ball thrusts ; pre-loaded bearings 8

CHAPTER 4. CARE AND MAINTENANCE OE THE LATHE. Care and respect necessary ; treatment after accidental damage ; readjustment of damaged lathe ; regular inspection, cleaning and oiling ; taking up wear ; yearly overhaul 17

CHAPTER 5. ACCESSORIES. Chucks : split, box, and 15 other types described and most of them illustrated ; table of over 40 chucks for machines of different makes, giving dimensions and thread capacity of each ; table of chuck sizes and equivalents in metric, inches—decimal and fractional—and in wire gauge ; step chuck table giving diameter of steps in mm. ; turning arbors ; T-rests, roller rests, slide rests, and saw plate. Tail stock accessories ; runners ; drill stocks ; rose cutters ; sinkers and taps ; Jacot drum ; pivoting attachment ; lapping attachment. Various other accessories : mandrel ; topping tool ; wheel cutting attachment ; screw head tool, etc. Motors with various methods of fitting belt drive ; pulley transmission ; pedal speed controllers and switches ; hand wheel drives treadle drives and other forms of pulley countershaft transmission. Other accessories : boring chuck ; lathe eye glass ; balance pivot polishing tool ; lathe light ; utility set 19

xi

CHAPTER 6. DEAD CENTRE LATHES, PIVOTING AND JACOT TOOLS. Dead centre lathes described and illustrated ; using lathes for turning between centres ; merits of lathes and " turns ". Pivoting : special tools ; burnishing pivots ; fitting new pivots ; jacot tools for bow or spool propulsion 57

CHAPTER 7. CUTTING TOOLS AND HOW TO USE THEM. Design of cutting tools ; clearance angles ; finishing the cutting edge ; whetting a slide rest tool ; fixing slide rest tools for cutting. Hand cutting tools ; types of graver ; holding the graver ; whetting a graver ; cutting angles ; use of the square-nosed graver 63

CHAPTER 8. WORKING WITH THE LATHE. Fitting up the job ; using three jaw and wax chucks ; correct tool position for turning ; speeds for turning and drilling ; detailed instructions for making a spring barrel and cap ; centring work on a wax chuck ; cutting wheel teeth ; indexing on the dividing plate ; worm and index plate dividing system ; snailing ; lapping. Turning a barrel arbor ; turning between centres ; filing a square with the roller rest ; sawing a square ; drilling round bar ; polishing ; using the screw head tool ; using the topping tool. Turning balance staffs : turning in the split chuck without removal ; turning one end and then reversing ; turning between centres ; using the split chuck with a wax chuck. Pivoting 70

CHAPTER 9. CHOICE AND CARE OF THE MOTOR. The right horse-power ; constant and variable speed ; types and speeds of motors ; power supplies ; installation ; wiring. Faults and maintenance : failure to start ; brushes ; commutators ; overheating speed control 90

CHAPTER 10. LATHES OF THE WORLD. Large size specially drawn illustrations showing design and construction of every type of lathe on the market at the time of the first printing. All are shown set up, some also shown cased, and others with special drives. Each lathe has its special features described and main dimensions set out. A standard list of equipment is given to avoid needless repetition, also full specifications and lists of special equipment available 97

Chapter 11. LATHES TODAY 153

Lathe, Tool and Material Stockists 217

Index 231

DIRECTORY OF LATHE MANUFACTURERS
and Major Own-Brand Dealers

The following list of manufacturers is provided for information and clarification only. Some manufacturers will not supply the public direct (Myfords and Cowell are notable exceptions); therefore, readers are advised to apply for prices and details from their usual tool and material suppliers (see page 217) or check online using the websites given below.

AJAX	Ajax Machine Tool Co. Ltd, Unit 360 Ampress Lane, Ampress Park, Lymington, Hampshire SO41 8XN. www.ajax-mach.co.uk
ARS*	Atelier de Construction de Rennes, 22 Boulevard de la Tour, d'Auvergne, Rennes, France.
AXMINSTER	Axminster Power Tool Centre Ltd, Unit 10, Weycroft Avenue, Axminster, Devon EX13 5PH. www.axminster.co.uk
BERGEON	Bergeon & Cie SA, Avenue du Technicum 11, CH 2400 Le Loche, Switzerland. www.bergeon.ch
BOLEY	Boley no longer manufacture watchmaker's lathes. Current production is restricted to high precision CNC lathes for industry.
BOXFORD	Boxford Ltd, Wheatley, Halifax, West Yorkshire HX3 5AF. www.boxford.co.uk. Boxford's production is now concentrated on the educational market. However, they can provide spares and accessories for their current and discontinued lathes.
CHESTER	Chester UK Ltd, Clwyd Close, Hawarden Industrial Park, nr Chester, Flintshire CH5 3PZ. www.chesteruk.net
CLARKE	Clarke International, Hemnall Street, Epping, Essex CM16 4LG. www.clarkeinternational.com
CLH	G. Levitt & Son Ltd, Hill Rise Works, 104 The Village, Stockton-on-Forrest, York YO3 9UW. No longer produce lathes but parts can be made to order.
CORONET	No longer make watchmaker's lathes.
COWELLS	Cowells Small Machine Tools Ltd, Tendring Road, Little Bentley, Colchester, Essex CO7 8SH. www.cowells.com
DERBYSHIRE	F.W. Derbyshire Inc., 910 Boston Turnpike, Shrewsbury, MA 01545, USA. www.fwderbyshireinc.com
EMCO	UK agent: Pro Machine Tools Ltd, 17 Station Road Business Park, Stamford, Lincolnshire PE93 3DW. www.emcomachinetools.co.uk. American agent: Blue Ridge Machinery Inc., PO Box 536, 2905 Putnam Avenue, Hurricane, WV 25526, USA. www.blueridgemachinery.com

FAVORITE	Golay Buchel no longer manufacture lathes.
GAMMA*	Electroimpex, Budapest, Hungary.
GRIZZLY	Grizzly, Inc., 1821 Valencia Street, Bellingham, WA 98229, USA. www.grizzly.com
HOBBYMAT	Unitech-Maschinen GmbH, Clemens-Winkler-Strasse 6, 09116 Chemnitz, Germany. www.unitech-maschinen.de UK stockist: Essel Engineering, Maesiocyn, Tylwch, Llanidoes, Powys SY18 6JJ. www.esselengineering.co.uk
IME*	Ideal Machine Tool & Engineering Co. Ltd, 282 Kingsland Road, London E8.
LANCO*	Lane Cove Engineering Co., 405 Pacific Highway, Lane Cove, NSW, Australia.
LEINEN	Pratecma, Inh Thomas Schafer, Gunther-Irmscher-Strasse 10, 73630 Remshalden-Grünbach, Germany.
LEVIN	Louis Levin & Son Inc., 13550 Larwin Circle, Santa Fe Springs, CA 90670, USA. www.levinlathe.com
LORCH*	Lorch, Schmit & Co. GmbH, 6 Frankfurt am Main - Ost 1, Hanauer Landstrasse 135, Germany.
MANIX	see Toyo
MANHORA*	A. Moynet, 26 Rue de Renard, Paris IV, France.
MARSHALL	No longer in production.
MICRO-LUX	Micro-Mark. www.micromark.com
MOSELEY	No longer in production.
MYFORD	Myford Ltd, Wilmot Lane, Chilwell Road, Beeston, Nottingham NG9 1ER. www.myford.com
PAULSON	No longer in production.
PEATOL	Taig Tools, 12419 East Nightingale Lane, Chandler, AZ 85286, USA. www.taigtools.com UK stockist: Peatol Machine Tools, 19 Knightlow Road, Harborne, Birmingham B17 8PS. www.peatol.com
PEERLESS	No longer in production.
PRAZI	Unitech-Maschinen GmbH, Clemens-Winkler-Strasse 6, 09116, Chemnitz, Germany
PROXXON	Proxxon GmbH, Im Spanishchen 18–24, 54518 Niersbach, Germany. www.proxxon.com
PULTRA	see Smart & Brown
RECORD	see Toyo
SAKAI	see Toyo
SCHAUBLIN	Schaublin Machines SA, Rue Principale 4, 2735 Bévilard, Switzerland. www.smsa.ch UK agent: Schaublin Machine Tools Ltd, PO Box 36, Stockbridge, SO20 6WP American agent: DA Swiss Inc., PO Box 910, Southampton, PA 18966, USA. www.daswiss.com

SCOMEA*   Societe Commerciale d'Outillage et de Mechanique
              d'Aviation, 7 Rue Lauriston, Paris XVI, France.
SHERLINE   Sherline Products, Inc., 3235 Executive Ridge, Vista, CA
              92801-8527, USA. www.sherline.com
              UK agent: Millhill SuppliesLtd, Unit 37, Broton Drive,
              Broton Trading Estate, Halstead, Essex CO9 1HB.
              www.millhillsupplies.co.uk
SIEG   Shanghai Sieg Group. Sieg lathes are sold all over the
              world, often under a retailer's name.
SMART & BROWN   Bracehand Ltd, Unit 1, Stanford Bury, Shefford,
              Bedfordshire SG17 5NS. www.barrystarling.co.uk
SMITHY   Smithy Company, PO Box 1517, Ann Arbor, MI 48106-1517,
              USA. www.smithy.com
SOUTH BEND   South Bend Lathe Co., PO Box 2027, Bellingham, WA
              98227, USA. www.southbendlathe.com
STAR   M. Gentil & Co., Village 156, 2406 La Brevine, Switzerland.
STEINER   Horia SA, 23 Rue de l'Avenir, 2852 Courtételle,
              Switzerland. www.horia.ch
TAIG   see Peatol
TOYO   Woo Sung E & I Co. Ltd, 1119-3, Seokjeong-ri, Poseung-
              myeon, Pyeongtaek-si, Gyeonggi-do, 451-820, Korea.
              www.manix.co.kr.
              UK agent: Rejon Machine Tools, Mumby Lodge, Mumby's
              Drove, Three Holes, Wisbech, Cambridgeshire PE14 9JT.
              www.rejon.co.uk
              American agent: Progress Machine & Tool Corp., 645
              South Olive Street, Los Angeles, CA 90014, USA.
              www.progresstool.com
UNIMAT   see Emco
VECTOR*   Vector, Wiesenstrasse 3, 78083 Dauchingen, Germany.
WABECO   Walter Blombach GmbH., Am Blaffertsberg 13, 42899
              Remscheid, Germany. www.wabeco-remscheid.de
              Sole UK importer: Pro Machine Tools Ltd, 17 Station Road
              Business Park, Barnack, Stamford, Lincolnshire PE9 3DW.
              www.emcomachinetools.co.uk
              American importer: MDA Precision, 3290 Hecker Pass
              Highway, Gilroy, CA 95020, USA. www.mdaprecision.com
WARCO   Warren Machine Tools (Guildford) Ltd, Warco House, Fisher
              Lane, Chiddingfold, Surrey GU8 4TD. www.warco.co.uk
WISKUM   No longer in production.
WOLF, JAHN*   Wolf, Jahn & Co., 418 Bergestrasse, Frankfurt am Main,
              Germany.

* The address given is the last known

INTRODUCTION

Very few, if any, will dispute that the lathe has now become an essential part of the watch repairer's equipment. Garrard, when writing a series of articles in the periodical " Work," in 1896, said that he estimated that nine-tenths of the watchmakers and repairers in England still used the turns in preference to the lathe. Even today some of the fine craftsmen still prefer the turns for certain work Such men may possess a lathe, but for work requiring a finer sense of " touch " they prefer turns. Skilled men can be seen today in one of the largest Swiss watch factories, engaged on pivoting for baguette and ultra-flat watch movements, using the old-fashioned turns ; each man with as many as eight pairs of turns and each pair fitted up for a particular job, thus, in a manner, employing quantity production methods with this ancient tool. By adjusting runners and beds to accommodate certain dimensions, the necessity to " fit up " afresh for each operation is avoided and time is thus saved. Turns date back for a great many years. Goodrich, in his book " The Watchmakers' Lathe " traced the history of the lathe to the pre-Christian era and says that the true home of the lathe was Egypt. Such lathes were what are now called turns, since the work is made to rotate between dead centres and given a backward and forward motion by means of a bow.

The makers of hand-made watch cases still use what is termed a " pole " lathe, where the work is made to rotate backward and forward, not because they prefer to use antiquated tools, but that it is more convenient for their particular form of turning.

Once the user of a lathe has become accustomed to it, he will not rely so much on the turns ; there are many uses to which the lathe can be put. With its multitudinous accessories, jobs can be done quickly, more efficiently and more accurately than by other means. It is the purpose of this book to review a selection of modern watchmakers' lathes and their accessories and in addition to explain how jobs are done and to deal with the work in some detail.

The lathe proper as we know it is distinguished from other lathes as " Hollow Spindle " or " Live Spindle ". The hollow spindle lathe with split chuck was invented about 1858 by C. S. Moseley of U.S.A., then employed by the Boston Watch Company. Shortly afterwards (about 1859) he introduced an improved lathe for the American Watch Company and that lathe was the forerunner of the modern instrument.

At about this date, A. Webster, who was in charge of the machine shop of the American Watch Company, was instructed to reduce

1

staff owing to a trade depression and it was because of this that Webster started to make a business of manufacturing watchmakers' lathes to be sold at large, so to keep the staff of the machine shop employed. Before any of the lathes could be completed in quantity, business revived in the manufacture of watches and the manufacture of lathes was dropped.

Kidder and Adams, employed under Webster, decided to continue the manufacture of the Webster-designed lathe and left the employ of the watch factory. After several changes in ownership, the lathe factory subsequently came into the hands of John E. Whitcomb, who with G.F. Ballow, opened a factory in Boston known as Ballow, Whitcomb & Company. In 1889 Webster designed another and improved lathe known as the Webster-Whitcomb and it is this lathe that set the W.W. standard. Ambrose Webster joined John E. Whitcomb and Henry N. Fisher and formed the American Watch Tool Company in 1894.

F.W. Derbyshire became Factory Superintendent of the American Watch Tool Company in 1901 and left in 1911 to form his own business, which survives to this day. In 1913 he applied for, and in 1916 was granted, a patent on the rack and pinion operated collet holding tailstock.

It is interesting to note that Schaublin of Switzerland, manufacturers of very fine lathes for the engineering industry, created their first lathes on the English made Churchill lathe.

Chapter I

THE LATHE AND ITS COMPONENTS

All watchmakers' lathes* are basically simple, comprising a bed, headstock and a tool rest (see Fig. 1). The *bed* is the base of the lathe and must be both rigid and accurate because it is, in a way, the foundation upon which the machine is built up. It is made in round, flat, round with a flat, triangular, and other sections, and is mounted on one or two feet, or a clamp, for fixing to the bench.

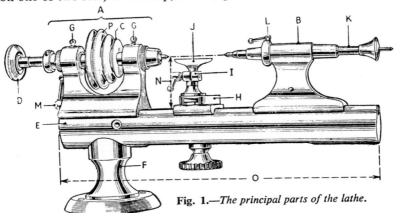

Fig. 1.—*The principal parts of the lathe.*

A. *Headstock.*
B. *Tailstock.*
C. *Pulley.*
D. *Draw-in spindle.*
E. *Bed.*
F. *Foot.*
G. *Oil caps.*
H. *T-rest shoe.*
I. *T-rest bush.*
J. *T-rest.*
K. *Runner.*
L. *Runner fixing lever.*
M. *Headstock fixing lever.*
N. *Height of centres.*
O. *Length of bed.*
P. *Index holes.*

At one end of the bed is the *fixed headstock*, which is by far the most important part of the lathe. It carries a *spindle* or *mandrel*, revolved manually or by a motor to cause the work to rotate. Accuracy of the work produced depends to a large extent upon the accuracy of manufacture of the spindle and its bearings and upon its freedom from wear.

At the other end of the bed is a *tailstock*, which may be moved along the bed and which carries the *back centre* or *runner*. In use, the tailstock is clamped in position on the bed to suit the length of the work being turned.

Also clamped to the bed, between the headstock and, if one is fitted, the tailstock, is a *tool rest*, a simple *T-rest* if only hand tools are to be used. Instead of this, and for a variety of purposes, a *slide rest*,

---

* AUTHOR'S NOTE: Here and throughout the text I refer to a small precision instrument, made to very high standards of accuracy, which is equally suited to the needs of the model engineer.

which carries a *tool holder* or *tool post*, can be fitted. Both the T-rest and the slide rest can be moved along the bed of the lathe to suit the work in hand.

The tool holder is mounted on a *cross slide*. The slide rest moves the cutting tool along the length of the bed to give *longitudinal feed* and the cross slide moves the tool across the bed to give *cross feed*. Both the longitudinal and traverse (or cross) feeds are independently controlled by hand. Longitudinal feed is used to reduce the diameter of a job and cross feed to *face* one end of it or to *part it off*, i.e. to cut it off.

The spindle in the headstock of a " simple " lathe such as the watchmakers' carries a *cone pulley* (larger lathes usually have intervening gears), which is driven by a belt. The different sizes of pulley give different turning speeds. The spindle is hollow and carries the *chuck* or *collet* which holds the work to be turned. An inside taper in the nose of the spindle and a corresponding outside taper on the chuck causes the chuck, as it is drawn into the spindle by a screw operated by hand at the opposite end, to be contracted and grip the work.

There are two main ways in which to hold work in the lathe. It can be gripped by one end in the chuck, as described, or it can be mounted *between centres*. The centres are used for bearings for the work. To make the work rotate with the spindle, a device known as a *carrier* is used.

A centre with a conical pointed end is known as a *male centre*, and one with a conical hole in the end is known as a *female centre*. When a small round rod is to be fitted between female centres, cones are turned on the ends so that the rod automatically takes up a central position, provided the cone pivots have been turned accurately ; when male centres are used, the ends of the work have to be indented to take the points of the centres.

The driving mandrel is sometimes made to carry a *face plate* with pump centre (i.e., a centre which will retract) instead of a chuck, mainly for work of irregular shape, which is fixed to the plate instead of being gripped in the chuck.

The tailstock is, on some lathes, screwed so that it can be used to hold and feed a tool such as a drill or boring tool into work held in the headstock. The work is thus rotated about the tool.

Lathe sizes are determined by three main dimensions :—

Spindle bore (which is usually 8 mm.),

Height of centres (i.e. from the lathe bed), and

Length of bed. Where the bed is detachable, the entire length is given, which includes that part occupied by the headstock. Where the bed is solid with the headstock the length of the bed is from the headstock to the end of the bed, i.e. where the tool rest and tailstock can slide, or if the tailstock is a fixture, between the centres.

Chapter 2

WHERE AND HOW TO MOUNT THE LATHE

However accurate a watchmakers' lathe may be, much of its value will be lost if it is mounted badly, in an awkward place, or in bad light. The question of height is an important one ; generally it is best to be able to look down on the work—not necessarily on the top, but very nearly. If the lathe cannot be mounted at a height that allows this to be done, the operator must arrange to sit higher. An adjustable stool solves the problem in a simple way, but many watchmakers prefer to sit on their lathe boxes placed on the stool they normally use, which gives some idea of the extra height required when the lathe is mounted on the bench.

A good light on the work is essential. Daylight is best to work in, but failing that there should be a strong top light from an electric bulb, with a shade used to direct the light on to the job and to protect the eyes. A low candlepower bulb strains the eyes and, generally speaking, fluorescent lamps are not suitable as the speed of the lathe sometimes synchronises with the frequency of the power supply and produces a stroboscopic effect which is very disturbing where accurate work is involved. This trouble can be minimised but not entirely eliminated by using double or treble fluorescent tubes.

The lathe must be firmly fitted to the bench and it will usually be found most convenient to have it on the left-hand side. In a small workshop where space is rationed, an ideal system is to have a lathe with one foot, which is screwed to the bench in a forward position to the left. A locking clamp in the foot allows the lathe to be swung to one side when not in use.

Such a convenient arrangement cannot be applied to a hand wheel driven lathe, whether of the under or overhand system, which is usually held in the vice or clamped to the bench and which often rocks up and down when driven at speed. An incidental objection to the hand-driven lathe is that when the lathe is removed from the bench, it is usually hung by its wheel underneath the bench top. From all points of view, there is no doubt that the motor-driven system is the best, followed by the treadle lathe. The handwheel drive has been long out-dated.

If the lathe is a left hand one, i.e. with the headstock on the right, then it should it be fitted to the right hand side of the bench. Some continental repairers prefer left hand lathes. There is little difference in their use, working tools being held in the same way. A few models with clamp fittings are universal.

Firm mounting of the lathe helps to reduce vibration, but the motor itself must not be forgotten as this may be the source of the movement. Make sure that the motor pulley lines up with the centre of the cone pulley on the lathe, or with any intermediate pulleys, and that the motor itself is firmly fixed. It is usually best to use rubber washers between the motor and bench to absorb any vibration.

Transmission pulleys should be fitted at the back of the bench and before being fixed finally in position should be tried with the belt on, to see that it rides well in all the pulley grooves. There should be no sign of belt ruffing which, if present, may result in the belt over-riding the pulley.

Belting can be another source of vibration and trouble, particularly if there is a large belt fastener which bumps over the pulley every time it goes round. This is soon reflected in the work produced. Two kinds of belting are in use to-day, leather and plastic, but there is every prospect of plastic superseding leather for two reasons ; the plastic material is quite circular in section, which ensures silent and smooth running, and it can be joined to form an almost seamless joint.* The plastic material gives an endless belt without fastener which produces no jolts and reduces vibration to a minimum.

* See Fig 72, page 48.

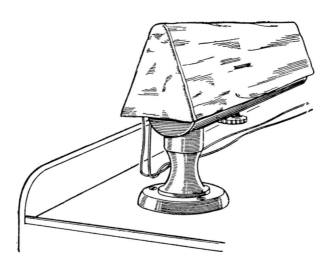

Fig. 2.—*Protective cover for lathe.*

Belt tension is important but some latitude is permissible. The tension should be light enough to turn the lathe under normal load without slipping. If it is very tight it may cause damage to the motor or lathe itself.

It is advisable to make a cover for a lathe which is fixed in position on the bench, a soft one made of American cloth or some similar material is quite suitable to keep off dust and is easily removed and replaced (Fig. 2). A lathe, to continue to give accurate results, must be treated with care. It is a relatively delicate instrument and should always be treated with respect in use and protected when not in use.

Chapter 3

SELECTING A LATHE

A position has been reached by the manufacturer of watchmakers' lathes where there is little to choose between them when it comes to fundamentals. There are points of refinement and slight differences in design, but for stability and general construction none is far superior to another. A general survey and examination of the lathes reveal good points in most. One lathe may be a little better finished than another, but off-set against that the other lathe may have some refinement which appeals to the prospective purchaser. So it is not possible to recommend any particular make. Therefore it is proposed to describe and illustrate each make in alphabetical order in Chapter 10 and to deal with the accessories in Chapter 5. Some manufacturers, especially the British, do not make all the accessories it is possible or desirable to make, but new accessories are constantly being added to their lists.

Accessories made by one manufacturer are not always interchangeable with the lathes of other makers ; this is a decided disadvantage to the owner of a particular make of lathe. The reason is not far to seek ; it is a matter of evolution. Each manufacturer claims some advantage of design and when it comes to accessories such as the slide rest, wheel cutting attachment, or lapping attachment, the question of adaptability arises. When buying a lathe therefore, if you have in mind to add some particular accessory and the accessory required is not included in the list to be found at the conclusion of the description of each lathe, enquiries should be made of the manufacturers about their future programme.

The matter of headstock accessories, such as chucks, split, wax, wheel, etc., is not of such great importance since most of these accessories are interchangeable provided they are of the same size, i.e. 6 mm. or 8 mm. The chuck manufacturers do however stress the importance of obtaining chucks with the correct thread pitch.

It will be observed when reading through the chapter dealing with lathes that most of them are made to take 8 mm. chucks.

Of lathe design, we are privileged here to publish the views of Samuel Levin, of Louis Levin & Son, the noted toolmakers of U.S.A.

A great deal has been written about the watchmakers' lathe and its uses. Every watchmaker, as well as the student and apprentice, accepts the fact that the lathe is his most important piece of equipment and that the variety of jobs he can do with it is limited only by the number of accessories with which it is furnished. Each manufacturer, of course, claims to make the finest, and advertisements are replete with beautiful illustrations which may or may not be faithful portrayals of the actual tools. There is, then,

8

some justification for a study of the lathe from the standpoint of its construction, rather than its uses.

Basically, the lathe is a device which revolves an object to be worked on while it is being cut. The process is known as turning. Even after the most rudimentary experience, one is aware of the fact that accuracy and good finish cannot be obtained unless the work is rigidly mounted in the lathe. Any looseness or springing produces chatter, and once chatter appears, there is no longer any chance to produce a good finish or maintain dimensional accuracy. Chatter also has a very deleterious effect on tool life.

Today, almost all leading makers of watchmakers' lathes make them according to the so-called W.W.* standards. What actually are these W.W. standards? When one speaks of a W.W. type lathe he means one which has a 50 mm. (1·394 in.) centre height, 60 deg. angular bed ways, 1·456 in. width on the top of the bed, an 8 mm. chuck body and a 40 deg. included angle on the chuck. There are other dimensions involved too, but these are the principal ones.

Whether these particular dimensions are the most ideal for a watchmaker's lathe can be argued without arriving at any definite conclusions. Around these basic dimensions each manufacturer has designed his own lathe and applied his particular standard of workmanship.

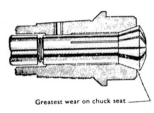

Greatest wear on chuck seat

Fig. 3.—*Where wear occurs.*

The heart of a lathe is the spindle and the manner in which it is mounted. The spindle must be hollow so that a wire chuck can be inserted at one end and a draw bar for tightening it at the other end. When a chuck is tightened and released it actually slides back and forth a certain amount on the conical seat in the spindle. Since this sliding takes place under great pressure, it is necessary to guard against undue wear at the points of contact. The wear is minimized by making the spindle of hard steel. In spite of the fact that hardness is so necessary at the chuck seat, some lathes with soft spindles are still being made (Fig. 3).

When making a hard spindle, the blank is made with a small amount of extra stock on the outside as well as the inside. This surplus material is removed by grinding after the piece is hardened and tempered. The reason for leaving the surplus material on the blank is to make allowance for warping when it is heat treated. Certain makers, who try to economize, harden only the end of the spindle and leave soft the entire portion from the cone bearing to the rear end. This is a cheaper way of making a spindle, but it does not produce one which is as good as a spindle that is hard from end to end, even where the shoulder of the draw bar rests.

Tightening a piece of work in a lathe chuck produces a considerable amount of strain on the spindle. The effect is as though one took a long slender rod and rested one end on the floor and with the palm of the hand pressed down on the upper end. The rod would, of course, start to buckle when the pressure became great. Exactly the same thing takes place in a lathe spindle. If it is made with too thin a wall, it will spring when a chuck

* W.W. stands for Webster Whitcomb, see page 1.

is tightened. Fig. 4 shows this condition. This leads to improper seating of the bearings, premature wear and even deflection of the spindle to a degree which may be readily noticeable. To make a spindle with a heavier wall means using more material and more labour, both for the spindle and

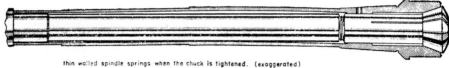

thin walled spindle springs when the chuck is tightened. (exaggerated)

Fig. 4.—*Thin walled spindle buckles.*

the bearings. Thus, in a sense, one can judge the quality of a lathe by the thickness of the spindle wall and by noting whether or not the spindle is hard all over.

To ensure a true running spindle, the chuck seat should be ground after assembly, with the spindle running in its own bearings. Particular attention should be given to the chuck key, which should not be too long or too wide, otherwise there may be trouble when inserting chucks.

Many attachments, such as index plates, screw cutting attachments, lever operated chuck closers, etc., must be mounted on the rear end of the spindle. Unless the lathe manufacturer provides the extra length on the spindle the watchmaker must forever forgo the possibility of using them on his lathe (Fig. 5).

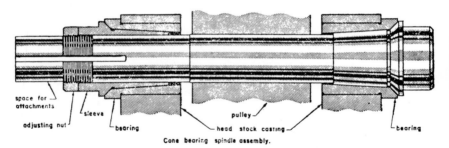

space for attachments

sleeve

adjusting nut

bearing

pulley

head stock casting

bearing

Cone bearing spindle assembly.

Fig. 5.—*Part section of cone bearing spindle.*

Two general types of bearing are used in lathes, sleeve bearings, as typified by the commonly used double cone bearings, and ball bearings which have just come to the fore. Each type will be discussed separately.

Early in the development of the watchmakers' lathe the double cone bearing was evolved in an attempt to equalize wear and simplify adjustment. How successful this arrangement has been may be judged from the fact that until recently practically all watchmakers' lathes and machinist's bench lathes used such bearings. Double cone bearings are currently made of either hard steel or bronze. Either will give satisfactory performance. The principal advantages of the hard steel bearing are that they require less frequent adjustment, and are less likely to become charged with abrasive, if one is not careful in using abrasive materials in the lathe. Soft bearings, however, will give years of good service. As proof, witness the many machines still in operation with babbitt soft metal bearings.

10

Lubrication of a cone bearing is usually accomplished by means of an oil groove in the bearing surface. The oil is applied at a hole which is uncovered by removing a dust cap or by means of an oil cup. Actually, an oil cup is of little benefit as the amount of oil which can be retained is governed by the capillary surface between the bearing and spindle. An excess amount of oil simply runs through and does no good.

Cone bearings are adjusted by a split nut on the spindle. Tightening this nut draws together the cones of the spindle and spindle sleeve, and presses them into the cones of the bearings. Thus, both side play and end play are eliminated at the same time. This adjustment must be made periodically as the bearings wear in. The spindle should be lubricated with a light spindle oil such as a sewing machine oil and occasionally it may be desirable to take the headstock apart for cleaning. If this is done, one should be careful to see that the key in the sleeve is in the key way of the spindle before pressing them together and that the pulley is so placed that the dog-point of the pulley screw will find its way into the hole in the spindle. These precautions should be carefully observed for many lathes have been badly damaged by disregarding them.

It is customary to drive a small lathe, such as the watchmakers' lathe, with a round belt. The actual form of the pulley groove is of some importance if belt slip is to be avoided. According to modern engineering practice, a 53 deg. groove is most desirable. Some pulleys are made with the angle of the groove as great as 90 deg. or more. These are inefficient because the belt must be tightened excessively in order to avoid slippage. Tightening the belt so much also leads to excessive wear of the bearings (Fig. 6).

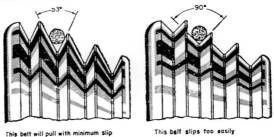

This belt will pull with minimum slip   This belt slips too easily

Fig. 6.—*Correct and incorrect pulley groove angles.*

Of the materials from which pulleys and also the draw bar knobs are made, a linen base laminated phenolic (plastic material) is the most serviceable. This material, from which timing gears for automobiles are also made, consists of layers of high grade linen impregnated with bakelite. It is strong and long wearing. Moulded pulleys, made of rubber or bakelite, are fragile and easily chipped.

While ball bearings have been used for precision spindles for a number of years, they are now coming into general use for watchmakers' lathes. The very words ball bearings have acquired such a connotation that their use automatically indicates quality. This is an erroneous concept. One should know that, just as all that " glitters is not gold," so a ball bearing does not necessarily mean a precision bearing.

Ball bearings were developed to reduce friction, and they are so well able to do this that they are now also known as anti-friction bearings.

It should be remembered, however, that to make a precision ball bearing spindle still takes the finest workmanship and engineering. None of the lathe manufacturers makes the actual ball bearings himself. These are made by the various ball bearing manufacturers who specialize in this field. It is of the greatest importance to know that, given the finest possible ball bearing, its performance will be governed by the manner in which it is built into the lathe and the care with which it is done. To make a precision ball bearing spindle requires the application of sound engineering principles, and a poorly executed ball bearing spindle is much worse than one having plain sleeve bearings.

When a load is applied to a ball bearing, the ball is somewhat flattened at the points of contact with the inner and outer races and its diameter is lessened on this axis because of the deformation. This means that a ball on the opposite side of the bearing cannot touch both inner and outer races, because a clearance space has been produced. Fig. 7 shows this condition clearly.

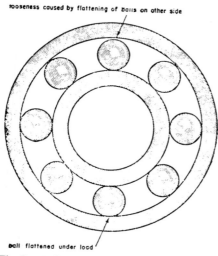

looseness caused by flattening of balls on other side

ball flattened under load

Fig. 7.—*Ball bearing deformation under load.*

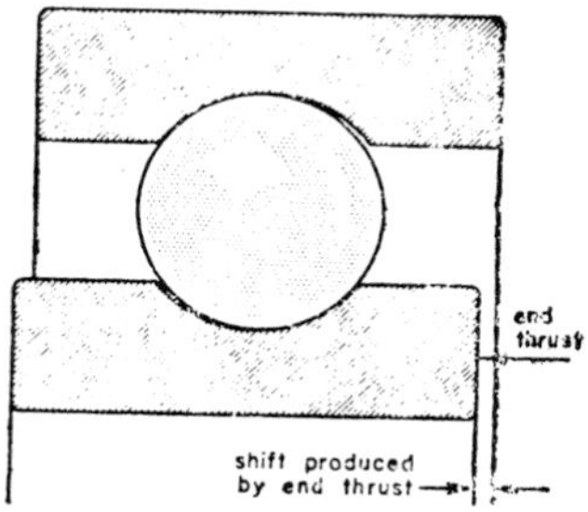

Fig. 8.—*Deformation caused by end thrust.*

end thrust

shift produced by end thrust

Similarly, end thrust against a ball bearing causes the races to shift axially because of the deformation of the balls under the applied load (see Fig. 8). Since the load on a bearing is seldom purely a radial load or pure end thrust, a combination of the two effects is produced. As a result of this brief analysis it is easy to see that by simply mounting a spindle on two ball bearings one does not have an arrangement which is satisfactory for a lathe. Such a spindle would have no rigidity and would chatter under even a very light load.

Some years ago ball bearing manufacturers developed the principle of pre-loading, which overcomes these objections to the application of ball bearings to precision spindles. This involved the use of bearings which are designed for heavy thrust loads and taking advantage of certain properties of a ball under a load.

Fig. 9 shows an angular contact ball bearing which is made for heavy thrust loads. Note that it has a wide shoulder on one side of the outer race but only a small shoulder on the other side. Because of this, it can withstand end thrust in only one direction. Bearings of this type are generally used in pairs when thrust in both directions must be resisted.

Let us now consider once more what happens to a ball when subjected to a load. As we have noted before, the ball tends to flatten out at the points of contact. However, because the load is applied to a ball, this flattening is not proportional to the load. Actually, there is a point beyond which any additional loading produces practically no additional deformation. It should be apparent that if it were possible to make ball bearings so that they would be constantly under a sufficient load, then the additional load caused by doing work in the lathe would cause practically no measurable deflection. This is accomplished in a pre-loaded bearing.

 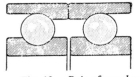 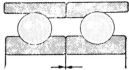

Fig. 9.—*Bearing for heavy thrust loads.*   **Fig. 10.**—*Pair of angular contact bearings.*   **Fig. 11.**—*Bearings shown in Fig. 10 pre-loaded.*

In Fig. 10 we have a pair of angular contact bearings placed side by side. Note that the inner races are made slightly thinner than the outer races, so that there is a space between them. Now suppose that, as in Fig. 11 a load is applied to both inner races to squeeze them together and that they could be held thus permanently. We would then have a pre-loaded bearing. An additional uni-directional load, such as might occur when turning or drilling in a lathe, will produce almost no deflection because the initial loading has already stressed the bearings beyond what can be expected from the work load. Furthermore, while the thrust increases the loading on one bearing, it relieves it on the other, so that any tendency for the bearing to deflect is practically nullified.

Fig. 12 shows a complete bearing and spindle assembly for a watchmaker's lathe. The pre-loading is accomplished in assembly by tightening the nut

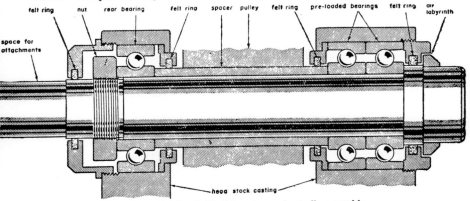

Fig. 12.—*Pre-loaded ball bearing and spindle assembly.*

13

on the spindle. This squeezes together the inner races of the pair of angular contact bearings at the front of the spindle. The rear bearing is subject to little stress and pre-loading is not necessary at this point.

It is possible to make a pre-loaded spindle as in Fig. 13. But, in this case the pre-load is taken by the headstock casting which, because it is cut out for the pulley, is not rigid enough. In spite of the fact that a headstock looks massive, it can be easily sprung and if the spindle design is faulty there will be chatter.

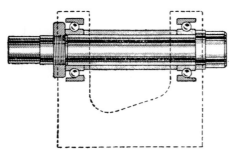

An unsatisfactory arrangement for pre-loading

Fig. 13.—*Another, less satisfactory, pre-loading method.*

The use of ball bearings makes the headstock a little bulkier. In any attempt to minimize this, a reduction of the thickness of the spindle wall so that smaller bearings can be used, is jumping from the frying pan into the fire, because by weakening the spindle its rigidity and accuracy are lessened.

Ball bearings are produced in various grades and the prices of the different grades may vary as much as tenfold. Ball bearings must be kept clean and it is, therefore, necessary to provide means of keeping the dirt out. This can be accomplished by placing a closely fitting felt ring on both sides of each bearing. And as an additional precaution, at the nose of the lathe spindle, a ring is placed on the spindle to create an air labyrinth which will create an outward current to carry particles of dust away from the bearing.

The additional labour and material required to produce a precision ball bearing spindle adds to the cost of a lathe and makes it more expensive than one with plain cone bearings. However, where greater rigidity, higher spindle speed or the elimination of the need for oiling are important, the extra cost is more than warranted.

Until just a few years ago, practically all standard watchmakers' lathes were supplied with the old style tailstock whose spindle was about 8 mm. in diameter and had a small taper hole at the working end. This type of tailstock is extremely limited in its application because of the difficulty of holding tools on a small taper shank. It is significant to note that in most cases this type of tailstock looks almost like new, after the rest of the lathe shows signs of use.

In 1945 Louis Levin & Son adopted a new design with a chuck holding spindle. The end of the casting facing the headstock was made with a substantial overhang to clear a slide rest.

Since the tailstock is now a most important tool, the buyer should consider its construction as much as he does the headstock. Here also, the spindle should be hard, preferably from end to end, and the wall of the spindle should be thick enough to obviate any danger of springing when a chuck is tightened. The spindle should be fitted closely enough so that there will be no side shake to destroy the accuracy of line up. This can be accomplished only if the hole in the tailstock casting has a smooth and precise

14

finish. The spindle clamp must be powerful enough to keep the spindle from turning when tightening a chuck.

The most sensitive tailstock is the one with a rack and pinion feed. With this arrangement one can use the smallest pivot drill and still have the necessary " feel " for delicate work.

While it is feasible to make an accurate micrometer stop for the tailstock spindle, it would add a great deal to the cost and its bulk would be objectionable because it tends to reduce the travel of the spindle. Merely providing a graduated screw does not make a reliable micrometer. The screw must be fitted accurately so that it has no play and any friction device or locking arrangement must resist the thrust of the spindle or it cannot be relied upon. If one takes these requirements into account, either the spindle must be made excessively long or its travel is reduced to an insignificant amount. Actually, it is much more practical to use a simple collar on the spindle and, when necessary, locate it with an ordinary feeler gauge.

By this time it is probably apparent to the reader that the quality of a lathe is dependent upon many details, no single one of which may be of paramount importance but all of which add to the precision or ease of operation. Among such details, for example one might mention that the binding levers for the headstock and tailstock should be on the sides and not on the ends of the castings where they may interfere with various attachments. It is easier to make the clamping bolts themselves out of smaller stock, but larger heads are an advantage because they have a greater gripping power. Likewise, the nut which tightens the T-rest to the lathe bed can be inexpensively made as a simple knurled disc. But a nicely machined nut with four ball end spokes is much easier on the hands and takes less effort to use. Where a watchmaker works in a restricted space he often swings his lathe aside to provide more working space on the top of his bench. To him it is a decided convenience to have a smoothly finished nut with large spokes instead of a commercial wing nut for fastening his lathe to the bench. And, we must not forget a well made tip over T-rest which has no play in the joint.

Without exception, watchmakers are almost as concerned about the appearance of a lathe as they are about its precision. In no other field is plating used on precision equipment. Where rust from handling is a danger, one simply wipes the tool with an oily cloth occasionally. Plating cannot be applied with absolute precision and, therefore, in order to maintain exact dimensions it must necessarily be applied as a thin layer. A heavy coating of plating destroys the accuracy of a tool and accomplishes nothing but a shiny appearance.

Plating is granular in structure and, therefore, somewhat porous. Unless treated with care it is not an absolute protection against rust. It is a good idea to wipe it with a slightly oily cloth occasionally. One need not use so much oil as to leave smears, just enough to leave a slight film.

The preparation for plating is as important as the plating itself. A good lathe is machined all over so that its form is smooth and concentric around the spindle. Edges, particularly on the bed, will remain sharp and not be buffed away. It is a known fact that the poorest tools are often the shiniest and have the fewest sharp corners. They are buffed until they glisten, with little attempt made to preserve the accuracy of working surfaces.

When speaking of tools, it is most appropriate to paraphrase the well known quotation, "No matter how well something is made, someone always finds a way to make it a little cheaper and a little worse."

15

While the design of a lathe may be of no particular interest to the average watch repairer, for the reasons mentioned earlier on, there are some points of vital importance to be learnt from the foregoing. One is the diameter of the driving belt. The owner of a lathe cannot alter the design of the grooves of the pulley, but he can see that the diameter of the driving belt is correct to suit the pulley, which is in effect, or at least to a large extent, the same as a correctly designed pulley. Touring the factory of a machine toolmaker in Switzerland, I saw the sensitivity of a measuring instrument illustrated in the following manner. A very substantial headstock-like piece, without pulley, was used. The size of the piece was about 3 ft. wide and the space between the bearings, where the pulleys would normally be situated, was about 1 ft., so the length of the bearings was about 1 ft. each. The rest of the testing piece was in proportion. The measuring instrument was fitted between the bearings which were then pressed together with the hands at arms' length. In this manner it is not possible to exert much force, but the instrument recorded that the bearings had been pressed closer together. The point to be made is this, Levin says that if the spindle sleeve is made with the wall too thin, it will buckle when a chuck is screwed up tightly with the draw in rod, and he is right. The average watchmakers' lathe looks substantially made but the instrument test just mentioned must be borne in mind. The lesson to be learnt here is *do not use force when tightening up a chuck*, it is not necessary. This matter will be referred to later, when discussing the split chuck.

Chapter 4

CARE AND MAINTENANCE OF THE LATHE

The care with which a lathe is treated and its correct maintenance, such as periodical cleaning, inspection and re-oiling is of the utmost importance. It adds to its life and preserves accuracy and expedition in its work.

Treat a lathe with the respect which every fine and expensive tool demands. Above all, do not handle it carelessly or allow it to be dropped. A dropped lathe is certainly a damaged lathe and it may possibly be ruined if dropped on a hard floor on a vulnerable point with the mass of the lathe behind it. Besides cracking the casting, the bed may be put out of truth or the bearings may suffer damage.

But should an accident happen, the lathe must undergo a rigorous testing before being put to work again, particularly with regard to the alignment.

To do this fit up a split chuck in the headstock and a male centre which is known to be true. Select one with a fairly long point. Fit a similar centre into the runner of the tailstock. Slide the tai'stock carefully towards the headstock so that the two points just meet. If the lathe has not suffered the points should meet exactiy.

With the points in this position turn the headstock slowly by hand and with a $\frac{1}{4}$ in. eyeglass closely observe that the points are central with no up or down movement. Should the least movement of the points away from each other be discerned while the headstock is rotating then the lathe is out of alignment.

While the headstock is rotating give the runner of the tailstock half a turn in either direction and again very carefully watch the points. If there is no up or down movement it can be assumed that the lathe is in alignment; should there be the least movement out of line the lathe will need adjustment.

As a general rule the adjustment of a damaged lathe is quite beyond the scope of the average watch repairer. The lathe should be returned to the maker if at all possible, failing this a machine toolmaker should be asked to re-adjust it. A good place for this kind of work to be done is the tool shop of a factory, where will be found special machines for similar work and above all testing and measuring instruments which are necessary to ensure a perfect job.

Regular inspection, cleaning and oiling will give a lathe an almost indefinite life. The headstock should be dismantled at least once in 12 months and for this the owner is advised to consult the makers' instructions where they exist, or to seek assistance from someone with

17

previous experience of the job. Having dismantled and disassembled the headstock, wash out every part thoroughly with benzine or petrol. Take particular care to dry all the parts, especially the inside of the casting. Thoroughly clean all oil cups, oil holes and oil ducts with a pointed piece of pegwood, with as much care and thoroughness as one would peg out a pivot hole.

If the bearings show signs of wear it is not advisable to attempt to repolish or to bed in the bearings oneself. If the wear is serious, return the headstock or the entire lathe to the maker or to a toolmaker. When the parts have been well cleaned and thoroughly well dried, reassemble and make sure the spindle has no end play, but is at the same time perfectly free. *This is the most important point in the assembly of a lathe.* Cone bearings prevent side play, the adjustment to take up the end play will take up the wear if any exists.

When the headstock has been assembled and runs perfectly freely in a dry state, apply oil to the oil ducts, make the headstock rotate and apply more oil until all the bearings are well served and a reserve of oil remains in the oil ducts or cups, if they are fitted. After this make it a habit to apply oil to the ducts at least once a month. A good plan is to decide a certain date when this should be done, either the first or last day of the month ; it is then less likely to be overlooked and there should be no doubt about the work having been done. But in all cases a little too much oil is better than too little. A lathe should never be run in a dry state. Where a special type of oil is specified to be used by the maker, use the maker's recommendation since oils, as every watchmaker knows, can be vastly different in effects although very much alike in appearance.

The advice to clean the lathe once in each 12 months and to lubricate it freshly once in each month applies to the lathe of the average watch repairer who would use the tool intermittently and at times after fairly long intervals. Of course it is assumed that the user keeps the lathe carefully put away in its case or keep it covered up (Fig. 2) and avoids leaving it where it can accumulate dust and particularly grit.

For a lathe which is used for quantity production or one which is used regularly, more frequent cleaning and certainly more frequent oiling is advisable. For a lathe used all day it should be the drill to oil it thoroughly every morning before starting work.

A good lathe carefully tended, almost cherished, will be found to be the watch and clock repairer's best friend. It will do fine work if it is looked after. It will do no work at all if it is damaged or neglected.

Chapter 5

ACCESSORIES

Chucks

Split ; Wax ; Box ; Step ; Ring Step ; Universal ; Brass Split ; Lantern ; Wheel ; Button ; Wood Screw ; Wood Turning ; Emery Wheel ; Circular Saw ; Carrier ; Balance ; Jacob's Drill.

Split Chuck

The word chuck has become peculiar to watchmakers ; to the engineer it is known as collet but to watchmakers it is just plain chuck, split chuck or wire chuck, etc. Of all the accessories to the lathe there is little doubt that the split chuck Fig. 14 is the most useful and certainly the most important, but for all this it is the most abused.

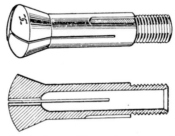

Fig. 14.—*Split chuck. Lower illustration shows chuck in section.*

The reason for this is that it is the one accessory which is in practically daily use and is among the least expensive to replace. To obtain the best results split chucks should be taken care of ; not thrown into a box with other odds and ends but kept either in a box provided with a tray and a hole for each chuck. Split chucks allowed to be maltreated become bruised and the prongs forming the chuck do not close evenly, with the result that they do not draw in an equal amount to each prong. A damaged chuck will not grip with an even pressure all round the circumference therefore preventing the work from running true.

Another very important point is cleanliness. A very small particle of dirt in the bore of the chuck, on the cone seating or between the prongs (the slits) can cause the chuck to run out of true. It is advisable to take the greatest care of split chucks, as much as if they were the most expensive part of the equipment. Crawford's, formerly the principal UK manufacturer of watchmakers' split chucks, ceased production some five years ago and now concentrate on industrial applications. Overleaf is a chart issued by Crawford's showing the different characteristics of many watchmakers' chucks.

19

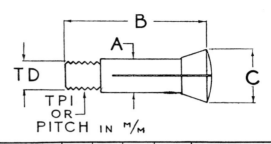

TD

TPI
OR
PITCH in ᴹ/ᴍ

Machine & Maker's Reference	A mm.	B mm.	C mm.	Dia. T.D. ins.	THREAD CAPACITY		
					Pitch T.P.I	Right Thro'	Part Thro'
Accro	6	30	10·7	0·199	·700 mm.	30	50
Adams Geo., 2¼ in. ...	8	34·5	13·2	0·268	·625 mm.	43	70
Bergeon	8	34·5	13·2	0·270	40 T.P.I.	43	70
Boley, 6½ mm. ...	6½	30	11·0	0·213	·625 mm.	35	52
Boley, 8 mm. ...	8	32	12·2	0·268	·625 mm.	43	70
Boley Leinen ...	8	34	12·8	0·268	40 T.P.I	43	70
Boydon	10	44·5	14·8	0·389	1·000 mm.	69	86
B.T.M.	8	32	12·2	0·268	·625 mm.	43	70
C.L.H., 8 mm. ...	8	34	12·5	0·275	·625 mm.	43	70
Coronet Diamond + Ruby	8	32	12·2	0·268	·625 mm.	43	70
Coronet Jewel ...	8	32	12·2	0·268	·625 mm.	43	70
Cowells, 8 mm. ...	8	34	12·5	0·275	·625 mm.	43	70
Craftsman, 6 mm. ...	6	30	10·7	0·199	·700 mm.	30	50
Derbyshire, 50 mm. ...	8	34	12·8	0·268	40 T.I.	43	70
Derbyshire	10	41·5	14·0	0·392	1·000 mm. BUTT.	59	90
E.H.J.	8	32	12·2	0·268	·625 mm.	43	70
Hinchcliffe, 8 mm. ...	8	34·5	13·2	0·270	40 T.P.I	43	70
I.M.E. 6 mm. ...	6	30	10·7	0·199	·700 mm.	30	50
I.M.E.	8	34	12·5	0·275	·625 mm.	43	70
I.M.E. Model 100 ...	10	42	14·5	0·354	1·000 mm.	63	80
Lane Cove (Lanco) ...	6	30	10·7	0·199	·700 mm.	30	50
Lane Cove (Lanco) ...	8	34	12·5	0·275	·625 mm.	43	70
Lorch, 6 mm.... ...	6	30	10·7	0·199	·700 mm.	30	50
Lorch, 8 mm.... ...	8	34	12·5	0·275	·625 mm.	43	70
Marshall Peerless ...	·312	34	12·6	0·268	·625 mm.	42	68
Nordan	8	34	12·5	0·275	·625 mm.	43	70
Pultra, C.S.1	6	30	10·7	0·199	·700 mm.	30	50
Pultra, C.1 and C.E.1	8	32	12·2	0·268	·625 mm.	43	70
Pultra, C.5 and C.F.1	10	44·5	14·8	0·389	1·000 mm.	69	86
Pultra, No. 10 ...	8	32	12·2	0·268	·625 mm.	43	70
Reliance	8	34	12·5	0·275	·625 mm.	43	70
Simplex	6	30	10·7	0·199	·700 mm.	30	50
Star	8	34	12·5	0·275	·625 mm.	43	70
Swan, 3 in.	8	34	12·5	0·275	·625 mm.	43	70
Taylor, 6 mm. ...	6	30	10·7	0·199	·700 mm.	30	50
Taylor, 8 mm. ...	8	34	12·5	0·275	·625 mm.	43	70
T.C.M.	6½	30	10·8	0·212	40 T.P.I	35	52
Webster-Whitcomb	8	32	12·2	0·268	·625 mm.	43	70
Wolf Jahn, 6 mm. ...	6	30	10·7	0·199	·700 mm.	30	50
Wolf Jahn, 6½ mm. ...	6½	30	10·8	0·212	40 T.P.I	35	52
Wolf Jahn, 8 mm. ...	8	34·5	13·2	0·270	40 T.P.I	43	70

When seeking a replacement:

1. Ensure that the new split chucks are made from the highest quality steel and are correctly hardened and tempered.

2. Most 8 mm split chucks look alike but, owing to thread and other variations, are not always interchangeable. If the wrong chuck is used, although it may appear to fit the lathe, it will cause excessive damage and will probably not run true.

3. When in doubt always supply the stockist with a sample. Give the name of the maker of the machine for which the chuck is required. Quote the reference number if known.

4. When a listed chuck is needed, check the dimensions, paying particular attention to the thread.

5. Provide the particulars of the bore sizes required, making it clear whether they are in millimetres, drill sizes or fractions of an inch.

6. Bore size as specified up to maximum capacity of collet type.

7. Collets can be obtained for most sizes and types of machine upon request and receipt of the sample.

Many years ago (about 1913) the American chuck makers, Hardinge Brothers, introduced a split chuck with a flat face. The theory put forward in favour of these chucks, know as Dale chucks, was as follows:

In the two sectional views here shown, Fig. 15, the difference between the old style round-faced and the new style flat-faced chuck is readily

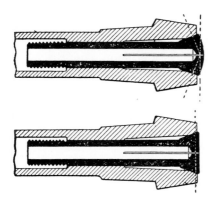

Fig. 15.—" *Dale* " *split chuck.*

apparent. The lines terminating in the centre of inside bearing of chuck which holds the work, show the direction of pressure on both inside and outside of chuck when in use and its relation to the spindle. The old style is practically a shoulder chuck up to No. 10 since all, or most of the bearing is outside of the spindle, and the truth of the chuck is dependent upon the strength of each section ; the weakest of the three will spring most. In most designs and all chucks of small diameters, each section springs easily. With the flat face the bearing is under the head and the pressure direct, as it should be.

In spite of this opinion the round face chuck has survived and appears to be satisfactory.

The range of chucks is decided upon by the lathe manufacturers and they start at No. 2 (0·28 mm.) to No. 70 (7 mm.) rising in increments of 0·1 mm. If required, a full range could number 69 chucks. More economical ranges are available, but it is always advisable to possess as full a range as possible.

To use the Split Chuck

When selecting a split chuck find one that fits the material as closely as possible. Do not force the prongs open by trying to use a chuck which is too small, the work should just fit into the chuck. On the other hand do not use a chuck which is too large, requiring drawing in to the full extent to grip the work. The objection to these two points is illustrated in Figs. 16 and 17. If the chuck is too small the

Fig. 16.—*Hole in chuck too small.*

Fig. 17.—*Hole in chuck too large.*

work is gripped at the back of the bore and an even parallel grip cannot be obtained. If the chuck is too large ; the work is gripped at the front part of the bore only.

In both these instances the work will " give ", maybe very slightly, but sufficient for the resulting work to be out of true. A correctly selected chuck needs only a slight tightening of the draw-in tube to grip the work ; not wrenched and screwed up as tightly as possible. A useful table of chuck sizes and their equivalents is given here.

CHUCK SIZES AND THEIR EQUIVALENTS

Chuck No.	mm.	Inches (approx.)	Fraction of inch	Wire gauge	Chuck No.	mm.	Inches (approx.)	Fraction of inch	Wire gauge
2	0·2	0·008			14	1·4	0·0551		
		0·01					0·059		
		0·0118					0·0595		53
		0·0135		80			0·0625	1/16th	
		0·0139			16	1·6	0·0629		
		0·0145		79			0·0635		52
		0·0156	1/64th				0·0669		
4	0·4	0·0157					0·067		51
		0·016		78			0·07		50
		0·0178			18	1·8	0·0709		
		0·018		77			0·073		49
		0·0197					0·0748		
		0·02		76			0·076		48
		0·021		75			0·0781	5/64th	
		0·0216					0·0785		47
		0·0225		74	20	2	0·0787		
6	0·6	0·0236					0·081		46
		0·024		73			0·082		45
		0·025		72			0·0826		
		0·0257					0·086		44
		0·026		71	22	2·2	0·0866		
		0·027					0·089		43
		0·028		70			0·0905		
		0·0293		69			0·0935		42
		0·0295					0·0937	3/32nd	
		0·031		68	24	2·4	0·0945		
		0·0313	1/32nd				0·096		41
8	0·8	0·0315					0·098		40
		0·032		67			0·0984		
		0·033		66			0·0995		39
		0·0335					0·1015		38
		0·035		65	26	2·6	0·1024		
		0·0354					0·104		37
		0·036		64			0·1063		
		0·037		63			0·1065		36
		0·0374					0·1093	7/64th	
		0·038		62			0·11		35
		0·039		61	28	2·8	0·1102		
10	1	0·0394					0·111		34
		0·04		60			0·113		33
		0·041		59			0·1142		
		0·0414					0·116		32
		0·042		58	30	3	0·1181		
		0·043		57			0·12		31
		0·0433					0·122		
		0·0465		56			0·125	1/8th	
		0·0469	3/64th		32	3·2	0·126		
12	1·2	0·0472					0·1285		30
		0·0512					0·1299		
		0·052		55	34	3·4	0·1338		
		0·055		54			0·136		29

Chuck No.	mm.	Inches (approx.)	Fraction of inch	Wire gauge	Chuck No.	mm.	Inches (approx.)	Fraction of inch	Wire gauge
34		0·1378			50		0·201		7
		0·1405		28			0·2031	13/64th	
		0·1406	9/64th				0·204		6
36	3·6	0·1417			52	5·2	0·2047		
		0·144		27			0·2055		5
		0·1456					0·2087		
		0·147		26			0·209		4
		0·1495		25	54	5·4	0·2126		
38	3·8	0·1496					0·213		3
		0·152		24			0·2165		
		0·1535					0·2189	7/32nd	
		0·154		23	56	5·6	0·2205		
		0·1562	5/32nd				0·221		2
		0·157		22			0·2244		
40	4	0·1575					0·228		1
		0·159		21	58	5·8	0·2283		
		0·16		20			0·2323		
		0·1614					0·234		A
42	4·2	0·1654					0·2344	15/64th	
		0·166		19	60	6	0·2362		
		0·1693					0·238		B
		0·1695		18			0·2401		
		0·1719	11/64th				0·242		C
		0·173		17	62	6·2	0·2441		
44	4·4	0·1732					0·246		D
		0·177		16			0·248		
		0·1772					0·25	1/4	E
		0·18			64	6·4	0·252		
46	4·6	0·1811					0·2559		
		0·182		14			0·257		F
		0·185		13	66	6·6	0·2598		
		0·1875	3/16th				0·261		G
48	4·8	0·189		12			0·2638		
		0·191					0·2656	17/64th	
		0·1929					0·266		H
		0·1935		10	68	6·8	0·2677		
		0·196					0·2716		
50	5	0·1969		9			0·272		I
		0·199		8	70	7	0·2756		
		0·2008							

Wax Chucks

Wax chucks, made of brass, are in various sizes (Fig. 18). They are known in America as wax brasses. Their use is to enable the work to be cemented on to the chuck when it is not possible or convenient to hold the work in any other way. The method of use is first to secure the chuck in the headstock of the lathe. Then apply heat to the end or working surface of the chuck with a spirit lamp or other form of smokeless heat. Apply heat until shellac can be smeared on to the surface : the object is to apply a thin film of shellac. If a thick layer is applied the possibility of the work running true in the flat is more remote. Having made the shellac flow freely present the work to the chuck and apply more heat and while doing so press the work hard on to the chuck with the back of a watch brush or something similar. If the work is to run true and centrally hold a blunt pointed piece of pegwood in the hole or recess of the work, resting the pegwood on the T-rest and then make the work rotate fairly quickly holding thus until the shellac sets. The work will run perfectly true in the flat and round. A particular piece of work using the wax chuck and also the use of the wax chuck when turning a balance staff, etc. is described on pages 74 and 87.

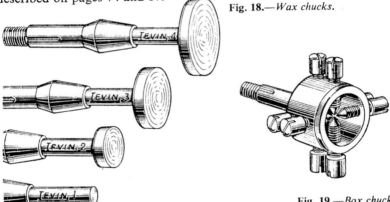

Fig. 18.—*Wax chucks.*

Fig. 19.—*Box chuck.*

Box Chuck

The box chuck (Fig. 19) is useful when turning a piece too large to fit up in a split chuck. The method is first to unscrew all eight screws until the ends of the screws are just flush with the inside of the chuck. Then screw the eight screws inwards an equal number of turns until the screws touch the work. Screw the screws up tightly an equal amount until the work is secure. Fit the chuck up in the headstock and make secure. Cause the work to rotate slowly and bring the T-rest up and test the work for truth. Hold the cutter up to the work and if the work is running true a full cut can be made but if the work is not true the cutter will touch the work for part of its diameter only. Try for truth at a point near to the chuck and also at the furthest point from the chuck. If the work is out of true near to the chuck, two sets of screws must be adjusted to make the work run true. For instance, as the cutter touches the work, hold the headstock fast and slightly draw the pair of screws furthest from the cutter and run the opposite pair in to tighten the work.

To make the work run true it may be necessary to adjust two pairs of screws at a time, because the screws may not come immediately opposite the cutter and it is desirable to move the work bodily away from the cutter. Continue thus until the work runs true or nearly so. Now test the other end for truth. If it is found to be out, adjust the screws at the back of the chuck only. For instance should the cutter touch the work in one place only hold the headstock at this point and withdraw the screw on the side nearest to the cutter and run the opposite screw in to tighten the work. It will be observed that the order of screw adjustment has been reversed ; a little thought and the method of adjustment will be found quite simple.

Step Chuck

The step chuck is useful to hold work of a circular disc nature, such as a wheel or barrel (Fig. 20). The chucks are made with steps and the diameter of one step to the next varies by an increase of 2 mm. Each chuck has nine steps so that a set of five chucks provides a good range of diameters, from 5·4 mm. to 23 mm. The care in selecting the correct chuck for the work is important, but not as vital as that employed when selecting a split chuck. The same care should be taken of these chucks as with the split chucks. They are susceptible to the same maltreatment and with similar results if so treated.

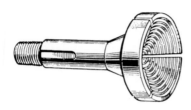

Fig. 20.—*Step chuck.*

Step Chuck Chart

Chuck No.	1	2	3	4	5
	5·4	5·8	6·2	6·6	7·0
	7·4	7·8	8·2	8·6	9·0
Step	9·4	9·8	10·2	10·6	11·0
diameters	11·4	11·8	12·2	12·6	13·0
in	13·4	13·8	14·2	14·6	15·0
mm.	15·4	15·8	16·2	16·6	17·0
	17·4	17·8	18·2	18·6	19·0
	19·4	19·8	20·2	20·6	21·0
	21·4	21·8	22·2	22·6	23·0

Ring Step Chuck

The ring step chuck is similar to the step chuck but reversed, the

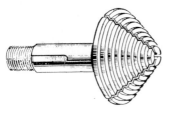

Fig. 21.—*Ring step chuck.*

steps being on the outside and when drawn in to the headstock the prongs of the chuck spread outwards (Fig. 21). It is useful for holding work of a ring nature, e.g. a watch barrel from the open end or a bezel, etc. As with the step chuck, ring step chucks are made in a range of five sizes.

Universal Chuck

A universal chuck is a general purpose chuck which can be used to grip work internally, such as a disc. By reversing the jaws it becomes a ring step chuck and can be used to grip rings, bezels and the like. Two systems are available, one (Fig. 22) where a key is used to operate the jaws, and the other (Fig. 23) where a knurled ring rotating edge is used for the same purpose. When the jaws are set as a ring step chuck, large diameter rod work can be gripped in the centre.

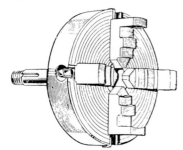

Fig. 22.—*Universal chuck, with key.*

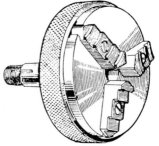

Fig. 23.—*Universal chuck, with knurled ring.*

Brass Split Chucks

Brass split chucks are sometimes referred to as jewel chucks (Fig. 24). These are small brass chucks to be inserted into a steel split chuck.

Fig. 24.—*Brass split chucks.*

They are made in sets of 20 with 5 mm. diameter body to fit a No. 50 split chuck and with a hole or bore ranging from 0·20 mm. to 0·32 mm. They are useful for holding small parts while turning, where the portion to be gripped is delicate, such as the thread of a jewel setting screw.

27

Lantern Chucks

There are two types of lantern chuck : one large, made of bronze (Fig. 25) supplied in sets of three, and the other, much smaller and made of steel (Fig. 26), also supplied in sets of three. The large lantern chuck is supplied with a steel chuck which fits into the headstock and the bronze lantern portion screws on to it. They are

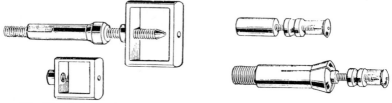

Fig. 25.—*Lantern chucks, bronze.* Fig. 26.—*Lantern chucks, steel.*

useful to hold work when it is necessary to work upon one end, such as the end of a screw. The small steel lantern chucks fit into a split chuck held in the headstock and they are useful for holding a seconds hand while turning the pipe and also while working on the ends of small screws, etc.

Wheel Chuck

Wheel chucks made for holding unmounted wheels, etc. are shown in Fig. 27. The locking nut contacts a cone-shaped piece, which centres the wheel. It can be used to hold a wheel in the headstock while cutting teeth and many other purposes.

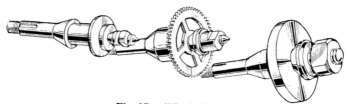

Fig. 27.—*Wheel chucks.*

Button or Crown Chuck

A button or crown chuck is a chuck with a step made to take keyless buttons (Fig. 28). The diameters of the bores range from 5 to 14 mm. available in sets of 10. Another chuck for the same purpose is the universal crown chuck (Fig. 29). The chuck is supplied with four screw caps of varying depths and hole apertures to take keyless buttons of various sizes. Both these systems of crown chucks are useful to hold the button while working upon the pipe or hollowing out to make it fit a pendant.

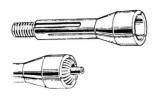

Fig. 28.—*Button or Crown chuck,*
reversed.

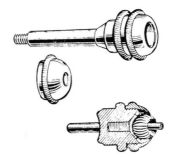

Fig. 29.—*Button or Crown chuck, with screw cap.*

Wood Screw Chuck

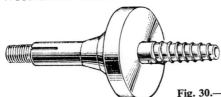

The wood screw chuck is fitted with a wood screw (Fig. 30), to take wood, while turning to make laps, etc.

Fig. 30.—*Wood screw chuck.*

Wood Turning Chuck

A three point wood turning chuck (Fig. 31) is made for wood turning, not only does this chuck support the work but also causes it to rotate while working, it is necessary for the work to be supported at the tailstock end, usually by a female centre.

Fig. 31.—*Wood turning chuck.*

Emery Wheel Chuck

The emery wheel chuck is fitted with an emery wheel (Fig. 32) and is used for grinding or whetting a cutter, and is useful for other purposes.

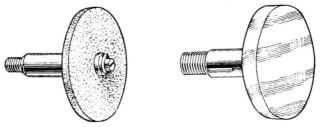

Fig. 32.—*Emery wheel chucks.*

Circular Saw Chuck

The circular saw chuck is a chuck fitted with a circular saw (Fig. 33) which is useful for cutting metal, when used in conjunction with a saw table as Fig. 45.

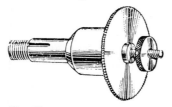 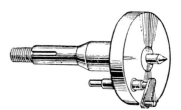

Fig. 33.—*Circular saw chuck.*　　　　Fig. 34.—*Carrier chuck.*

Carrier Chuck

The carrier chuck is supplied with male and female centres (Fig. 34) for dead centre turning and when using the Jacot drum fit-up and also turning between centres. The illustration shows a male centre.

Balance Wheel Chuck

The balance chuck is designed to hold balances (Fig. 35) and is provided with three plates for different size balances and is used to hold the balance while polishing the pivots. This chuck serves, up to a point, the purpose of a Jacot tool ; but of the two, the Jacot tool is to be preferred to the balance chuck, but no doubt this chuck has its uses.

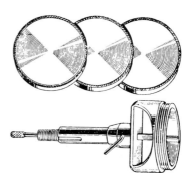

Fig. 35.—*Balance chuck.*

Drill Chuck, Jacobs

A Jacobs chuck for drills is designed for use in the headstock (Fig. 36). The jaws are opened and closed by means of a geared key so that the drill can be gripped tightly without injury to the chuck.

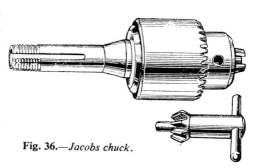

Fig. 36.—*Jacobs chuck.*

When fitting up all forms of chucks into the headstock, make sure the "feather" or key-way is in position correctly before tightening up. It is also important to keep the key-way clean.

Turning Arbors

Turning arbors are tapered steel arbors (Fig. 37), used for turning such pieces as collets, bushes, etc. Used in the lathe between centres with the carrier chuck (Fig. 34).

Fig. 37.—*Turning arbors.*

RESTS

T-rests ; Roller rests ; Slide rest ; Saw plate.

Together with the split chuck the T-rest (Fig. 38) is no doubt the most useful of all accessories, in fact, it is essential. The T-rest should be

used only as a support for the tool. It should not be used as a steadying point for the file, burnisher or emery buff—a roller rest is better for this purpose. If when rounding up the head of a screw the T-rest is used to support the file, nicks are cut into the rest and this is objectionable, because when turning, the graver or cutting tool should be able to slide up and down along the top edge of the rest without hindrance.

Fig. 38.—*T-rest.*

The edge of the T-rest upon which the tool rests should be smooth and not dead hard. If it is dead hard the tool is inclined to slip ; since two hard surfaces in direct contact is not good when one, the cutter, is held by hand. The edge should be let down to a fairly low temper, beyond the blue, so that when the cutter is held down firmly on to the rest it is inclined to grip it. If the edge of the rest does become marked, re-dress it with a very fine file; file lengthways of the rest, and thus keep the edge even and avoid serrations the file would make if used at right angles to the top edge. T-rests are usually tempered to a fairly low temper which allows them to be filed and also facilitates the grip.

Tip-over T-rest

The tip-over T-rest (Fig. 39) is a variant of the T-rest. Without removing the rest, and thus disturbing its setting, the rest can be swung back out of the way while measurements or comparisons are made, as, for instance, when turning a balance staff, in making a measurement, or holding the old staff against the new one for comparative measurements. Instead of unscrewing the T-rest it is just lifted up and over out of the way. Setting the T-rest at the correct position takes time and the correct position is an important part of turning.

Fig. 39.—*Tip-over T-rest.*

Fig. 40.—*Roller rest, single.*

Roller Rest

A roller rest is a useful accessory when using the file, burnisher or emery buff or any other appliance that would cut or injure the top surface edge of the T-rest (Fig. 40). Quite apart from saving the T-rest the roller is more efficient for its purpose.

Double Roller Rest

The double roller rest (Fig. 41) is used to facilitate filing flat surfaces, in fact, if correctly used, it is not possible to file other than dead flat. The work to be filed is held in the lathe and the headstock locked by means of the index plate. The double roller is adjusted in height so that if the file is laid across touching both rollers and then is lowered so that the end of the file touches the work and is in turn lowered again, the amount the work is to be filed is equal to the amount the rest is lowered the second time. If the file is now operated until both rollers contact the file, the surface filed must be dead flat.

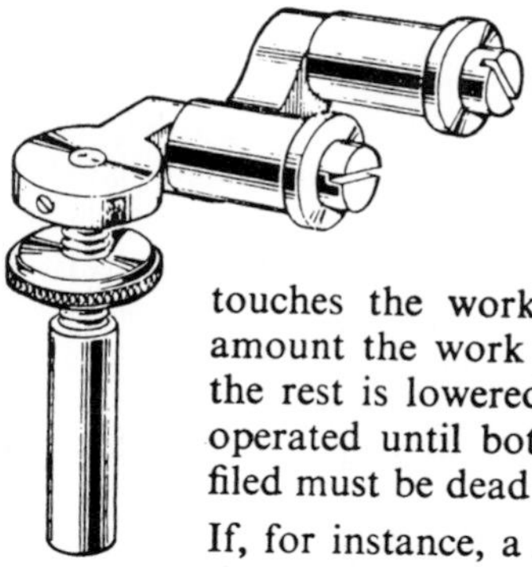

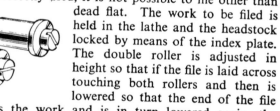

Fig. 41. *Double roller rest.*

If, for instance, a square is to be filed on a round rod, the first flat is filed as described, the headstock is made to rotate a quarter of a turn and locked, another flat is filed and so on until four flats have been filed. Examine the square, without removing from the headstock, to see that a full square has been obtained. The corners may be rounded, in which case the rollers are lowered a little and the filing is proceeded with as before. Continue thus until the correct sized square is obtained. A square filed in this manner must be perfectly square and the flats must be flat as the device will not allow otherwise. See page 81.

Slide Rest

There are various designs of slide rests : 2 slide and 3 slide. Fig. 42 is a 2 slide rest by Derbyshire. All are made to serve the same purpose, i.e. to hold the cutter and make it traverse automatically either longitudinally or laterally. There are many uses to which the

Fig. 42.—*Slide rest and cutting tools, by Derbyshire.*

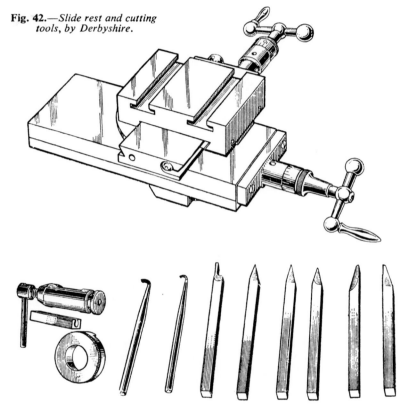

slide rest can be put ; to face a plate, cut recesses, turn an arbor, etc. The illustration (Fig. 43) is a 3 slide rest, made by Derbyshire. In addition to the usual longitudinal and lateral movement another slide moving laterally is provided. It is operated by a knurled nut and enables work of great accuracy to be done. Fig. 44 is a 3 slide rest by Paulson.

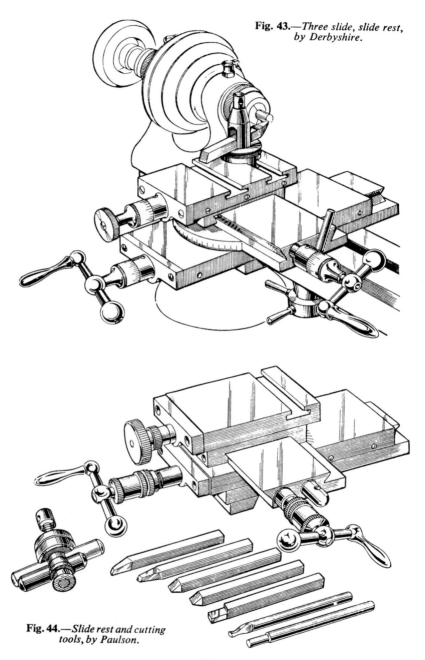

Fig. 43.—*Three slide, slide rest, by Derbyshire.*

Fig. 44.—*Slide rest and cutting tools, by Paulson.*

Saw Table

The saw table (Fig. 45) is used in the T-rest holder. This table is brought up to the circular saw, which is held in the headstock. The

Fig. 45.—*Saw table.*

slot in the table must be central and parallel to the saw, otherwise the saw will not be free to rotate. The height of the table depends upon the thickness of the material to be cut and the work should be at such a height with relation to the saw that the saw cuts through the centre of the thickness of the work. Fig. 46 shows an application of a saw table in use with a double circular saw. Generally speaking fit-ups of this description are only justifiable when there are a number of the same jobs to do, i.e. production work.

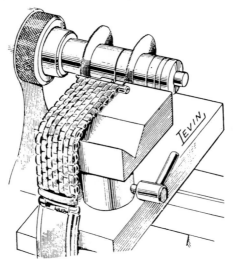

Fig. 46.—*Saw table for double circular saw.*

TAIL STOCK ACCESSORIES

Runners ; Drill stocks ; Rose cutters ; Sinkers and Taps ;
Jacot drum ; Pivoting attachment ; Lapping attachment.

Runners

Runners are made for all purposes (Fig. 47).

(16) Runner for turning small pivots : one end dotted on the extreme edge and the dot marks are used as centres, so as to expose as much as possible the work being turned. The other end is for filing a centre.

(17) For turning pinions : one end has pivot guard.

(18) For turning cylinders : one end has star with 6 centre marks.

(19) Eccentric with pivot guard : one end triangular with 2 pivot guards and one centre mark.

(20) Two concentric pivot guards.

(21) Two eccentric pivot guards.

(22) Concentric point and centre guard.

(23) Concentric point and centre for general watch work.

(24) Eccentric point and eccentric pivot guard.

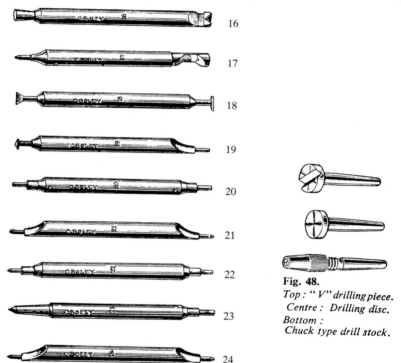

Fig. 47.—*Tailstock runners.*

Fig. 48.
Top : " *V*" *drilling piece.*
 Centre : Drilling disc.
Bottom :
 Chuck type drill stock.

Drill Stocks

There are various forms of drill stock. The one illustrated in Fig. 48 made by G. Boley, is the hollow runner type. The drill fits into the chuck type drill stock (bottom) a rod running through the runner to eject the stock. The flat drill disc (centre) is used in the hollow runner when the drill is fitted into the headstock and the work held between them. The V-shaped piece (top) fits into the hollow runner and the drill into the headstock and the round rod to be drilled laterally is held centrally in the V-shaped notch.

Rose Cutters

Rose cutters are useful for cutting recesses and making pieces where a pipe or pivot shaped piece is required Fig. 49. They can be used in the tail stock with the work made to rotate in the headstock, or, held in a split chuck in the headstock and the work held stationary.

Fig. 49.—*Rose cutters.*

Sinking Tools

Sinking tools are for cutting a recess or a part-through hole type of cut. Those shown in Fig. 50 can be fitted into the tail stock runner and the work made to rotate in the headstock, or used in the same manner as the rose cutters.

Fig. 50.—*Sinking tools.*

Taps

Taps are provided for use in the lathe. They are fitted into the tailstock runner and the work in the headstock. When in use the work is made to rotate considerably slower than when drilling. It is better to make the headstock rotate by hand.

Jacot Drum

The Jacot drum, as its name implies, is a form of Jacot tool (Fig. 51).

It is not customary to use this fit-up for polishing watch pivots. The Jacot tool to polish watch pivots is described under dead centre lathes (page 62). The lathe Jacot drum is for clock pivots. The drum fits into the fitting as in Fig. 52. The bed selected is made central by means of the pump centre and the drum, which is also used to hold the drilling attachment, is made secure ready for use.

Fig. 51.—*Jacot drum.*

Fig. 52.—*Self-centring drilling attachment.*

Pivoting Attachment

The pivoting attachment consists of the drilling attachment (Fig. 52), the centring plate having a series of holes with the front surface chamfered accurately. If a hole is selected the exact size of the drill to be used, the hole made central with the pump centre, made secure and the pump centre replaced by the drill stock, then a hole can be drilled in the centre of a rod, such as an arbor. Larger plates (Fig. 53) are also supplied which are used in the same apparatus.

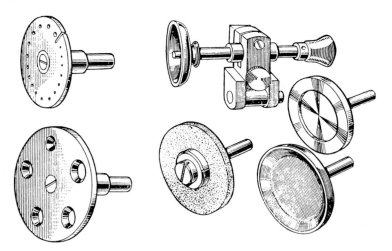

53.—Self-centring drilling plates.

Fig. 54.—*Lapping attachment to fit on to the tailstock, by Lorch.*

Lapping Attachment

There are one or two methods of fixing a lapping attachment. This system by Lorch, (Fig. 54), is where it is either fitted on to the runner of the tailstock or, with the addition of a fitting, clamped into the bush of the T-rest holder. This polishing equipment has many uses including polishing pivots, heads of screws and similar work, also for snailing work, such as flat keyless wheels, etc. Three laps are provided ; the hollow lap, where the edge only is used, is made of bell

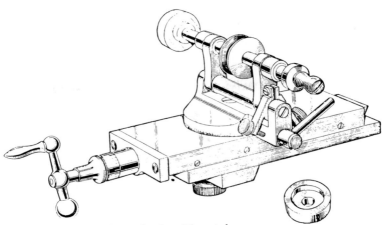

Fig. 55.—*Lapping attachment fitted to slide rest, by Derbyshire.*

metal ; another is of iron and the last of boxwood. Another and more elaborate polishing accessory (Fig. 55) by Derbyshire, is fitted to the slide rest and is used for similar purposes as the more simple apparatus just described, and in addition the tool can be set at an angle for polishing a bevel, etc. Another system (Fig. 56), fitted to the slide rest and is made by Paulson and is primarily intended for polishing pivots. Boxwood and bell-metal laps are provided.

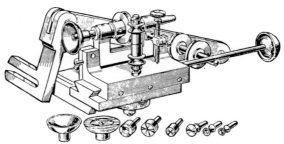

Fig. 56.—*Lapping attachment fitted to slide rest, by Paulson.*

OTHER ACCESSORIES

Mandrel ; Face Plate ; Topping Tool ; Wheel Cutting ; Screw Head Tool ; Batch-Production Equipment ; Slide Rest ; Drilling ; Motors and Other Transmission of Power ; Switch Motors ; Boring Chuck.

Mandrel

The mandrel is another name for the revolving spindle of a lathe, but watchmakers generally associate the word mandrel with the complete tool. A face plate (Fig. 57) added to the watchmakers' lathe converts the lathe into a "mandrel". There are many uses to which the mandrel can be put, from facing a plate to using it as an uprighting tool. Whether used with the T-rest or the slide rest the mandrel is an indispensable part of the watchmaker's equipment. Fig. 58 shows the face plate fitted to the head stock.

The mandrel or face plate has a spring-loaded centring rod known as the pump centre. A work piece with a true hole through it is centred about the hole by the tapered end of the pump centre.

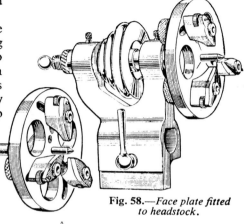

Fig. 57.—*Face plate.*

Fig. 58.—*Face plate fitted to headstock.*

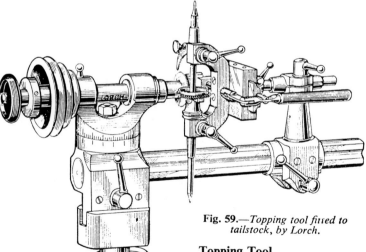

Fig. 59.—*Topping tool fitted to tailstock, by Lorch.*

Topping Tool

The topping tool is sometimes referred to as "rounding up" tool. This name also is generally associated with a complete tool, which is used

to alter the shape of wheel teeth or to reduce the diameter of a
toothed wheel by cutting each tooth space deeper. There are two or

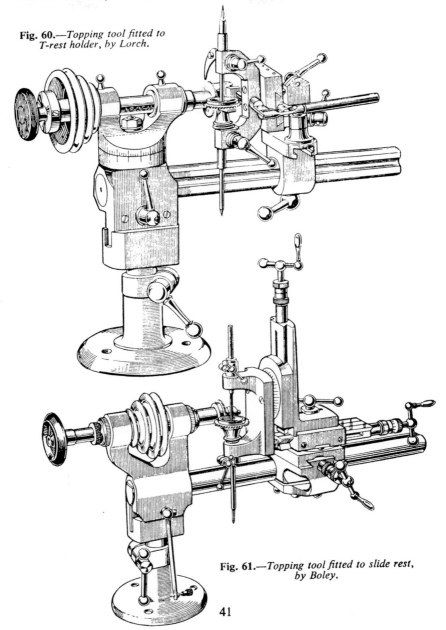

Fig. 60.—*Topping tool fitted to
T-rest holder, by Lorch.*

Fig. 61.—*Topping tool fitted to slide rest,
by Boley.*

three methods of fitting this tool to the lathe. Fig. 59 shows it fitted to the runner of the tailstock by Lorch, Fig. 60 to the T-rest clamp by Lorch, and Fig. 61 to the slide rest by Boley. The method of using it is precisely the same as when using the ordinary topping tool.

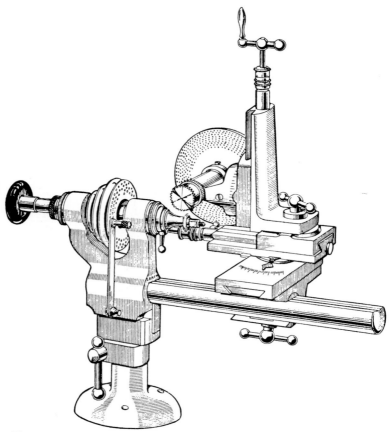

Fig. 62.—*Wheel-cutting attachment with cutter held in headstock, by Boley.*

Wheel Cutting

There are two systems of wheel-cutting accessories ; one where the wheel is held in the headstock with the count plate and the cutter in the slide rest, and the other where the cutter is attached to the headstock and the wheel and count plate to the slide rest attachment. Both are illustrated in Figs. 62-63.

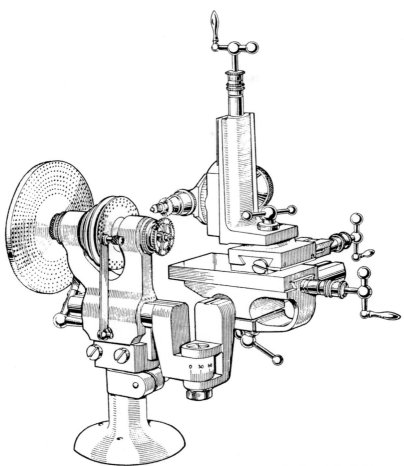

Fig. 63.—*Wheel-cutting attachment with wheel held in headstock, by Boley.*

Screw Head Tool

A useful adjunct to the lathe is the screw head tool (Fig. 164) for polishing the heads of screws, etc., dead flat.

Screw Cutting Attachment

The screw cutting attachment (Fig. 182) is made by Derbyshire and fitted to their 12 in. bed lathe. It is provided with 14 gears to cut both English and metric threads and is mounted on the top slide of the slide rest.

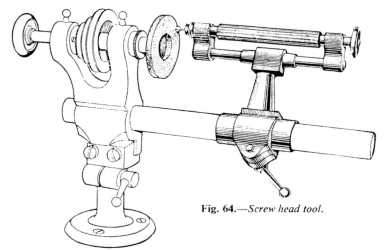

Fig. 64.—*Screw head tool.*

Batch-Production Equipment

There are several attachments to the lathe which facilitate the production of parts when production in quantity by repetition is required. These can hardly be referred to as mass production, since machines are made which are capable of producing the most complicated pieces wholly and completely automatically. When once the machine has been set it requires only to be fed with the " raw " material and one operative can tend as many as twelve machines. Where a comparatively small number of the same parts are required it would not be economical to set up and make cams, etc., for an " automatic " to do the work.

To secure chucks, in place of the usual draw in spindle, the device (Fig. 65) is useful. This system is by Derbyshire, and it is fitted to

Fig. 65.—*Automatic chuck closer, by Derbyshire.*

their Magnus 12 in. bed lathe with ball bearing headstock. The system is spring bound and the opening and closing of the chuck is almost instantaneous. Another system (Fig. 66) is by Boley. The fixing

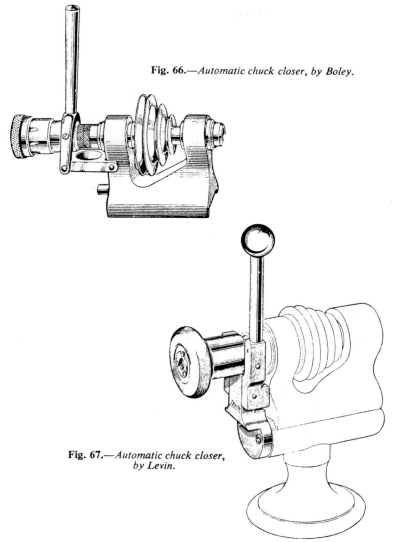

Fig. 66.—*Automatic chuck closer, by Boley.*

Fig. 67.—*Automatic chuck closer,*
by Levin.

and release of parts held in the chuck is effected by a lever while the work is in motion. Another system by Levin is illustrated in Fig. 67.

Slide Rest

A useful slide rest (Fig. 68) by Levin is provided with stops and levers to operate the slides and when once set can be worked by a semi-skilled operative.

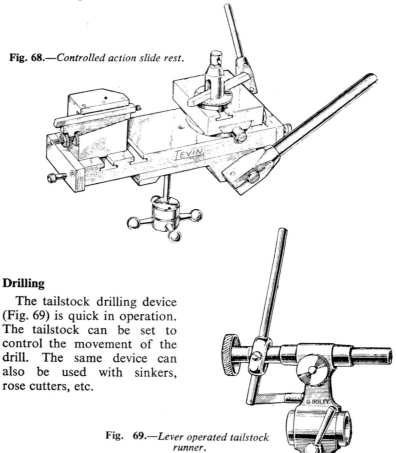

Fig. 68.—*Controlled action slide rest.*

Drilling

The tailstock drilling device (Fig. 69) is quick in operation. The tailstock can be set to control the movement of the drill. The same device can also be used with sinkers, rose cutters, etc.

Fig. 69.—*Lever operated tailstock runner.*

Motors and other Transmission of Power

Motors ; hand wheels ; foot wheels ; pulley transmission

The methods of propulsion of the watchmaker's lathe are as numerous as are the accessories to it. There is little doubt that the electric motor is to be preferred to the hand or foot methods. It may take a little practice to become familiar and confident with it, but once this initial difficulty has been overcome, other means must take second place. It is more speedy and leaves both hands free. For the average watchmaker's work a $\frac{1}{16}$th or $\frac{1}{20}$th h.p. motor is all that is required and in the majority of cases a pulley attached to the spindle of the motor with a belt running direct from this pulley on to the pulley of the lathe as in Figs. 70-71 meets most requirements. For heavier work, such as clocks, up to a $\frac{1}{4}$ h.p. motor will be necessary.

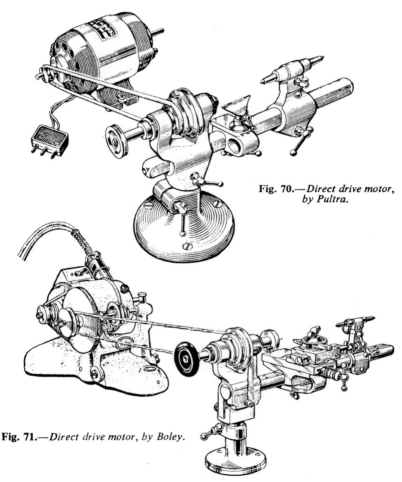

Fig. 70.—*Direct drive motor, by Pultra.*

Fig. 71.—*Direct drive motor, by Boley.*

A round leather belt joined with a staple or a plastic belt can be used for driving. The round plastic belt is noiseless in use and has no joint. The method of fitting plastic belts is as follows. Cut the belt to the

47

required length and to join, heat the blade of an old table knife or a similar piece of metal, place the knife in the vice and hold both ends to it as in Fig. 72. When the ends of the belt melt and a small ring is formed, but before this ring burns, join the ends. Make sure the ends are joined centrally.

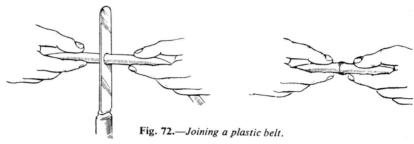

Fig. 72.—*Joining a plastic belt.*

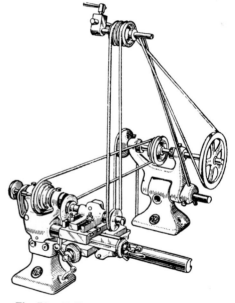

Fig. 73.—*Pulley transmission, by Bergeon.*

There are occasions when a different arrangement is necessary, as when using the polishing attachment or where a secondary drive is required. The illustrations (Figs. 73-74-75) speak for themselves. There are two methods of starting and stopping the motor, one by a hand switch and the other by a variable speed foot switch, and of the two the latter is to be preferred (Fig. 76). The drawback to the foot switch is that if the motor is to be kept running for any length of time, say for more than ten minutes, the foot control absorbing the current not required heats up. On the other hand, the average watch repairer stops and starts every few minutes to observe the progress of his

48

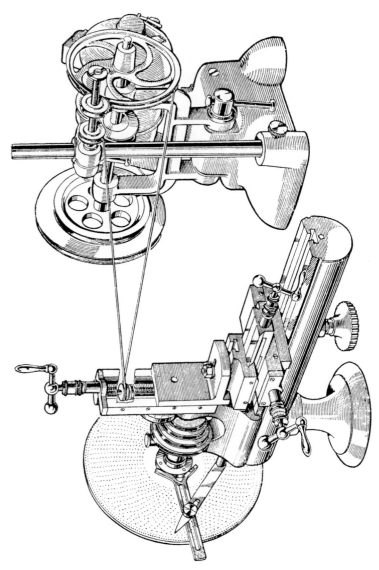

Fig. 74.—*Pulley transmission, by Paulson.*

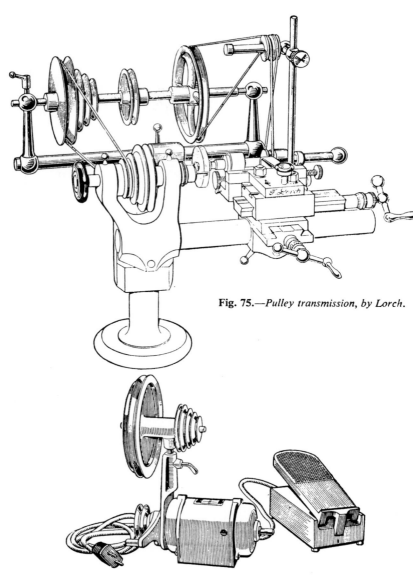

Fig. 75.—*Pulley transmission, by Lorch.*

Fig. 76.—*Foot motor switch, by Favorite.*

turning. The advantage of the foot switch is that both hands are free, the right hand, say, operating the cutting, and the left hand at rest. For short runs of the motor with the hand switch one is rather inclined to hold one hand on the switch all the time, a tiring position.

There are several switch motors on the market (Figs. 77-78-79). Where electric power is not available a hand wheel or foot wheel can be used. Figs. 80-85 show a variety of hand and foot wheels.

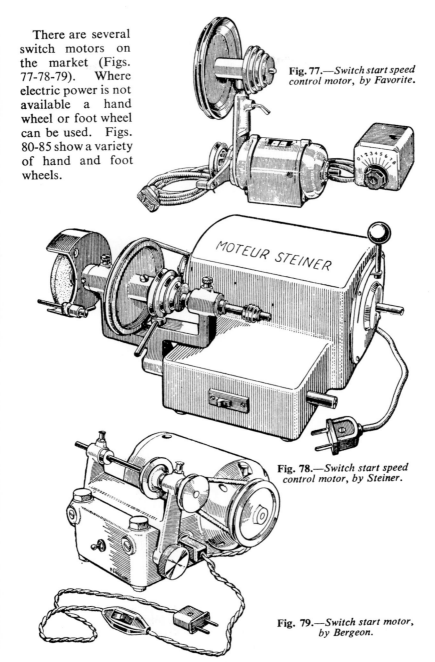

Fig. 77.—*Switch start speed control motor, by Favorite.*

Fig. 78.—*Switch start speed control motor, by Steiner.*

Fig. 79.—*Switch start motor, by Bergeon.*

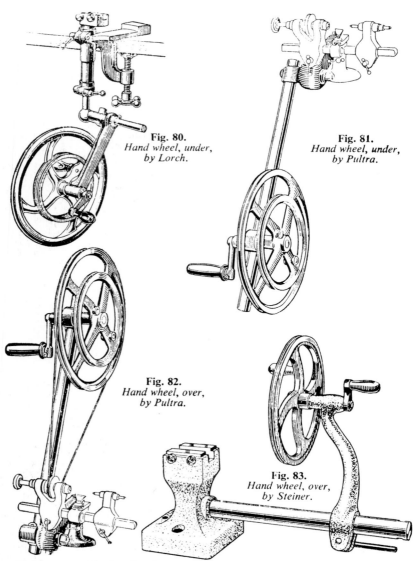

Fig. 80.
Hand wheel, under,
by Lorch.

Fig. 81.
Hand wheel, under,
by Pultra.

Fig. 82.
Hand wheel, over,
by Pultra.

Fig. 83.
Hand wheel, over,
by Steiner.

Pulley transmission is always interesting and an example is shown here (Fig. 86). Say the maximum speed of a motor is 1,500 revs. per minute, if you employ a pulley on the motor three times the diameter of the pulley on the lathe spindle, the speed of the last pulley will be 4,500 r.p.m. If therefore a multiple of pulleys were used far greater speed would be obtained, but there are limits to the practicability of

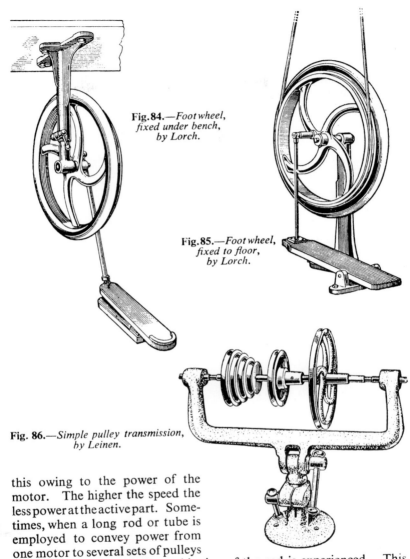

Fig. 84.—*Foot wheel, fixed under bench, by Lorch.*

Fig. 85.—*Foot wheel, fixed to floor, by Lorch.*

Fig. 86.—*Simple pulley transmission, by Leinen.*

this owing to the power of the motor. The higher the speed the less power at the active part. Sometimes, when a long rod or tube is employed to convey power from one motor to several sets of pulleys operating a series of lathes, whipping of the rod is experienced. This is often due to lack of poise of the rod—not exactly cylindrical—or, some of the pulley sets attached to the rod are not in poise. To eradicate this trouble can be difficult and a careful examination of all the component parts for poise or balance and alignment of bearings is essential.

Boring Chuck

The boring chuck is used in the tailstock (Fig. 87). The cutter is secured in the chuck by the Allen screws and it can be moved laterally by means of a micrometer screw. The purpose of this chuck is to make a cut similar to that made with a slide rest, but in one cut only, i.e. to bore. It is useful for sinking or recessing, and is of inestimable value in semi mass-production work.

Fig. 87.—*Boring chuck, by Levin.*

Lathe Eye Glass

A useful adjunct to the lathe is the fixed eye glass. As Fig. 88 shows, it can be fixed in any desired position and is convenient especially for repetition work. The model shown is made by Paulson.

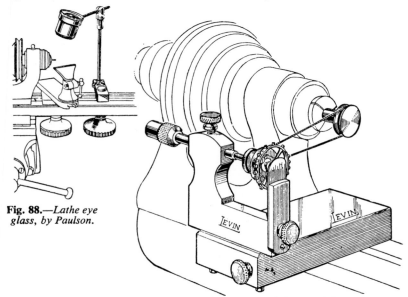

Fig. 88.—*Lathe eye glass, by Paulson.*

Fig. 89.—*Balance pivot polishing tool, by Levin.*

Balance Pivot Polishing Tool

The balance pivot polishing tool (Fig. 89) is used for polishing the ends of balance pivots and is made by Levin.

Lathe Light

The lathe light (Fig. 90) can be fixed in any convenient position and is useful for close work.   Made by Boley.

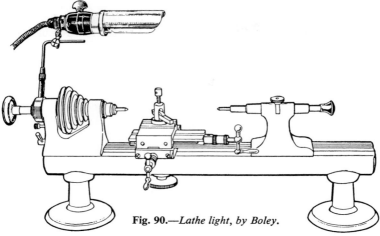

Fig. 90.—*Lathe light, by Boley.*

Utility Set

The utility set accessory (Figs. 91-92-93) by Levin can be used for a number of purposes.   Where it is required to cut, polish or grind a surface at right angles or parallel to another.   The illustrations show two purposes for which this accessory is useful.

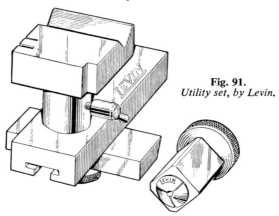

Fig. 91.
Utility set, by Levin.

The illustrations of accessories given can, because of their multiplicity, be only representative and for this reason names of the makers of some of the more complicated accessories are given. This will give an indication of the types of accessories available and in the latter part of the book, when dealing with the various makes of lathes, the addresses are given and it is suggested that enquiry be made to the maker or supplier for any further information relating to a particular accessory or requirement. Lathe manufacturers are constantly adding to their list of accessories.

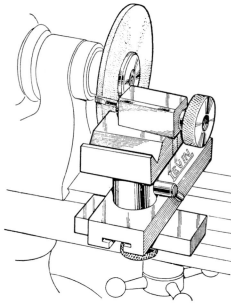

Fig. 92.
Grinding with utility set.

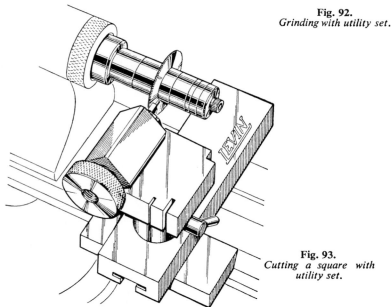

Fig. 93.
Cutting a square with utility set.

Chapter 6

DEAD CENTRE LATHES, PIVOTING AND JACOT TOOLS

The dead centre lathe is used where the work to be turned is to be
made to rotate between centres and not held in the headstock with
hollow or " live " spindle. The dead centre lathe is really the equivalent
of turns. Turns, to use a familiar term, are still in use and some of
the lathe manufacturers have arranged so that by an adaptation of their
parts, turns can be produced. As an example, Lorch supply a bed and
two tailstocks with runners and T-rest (Fig. 94). Steiner supply in

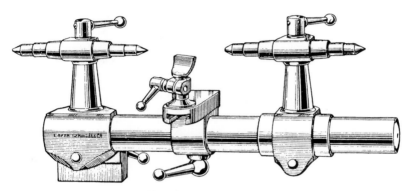

Fig. 94.—*Turns, by Lorch.*

their full combination a separate tool which consists of the bed and two
tailstocks, with a set of accessories as in Fig. 95. A feature of this

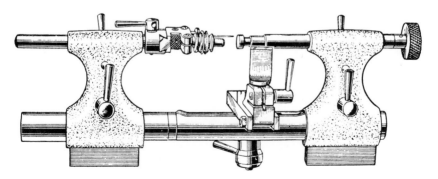

Fig. 95.—*Turns, by Steiner.*

equipment is the slide runner (Fig. 96) for centring in all directions. This is useful when using the eccentric runners or the Jacot drum in the tailstock, for pivot work.

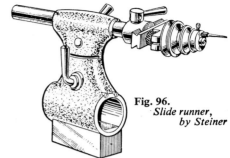

Fig. 96.
Slide runner,
by Steiner

The majority of lathes can be converted into dead centre lathes, provided the bed is suitable and two tailstocks are used.   All lathes can be used for turning between centres if a centre is secured in the headstock and the work made to rotate independently of the headstock.

There is a deal of controversy over the merits of turning between centres and of the use of the live spindle.   There can be no doubt that correct turning between centres must be true.   Turning the work complete without removing from the chuck must be true.   Turning part of the work and then removing and replacing in the chuck can be true, provided the greatest care is exercised in selecting the split chuck in the first place and that the greatest care has been taken of the chucks to ensure that they open and close accurately.   For speed there can be little doubt that the split chuck is the best and, for most commercial purposes, satisfactory.   There are four methods of turning a balance staff in the lathe—(1) held in the split chuck, partly turned and then

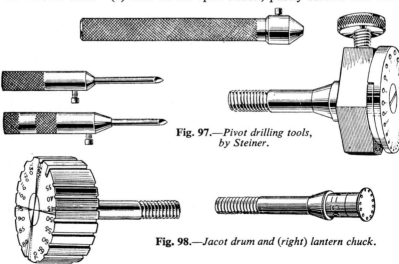

Fig. 97.—Pivot drilling tools,
by Steiner.

Fig. 98.—Jacot drum and (right) lantern chuck.

reversed, (2) held in the split chuck and completely turned with one holding, (3) turned between centres, (4) turned in the split chuck and finished in the wax chuck. These methods are fully explained on page 84.

PIVOTING

Steiner make an apparatus (Fig. 97) for drilling up an arbor to fit a new pivot. For the same tool the Jacot drum and the lantern chucks for rounding up ends of pivots (Fig. 98) are supplied. Their use is precisely the same as that of the ordinary pivoting tool (Fig. 99).

Another very useful tool for pivoting and for use as a Jacot tool is made by Lerrac (Fig. 100). The body of the tool is in bronze, designed to avoid any deformation. A screw arrangement (1) permits the correction of slight errors of alignment, horizontal or vertical, of the runner.

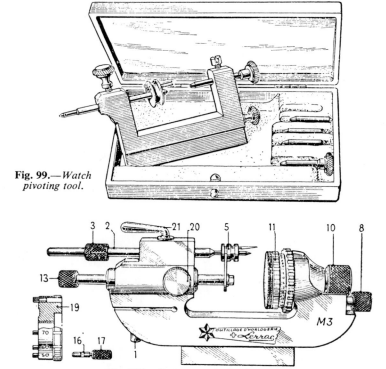

Fig. 99.—*Watch pivoting tool.*

Fig. 100.—*Lerrac watch pivoting tool.*

Made from special non-deforming steel the Jacot drum (11) makes the wear of the beds practically negligible. The beds are of sizes from 4/100 to 36/100 mm. Highly finished, they allow the polishing of the smallest pivots. A part of this drum is ground away so as to serve as a lantern for rounding the ends of pivots. Holes are drilled to suit pivots from 4/100 to 40/100 mm. This part is tempered so as to prevent it from being too brittle. Two cones are provided to take up wear of the runner, the ends of which are hardened and tempered.

For burnishing pivots. 1.—Unscrew the screw (20) and the lever (21) bring the point of the runner (2) up to the drum (11), release this from the locking spring by turning the milled head (8). Turn the drum until the required notch comes opposite the end of the runner. Lock the drum in this position by turning the milled head (8) in the contrary direction.

2.—By means of the knob (13) withdraw both runners together, then adjust the distance between the end of the runner and the drum, with the pivot in the centre of the runner (2) ; hold the wheel or pinion with the right hand by means of balance spring tweezers (preferably curved). The adjustment for the length of the arbor having been made, secure the runner (2) by means of the lever (21), and then adjust the position of the carrier pulley (5) by means of the runner (13). Fasten the latter by the screw (20).

To change the ends of the runner. Secure the two runners (by screw (20) and lever (21)), pull off the protecting shield (3), unscrew lever (21), pull out the runner and reverse it ; the driving pulley (5) will remain in its place, held by the extension bracket on end of runner (13).

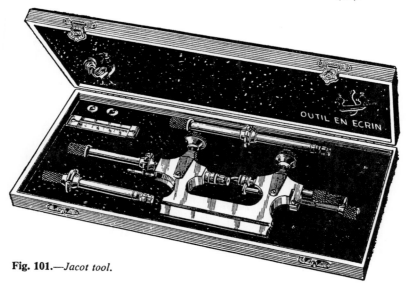

Fig. 101.—*Jacot tool.*

For fitting a new pivot. Before fitting the pivot-drilling plate (" cone plate ") in position, select a drill which has exactly the same diameter as the appropriate hole in the plate. To change the plate for the drum, unscrew the screw (10). The screw (10) should not be unscrewed except for changing the drum for the plate, or vice versa. The adjustment for the length of the arbor is made in the same way as for pivot burnishing. Drill-holders are supplied for drills having a diameter of shank 0·6 mm. and 1·0 mm. If the drill has a shank 1·5 mm., slip the piece (17) directly on the shank of the drill, and insert a tube into the back of the hole opposite the appropriate cone.

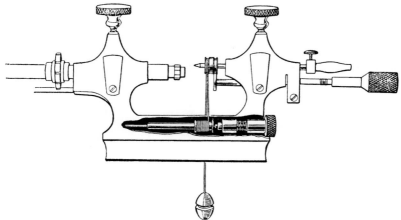

Fig. 102.—*Jacot tool with spool propulsion built in, by Steiner.*

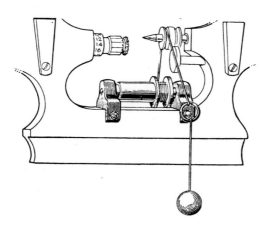

Fig. 103.—*Jacot tool with spool propulsion attached, by Steiner.*

61

The Jacot Tool

The Jacot tool is used solely for the purpose of polishing pivots (Fig. 101). The usual method of propulsion is by means of a bow. Two methods of propulsion of fairly recent introduction are illustrated here. Fig. 102 is built into the tool and Fig. 103 is an attachment which can be added to an existing tool. Both methods are known as " spool winding." (It will be noted that the illustrations of Jacot tools are continental in style, i.e., the pivot bed is on the left).

Although referred to as pivot polishing, the operation carried out with the Jacot tool is actually burnishing. Select a groove on the runner of the tool so that the pivot rests in the groove or bed a little more than half its diameter. Fit up the staff or arbor with one end in a runner and the other resting in the bed selected. Make sure that the pivot can turn freely in the bed. With balance staff pivots, bring up the runner so that only the part of the pivot with straight sides rests in the bed and the conical part is free.

Apply oil to the pivot in the runner and use a Jacot tool pivot burnisher, which is a hand tool with the left edge on both sides rounded, smeared with oil. The rounded edges are to burnish the radii at the root of balance staff pivots simultaneously with the pivot.

The method is fairly rapid so the pivot should be tried in its hole at frequent intervals.

Chapter 7

CUTTING TOOLS AND HOW TO USE THEM

A good cutter is essential if good work is to be produced on the lathe, because the work done reflects the cutting edge of the tool. If the cutting edge is ragged, it makes a ragged cut ; if it is keen and even, it makes a clean cut.

To consider the slide rest tool first ; the cutter is really a wedge which divides the metal. There are one or two fundamental facts that control this operation. If a thin wedge is used, the material is divided more easily than if the wedge is thick. The first can be said to be sharper and would use less power to do a given job, but other factors such as strength, resistance to wear, and heating have also to be considered. Strength, for example, is determined by the work the tool has to do ; whether it has to cut a hard metal, such as steel, or a soft metal, such as brass. A compromise has to be reached in tool design, and for general purposes the tool illustrated in Fig. 104 will meet most demands of the watch repairer.

When machines are required to run for hours on end, the angles of rake and clearance are of the utmost importance since they control the durability of the cutting edge, and such factors as the rate of feed, cutting speed, vibration of the cutting edge (chatter) due to springing, and temperature of the cutting edge, which, if excessive, destroys the temper of the edge. Engineers study these fine points to obtain cuts consistent in amount and quality and also introduce cooling mediums such as soluble oil, or soapy water, flowing over the cutting edge to carry the heat away.

The ideal cutter from the point of view of cutting only is a thin one, but as this is not practicable it is advisable to get as near to it as possible. If a cutter were made as shown in Fig. 105, the cut would be clean and easily made, but as there is little body at the cutting edge, heat would

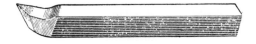
Fig. 104.

Fig. 105.

not be carried away by the mass of metal and also there would be chattering caused by the edge springing inward. If the metal to be cut were very soft and ductile so that it would tend to cling to the edge of the cutter, as would copper or aluminium, a cutter of this shape or something like it would be suitable.

The tool shown in Fig. 104 is a good general compromise. Fig. 106 shows : A, top rake ; B, clearance ; C, top face ; D, bottom face. The angle of clearance should be from 5° to 10° for metals the watch or clock repairer is likely to deal with. A smaller angle would be used for a tool for hardened and tempered steel. The top rake angle (A) should be about 5° or less for very hard materials.

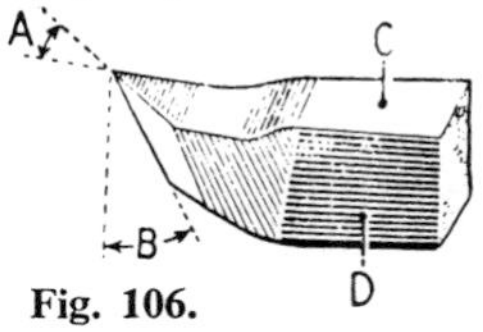

Fig. 106.

Slide rest tools can be purchased or made to almost any shape for various purposes, but the rules controlling the actual cutting edges are the same. The tool can be made from round or square section carbon steel, filed to shape. The cutting end should be hardened and then tempered to a pale straw colour. Fig. 107 shows some cutting tools for various purposes.

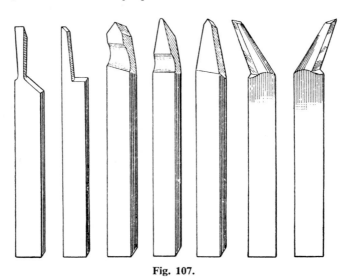

Fig. 107.

Finishing the cutting edge is important : a rough edge will produce a rough cut, unless the work is made to rotate at an extremely high speed and the cutter is traversed slowly, which is not at all economical. For general work the whole of the cutting edges should be finished with an Arkansas stone—the whole of the edge as shown

Fig. 108. at AB in Fig. 106, not just the actual edge as shown in Fig. 108 otherwise the object of angles would be defeated.

To whet or sharpen the cutting edge of a slide rest tool is not as simple as it would at first appear. An ordinary hand graver is simpler to

prepare. The slide rest tool is shorter and thicker and the surface to be treated is, by comparison with the rest of the tool, small. A convenient method is to hold the tool in the left hand against the filing block held in the vice (Fig. 109) and with an Arkansas stone held in the right hand proceed to dress the cutting edge, giving the slip a circular motion to keep the surface of the cutting edge flat.

Observe the whole of the edge frequently and adjust the position of the Arkansas slip to achieve this object. To whet a slide rest tool well requires time and some practice. To protect the edges, it is advisable to keep the cutters with the cutting edges downwards in partly drilled holes, which fit the shanks of the tools fairly tight, in a block of wood.

When a particularly fine or polished cut is required, the cutting edges are polished with an iron polisher charged with diamantine. The cutter is held as shown in Fig. 109 and in place of the Arkansas slip, the iron polisher is used.

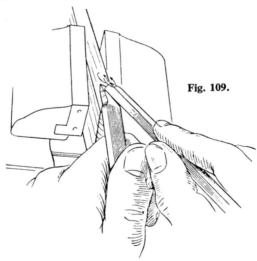

Fig. 109.

The polisher should be rectangular in section and about 6 in. long. It may be made of mild steel instead of iron. Before using, it is cleaned by filing, leaving a cross grain for the retention of the polishing material.

Diamantine is sold in small bottles which must be kept corked when not in use to exclude dust. It is a fine white powder—actually alumina—and is made up by taking as much as will cover a circle of about $\frac{1}{2}$ in. diameter and place it on a polishing block, a piece of zinc about 3 in. square by $\frac{1}{4}$ in. thick which has been scraped on top with a knife.

Mix the diamantine on the block with one drop of clock oil using a *very clean* knife blade. Apply plenty of pressure and turn the powder over and over until it has the consistency of putty.

To charge the polisher, just dab it on to the diamantine on the polishing block. It is only necessary for a small amount to be used ; just damping the polisher with the diamantine " putty " is sufficient.

Cleanliness must be emphasised again. The bottle of diamantine must be kept corked. The zinc block should be kept in a paper cover when not in use and should be scraped before it is charged with diamantine. The polisher must be cleaned by filing before charging.

Method of Fixing Tool

The cutting tool should be held in the post of the slide rest so that the cutting end is as short as possible. Just sufficient of the tool should project for freedom of the work ; thus springing of the shank or body of the tool is eliminated as much as possible. The tool must be gripped in the post *very firmly*. The actual cutting edge should be at such a height in relation to the work that the cut is made a little above centre. These points must be observed to obtain a clean cut devoid of chattering :—

Work held firmly.
Tool short and very firm.
No side play in the slides of the slide rest.
No end play in the head stock, if the work is held in a chuck.
No end play of the work if held between centres.
Relatively slow movement of the cutter.
Attention to the correct rake of the tool.
Avoidance of flexible work owing to excessive length or thinness.
All these points add up to one thing—*firmness.*

Hand Cutting Tools

The principal hand cutting tool is the graver. This is used by holding it firmly down on to a T-rest. The cutting end of the graver is formed at the correct angle when the graver is purchased and the two most popular for watch and clock work are the lozenge (Fig. 110) and the square nose (Fig. 111). For watch work, the lozenge is the

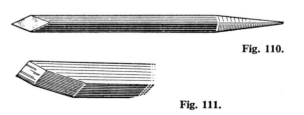

Fig. 110.

Fig. 111.

66

most useful, and practically all forms of turning can be done with it. The method of holding is shown in Fig. 112. The first finger is held down firmly on the graver and the object is that the graver must not be allowed to give way to the work being turned. It must *cut*, and cut cylindrically and true. If the graver is held loosely and is pushed out of the way by the work, it will just follow the shape of the work, whatever it may be and not cut true. A comparatively long surface like that of a balance staff is best cut with the edge of the graver held at an oblique angle as shown in Fig. 113. It will be found that the edge will stand up to the work better than if the point only were used.

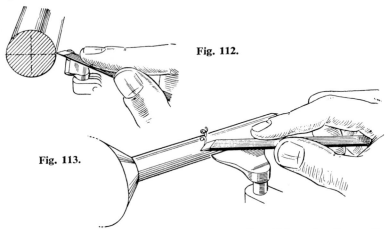

Fig. 112.

Fig. 113.

When whetting the graver, as shown in Fig. 114, make the surface travel along a long oval and use considerable downward pressure to keep the surface being ground flat by avoiding any rocking. If the stone is tilted slightly and held as shown, it will give slightly under the pressure, which helps to keep a flat surface. The feather edges thrown up are removed by holding the graver flat on the stone and just giving one or two rubs only, at A and B, Fig. 115.

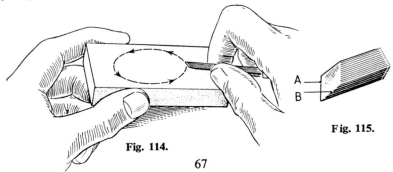

A
B

Fig. 115.

Fig. 114.

To test a graver for sharpness, touch the point on the thumb nail as in Fig. 115. It should cling. Finally, before using, dig the point of the graver into soft wood, such as the leg of the bench, to ensure that all traces of the feather edges are removed. If a feather edge is present, it will not cut, but will tend to burnish the surface of the work. A burnished steel surface can be troublesome to remove. Usually the edge of the graver held obliquely as in Fig. 112 is effective.

The position of the graver is important. For good work it must be comfortable, that is, it must cut with ease. This is determined by the height of the cutting edge or point on the work. The illustrations, Figs. 116, 117, 118 and 119, show this clearly. The work it is possible to do with a simple graver is legion with the watchmaker, but so much

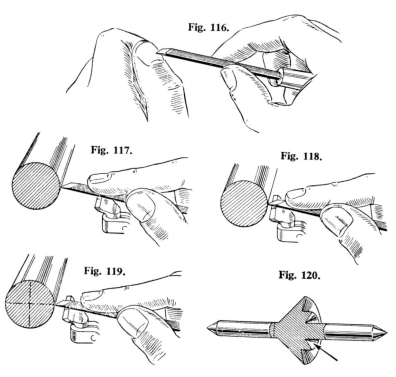

Fig. 116.

Fig. 117.

Fig. 118.

Fig. 119.

Fig. 120.

depends upon the skill of the craftsman, it is necessary to spend many hours practising to become really proficient. There is hardly any part of a watch or clock repairer's work that needs as much practice as turning. The undercut in the balance staff (Fig. 120) and similar jobs are done with a lozenge shaped graver.

The Square Nose Tool

The square nose tool (Fig. 111) is used for larger work, such as clock and model engineer's work. The point is stronger than that of the lozenge shaped tool and the flat cutting edges are more robust. With this tool the flat edge can be used at an oblique angle, too, as explained when the use of the lozenge shaped graver was described.

Whether the slide rest tool, the lozenge, or the square nosed graver is used, the finish of the cutting edge determines the work. For roughing out, the finish as left by an Indian stone after sharpening is satisfactory. For a finer finish use an Arkansas stone, and from this finish the work is immediately ready for burnishing, as for pivots, or polishing with oilstone dust and oil and then finishing with diamantine, as for arbors.

To finish brass with a polished surface straight from the cutter, polish the cutting edge of the cutter with diamantine as explained for the slide rest tool, using the zinc block for the lozenge or square nosed tool.

Often a finer cut can be obtained when using the hand tool by just damping the end of the tool in the mouth.

When using a hand tool, as with a slide rest tool, great care must be taken to see that there is no possible cause of vibration. The work must be rigid, with no play between the centres or in the headstock, if a chuck is used.

If an emery wheel is used to grind (or whet) a tool, great care must be taken to avoid the tool becoming too hot as this will take the temper out of the steel and soften the cutting edge so that it will not cut. If the wheel is a dry one, have a bowl of water handy and keep dipping the tool in this to keep it as cool as possible. If a tool has been overheated by grinding, the edges will become discoloured. If the discoloration is only on the extreme edges, that part should be ground carefully away, retaining the tool shape and angles and avoiding further overheating. If the discoloration is bad, the tool will have to be heat-treated again.

A useful handle for all hand cutting tools is the one illustrated in Fig. 121. It is a short length of cane and the cutter is burnt into the handle, making sure not to let the heat run up the tool too far.

Fig. 121.

69

Chapter 8

WORKING WITH THE LATHE

In order to incorporate the fullest use of the lathe and its accessories we propose to make a barrel and barrel arbor. The work is of no

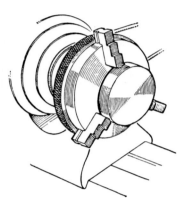

Fig. 122.—*Disc fitted up in three-jaw chuck.*

particular size and for no particular purpose. It has been selected because in its making the slide rest, wheel cutting, topping, lapping, drilling, square filing, to mention some accessories, will be used. A balance staff, employing four methods, will be made and finally the method of fitting a new pivot will be explained.

To make the barrel, procure a piece of brass of the necessary thickness, i.e. thick enough to make the barrel of the requisite height. This can be cut from a length of rod of the required diameter or from a piece of plate. Having cut the disc fit up in the 3-jaw chuck (Fig. 122), use the jaws in the reverse

way round and grip the disc so that it is held by the sides of the jaws only and does not touch the bottom of the chuck. The top and bottom of the disc may not be true and it is necessary to face these two surfaces so that they are true. Use the slide rest (Figs. 42-44) and run the cutter across the surface so that a full clean cut is made. Reverse the disc in the chuck and face the other surface. While the disc is in the chuck drill a hole through, smaller in diameter than the size of the barrel arbor pivot is to be.

If the disc is to be cut from a plate, cut the plate to a reasonable size first, then cement on to a wax chuck (Fig. 18) with shellac. Fit the chuck up in the lathe and heat the end of the wax chuck with a spirit lamp or some other form of smokeless heat ; continue to apply heat until it is possible to smear a thin film of shellac over the whole of the flat surface of the chuck. If the barrel is fairly large it will be better to cement the disc to the chuck before fitting up in the lathe as it may take some considerable heat to make a thick disc adhere to the chuck. In these circumstances, place the disc on a plate over a gas ring and when hot enough smear the surface of the disc with shellac. If the chuck is placed on the plate a little while before the shellac is applied to the disc, it will be hot enough to ensure a good adhesion. Place the chuck on the disc and use some considerable pressure to ensure that the

70

chuck makes close contact with the disc. Turn off the heat and allow to cool, still applying pressure.

To come back to the heated chuck in the lathe, present the disc to the chuck and hold it in position with the back of a watch brush, apply more heat until the disc is hot and so press the disc hard on to the chuck, remove the heat and allow to cool with the pressure still applied. It is important that as thin a film of shellac is used to ensure that the disc contacts the chuck as closely and evenly as possible. If a thick layer of shellac is used and the work not pressed hard on to the disc, it could quite easily be high on one side and down on the other, and this would result in the work being turned out of true and the disc would be of unequal thickness. On the other hand, if a thick layer of shellac is used and the work made to rotate while the pressure is applied it would true itself during cooling.

It is now necessary to turn a groove in the disc down to the wax chuck surface with the aid of the slide rest. A light tap with a hammer

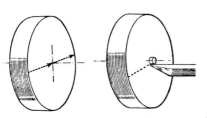

will cause the unwanted metal to fall away from the chuck, leaving the disc still cemented in position. While the disc is cemented to the chuck it is possible to turn the barrel to shape with the slide rest. The height of the cutter on the slide rest is important and it should be exactly in the centre of the work. If the cutter is drawn

Fig. 123.—*Correct position for cutter, and (right) Cutter too low, leaving "pip" in centre.*

across the work, from the centre inwards, when the headstock is revolving in the usual direction, or from the near-side edge towards the centre, no pip will be left in the centre of the disc. Should the cutter be too high or too low a pip will be left (Fig. 123).

For all ordinary hand work of a light nature such as the operator is likely to encounter, the shape of the cutter is as in Fig. 124 and it is

used with the point following so that little of the flat cutting edge is presented to the work. The condition of the edge of the cutter and the speed the work is made to rotate and the speed with which the cutter is made to traverse control the fineness of the surface cut.

Fig. 124.—*Slide rest tool cutters.*

If the cutter is whetted on a fine Arkansas stone, the edges polished on a zinc block with diamantine and the work made to rotate at considerable speed with the cutter traversing at a very slow speed, the surface cut will be fine and polished. If the point of the cutter only is used

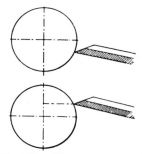

and the work made to rotate at a very high speed and the cutter to traverse at a very slow speed, then a series of fine spiral lines would result, which would be tantamount to a fine cut.

The cutter should be presented to the work at the centre line or slightly above it, not as in Fig. 125. The tool should be horizontal for a slide rest tool (Fig. 140) or a hand graver can be held at a

Fig. 125.—*The graver should not be held too high or too low.*

slight upward tilt.

Engineers pay great importance to speeds, especially when automatic machines are used, whether for turning arbors, etc., or cutting teeth and the leaves of pinions. There are three reasons for this : the wear of the tool, heat generated during cutting, and the finished surface. The operator need not concern himself with these matters, mainly owing to the duration of his work in operation, but should he require a guide as to the correct speed for production work, we give here a useful table of speeds for different metals.

SPEEDS FOR TURNING AND DRILLING

Tempered steel — Surface speed 3 to 5 metres per minute
Soft steel   —   ,,   ,,   7 „ 9   ,,   ,,   ,,
Hard brass   —   ,,   ,,   13 „ 20   ,,   ,,   ,,
Soft brass   —   ,,   ,,   30 „ 40   ,,   ,,   ,,

Averages

Tempered steel — 4 metres per minute
Soft steel   — 8   ,,   ,,   ,,
Hard brass   — 16   ,,   ,,   ,,
Soft brass   — 32   ,,   ,,   ,,

The following table is based on the above *average* speeds :

Diameter of work (millimetres)	Rev. per minute, Tempered steel
5	255
4	320
3	425
2	640
1	1,275
0·5	2,550
0·4	3,200
0·3	4,250
0·2	6,400
0·1	12,800

Soft steel — multiply above figures by 2
Hard brass—   ,,   ,,   ,,   ,, 4
Soft brass —   ,,   ,,   ,,   ,, 8
Aluminium and light metal alloys — 60-120 metres/min. or approx. 2 to 4 times as fast as soft brass.

The engineer has at his disposal machines making 15,000 to 20,000 rev. per minute. A fractional horse power motor may make 1,200 to

72

1,500 r.p.m. and by using a large pulley on the motor and the smallest on the lathe, perhaps 5,000 to 6,000 rev. per minute are possible at the cutting surface. As an example, if the disc is 1 in. in diameter and the work is rotating at 6,000 r.p.m., and the cutter is made to traverse evenly at the rate of 1 minute for the ½ in. from or to the centre, 6,000 spiral lines will be cut on the surface, which in effect will be an almost polished surface. So to produce a fine surface the work is made to rotate at a high speed and the cutting tool travels at a low speed.

Another important point to watch is that the cutter is as short as possible, to prevent chattering. Other causes of chattering are to traverse the point of the cutter first and to present too great a flat part of the cutter to the work. The correct method of setting the cutter is to use a fairly stout cutter, set at the correct height, by packing with metal if necessary and set the cutter into the holder as short as possible, making sure the cutter projects far enough from the holder to contact the full depth required. See that the cutter is held very firmly in position. Absolute rigidity of cutter and work is essential to avoid chattering.

The shape of the barrel is as in Fig. 126 and if the wax chuck is used it is possible to make the cuts without removing the disc from the chuck. When cutting out the bottom of the barrel it will be necessary to make two cuts, leaving the boss in the centre. One cut will be from the far

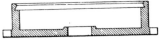

Fig. 126.—*General shape of the barrel.*

side to near the centre, the headstock revolving in a clockwise direction, and the other from the centre on the other side of the boss to the point where the first cut finished, the headstock revolving in an anti-clockwise direction. The lathe is reversed by crossing the belt drive.

The groove into which the cover snaps is best cut with the graver held on the T-rest (Figs. 38-39). The shape of the groove is shown in Figs. 126 and 129. Having formed the barrel as far as possible, remove the wax chuck from the lathe and allow the chuck to drop on to the bench from a height of say 6 in. : this will cause the barrel to dislodge from the chuck. Next fit the barrel into a step chuck (Fig. 20) open end into the chuck. Make sure the step into which the barrel fits is the correct size. It should just fit comfortably so that a slight turn of the drawn-in rod will tighten the barrel in the chuck and the barrel will seat down. Now run the cutter in the slide rest across the surface to face it.

The barrel made from a disc, cut from rod, is fashioned by fitting the disc into a step chuck and cut as explained. When the barrel is formed and the cover groove cut, reverse in the chuck and face the outside of the bottom of the barrel.

To make the cover, select a piece of sheet brass of the correct thickness. Cement this on to a wax chuck which is smaller in diameter than the finished cover is to be. Cut out a disc a little larger in diameter than ultimately required, then face the disc and drill a hole in the centre. Remove the disc from the chuck and re-cement to work on the other side. To make the disc run true, hold a rounded end pointer, larger in diameter than the hole, in the hole itself ; apply heat, and with the pointer held on the T-rest cause the work to rotate at moderate speed, press the pointer to the work and in this manner the disc will find its centre and run perfectly true. Remove the source of heat and continue to rotate and hold the work until cool and the shellac sets (Fig. 127).

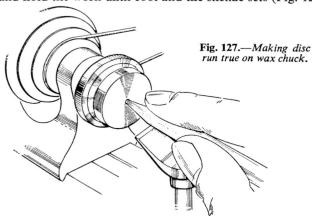

Fig. 127.—*Making disc run true on wax chuck.*

The disc is cut to shape as in Fig. 128. Turn the edge of the cover rounded with the graver held on the T-rest and reduce until it enters into the chamfered part of the snap groove of the barrel. Remove from the chuck, cut a notch in the cover so that it can be prised open. The cover should now snap into the barrel. If it does not, mount the cover on to a turning arbor (Fig. 37) and fit up in the lathe and with a fine file reduce the diameter slightly, retaining the same rounded contour. Then try in the barrel again. The fit should be as in Fig. 129.

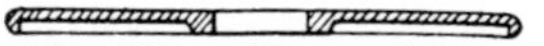

Fig. 128.—*Shape of barrel cover.*

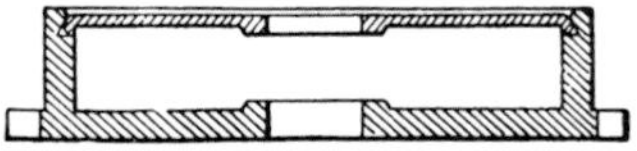

Fig. 129.—*Barrel completed, before cutting teeth, showing snap of barrel cover.*

The barrel is finished and the next work is to cut the teeth. For this purpose fit the lathe up either as in Fig. 62 or Fig. 63. The system as Fig. 63 will be used, but the instruction given here equally applies to whichever system is used. Fit the large index plate on to the lathe and then fit the barrel on to a wheel chuck (Fig. 27) and fit this up in the headstock. Select the cutter to be used and fit this on to the wheel cutting attachment on the slide rest. The index plate, also termed dividing plate, is divided into sets of holes into which the index is inserted. The arrangement of holes varies, sometimes from 30 to 360 holes in a circle. It must be decided which series of holes is to be used and this depends upon the number of teeth to be cut. If, for instance, 80 teeth are to be cut and there is not a circle with 80 holes, but there is a circle with 160 holes, then the headstock is stepped forward two holes at a time between each cut. There may be a circle of 240 or 320 in which case the headstock is stepped forward three or four holes respectively, between each cut. Obviously the less number of holes stepped over the better and if the plate has an 80 hole circle then this would be used, stepping forward one hole at a time. The up and down slide is adjusted laterally so that the cutter operates exactly in the centre of the wheel. To ensure this, fit up in place of the barrel a point in a split chuck, adjust the up and down slide laterally so that the point touches the centre of the cutter and do not touch this slide after the adjustment has been made (Fig. 130). The teeth cut will now be upright.

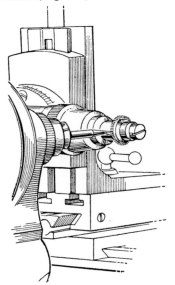

Fig. 130.—*Pointer in chuck to ensure cutter is central.*

The lower or lateral slide is next adjusted so that the cutter cuts into the wheel the correct depth and when once set this slide is not touched.

When all is set correctly and with the barrel in position fit the belt on to the pulley of the wheel cutting spindle. Lock the index plate with the index pin, cause the cutter to rotate with the highest speed, operate the middle slide to bring the cutter up to the work as slowly as possible and when a full cut has been made, withdraw the cutter clear of the work. Move the index plate the requisite distance and lock, bring the cutter up to the work again and when a full cut has been made the first tooth will have been formed. Continue thus until all the teeth are cut. Some important points to observe are that the middle slide only must be moved and in no circumstances touch the slides controlling the position of the cutter; lock the index plate firmly and accurately before making each cut. Fig. 131 shows a device, by Paulson, to ensure that the index pin contacts the circle of holes set to be used.

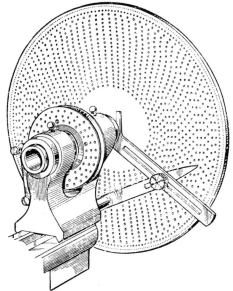

Fig. 131.—*Controlled index pin on dividing plate, by Paulson.*

There is a system used in place of the index plate employing a worm gear and a dividing plate. It has the advantage that any number of teeth can be cut, including all odd numbers but, unless provision is made to take up backlash, it is not satisfactory. In any case there is not such a system in production for the operator to purchase and for watch work the index plate system is to be preferred.

The worm and index plate system consists of a frame with a single worm pivoted in it. To the extended arbor of the worm a small dividing plate is fitted and operating on this plate is an index and pin. The plate has five circles of holes drilled with 7, 8, 9, 10 and 11 holes at equal distances apart. The frame is bolted to the headstock in such a position that the worm gears into a worm wheel which is fitted to the hollow runner of the headstock Fig. 132. There are two wheels, one of 70 and the other of 72 teeth. They are fitted friction tight and keyed on to the spindle to prevent slipping. Using the 72 wheel, for example, if we want to cut a wheel with 72 teeth, the worm is made to rotate one complete revolution, by means of the dividing plate, between each cut and by this means 72 teeth can be cut. For convenience of calculating make a fraction with the numerator equal

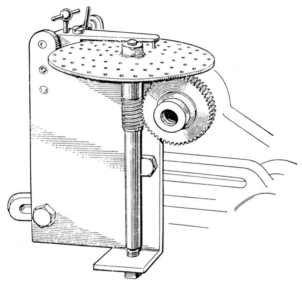

Fig. 132.—*Worm and index plate wheel cutting dividing system.*

to the number of teeth in the worm wheel and the denominator equal to the number of teeth to be cut. Instead of saying one revolution of the worm call it 72/72. To cut 144 teeth the plate is rotated half a turn between each cut since $72/144 = \frac{1}{2}$. To cut 36 teeth the plate is made to rotate two turns between each cut—$72/36 = 2$. Thus for 45 teeth = 72/45 which means the plate is rotated 72/45 turns. If there were a plate with 45 holes you could count 45 of them between each cut, but there is no such count. Therefore make the fraction into one which has a denominator equal to the number of holes in one of the circles such as 72/45=8/5. There is not a set of five holes but one of 10 holes so convert 8/5 to 16/10, count 16 holes or one complete revolution plus six between each cut and it is possible to cut a wheel of 45 teeth.

Other examples are these : 49 teeth, use the worm wheel of 70 teeth, $70/49 = 10/7 = 10$ holes of the seven index circle or one complete revolution plus three holes; 84 teeth $= 72/84 = 12/14 = 6/7 = 6$ holes of the 7 hole circle; 50 teeth $= 70/50 = 7/5 = 14/10 = 14$ holes of the 10 circle or one complete turn plus four holes. It will be seen that almost any number of teeth can be cut.

To overcome the backlash, a cord is wound round the chuck holding the wheel being cut, one end is fixed to the lathe and the other end has attached to it a heavy weight. This has the effect of straining the chuck in one direction with a constant force, thus taking up any backlash or freedom of the chuck.

During cutting the teeth a burr will be thrown up and this is removed with the hand graver. Remove all the wheel cutting apparatus including the index plate. Fit up the T-rest and with a sharp graver just touch each side of the wheel while it is revolving at a fair speed to cut the burr away cleanly. Now remove the barrel from the lathe. If making the barrel for a particular purpose open the holes to the correct size, make the arbor and finish the barrel, but as the purpose of this part of the book is to demonstrate the use of the lathe, for convenience, finish the barrel and open the holes later.

The next operation is snailing and the information given here equally applies to steel keyless wheels. Both the bottom and the cover of the barrel are snailed.

Fit the barrel, with its cover complete, into a step chuck in the lathe. Then fit one of the lapping attachments (Figs. 54, 55 or 56) up on the lathe. Fit into the lapping attachment the hollow lap. The diameter of the lap controls the extent of the curve snailed. For instance, a small lap will impart lines which are half circular while a large lap, say twice the diameter of the piece being snailed, will impart lines almost straight. A lap twice the diameter of the article being snailed gives quite a pleasing effect. To obtain the desired result it may be necessary to make a lap especially for the purpose. In these circumstances use a copper disc, like, say, a penny, half-penny or a farthing. Drill a hole in the centre to fit the arbor on the lapping tool, dome out on a lead block and then fit on to a wheel chuck in the lathe and turn true (Fig. 133). When all is ready charge the active edge of the lap with oilstone-dust and oil and present the lap to the work as in Fig. 134. Make the lap rotate quickly and cause the headstock to revolve slowly with the hand. The lapping attachment is pressed on to the work with the other hand, exert a light pressure. Do not cut deep lines but just scratch the surface more or less, to give it that pleasing radiating effect. Reverse the barrel in the chuck and snail the other end.

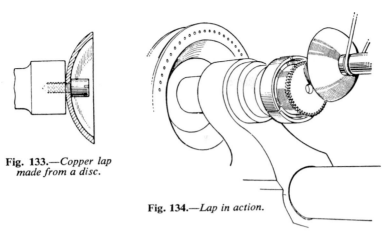

Fig. 133.—*Copper lap made from a disc.*

Fig. 134.—*Lap in action.*

The barrel is now finished and to make the arbor we shall employ as much lathe practice as possible. The arbor will have a winding square, a square to carry the ratchet wheel, a hole for a pin to hold the wheel in position. Fig. 135 gives an indication of the shape of the arbor.

Fig. 135.—*Barrel arbor finished.*

Fig. 136.—*Barrel arbor in the rough*

Procure a piece of carbon steel of the required length and diameter sufficient to cut the barrel hook from the solid, as indicated in Fig. 136. If the diameter of the steel is not large it can be fitted into a split chuck, in which case allow sufficient to project from the chuck to enable the whole arbor to be turned. Turn a cone pivot on the end and bring the tailstock up with a female runner to support this end of the rod while being turned. If the diameter is too large to be held in a split chuck the rod is fitted up between centres in the following manner. Secure the rod in the 3-jaw chuck (Fig. 22 or 23) with the jaws reversed, or in the box chuck (Fig. 19) and turn a cone pivot on each end. Fit the female centre with pulley (Fig. 137) in the headstock. Fit a carrier

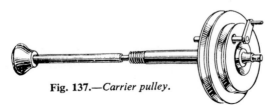

Fig. 137.—*Carrier pulley.*

79

on to the rod or arbor (Fig. 138). Next fit the slide rest into position and then the tailstock with female runner and commence turning as in Fig. 139. The height of the cutting tool in the slide rest is important. The cutting tool is as in Fig. 124. The cutting edge of the tool should

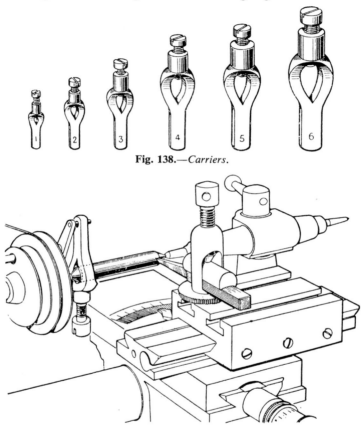

Fig. 138.—*Carriers.*

Fig. 139.—*Fit up in lathe to turn arbor.*

touch the work just a shade above the line of centres (Fig. 140). Fit the cutter short into the holder and make very fast. With all turning the work and the cutter must be very firm ; work cannot be turned true if held and cut loosely. Firmness eliminates chattering. When all is set, adjust the slide so that a light cut is made, then run the cutter along the whole length of the arbor, using the point of the cutter only.

Reduce the arbor to the shape as in Fig. 136. Take great care that all the shoulders are square and that there is no pip at the root of the shoulders. Make sure that the cutter has a good edge and a sharp point, then see that the work rotates at a moderate speed and the cutter traverses very slowly. To take one shoulder as an example, having reduced the diameter to nearly the correct size, make a fine cut and run the cutter down the face of the shoulder and then along

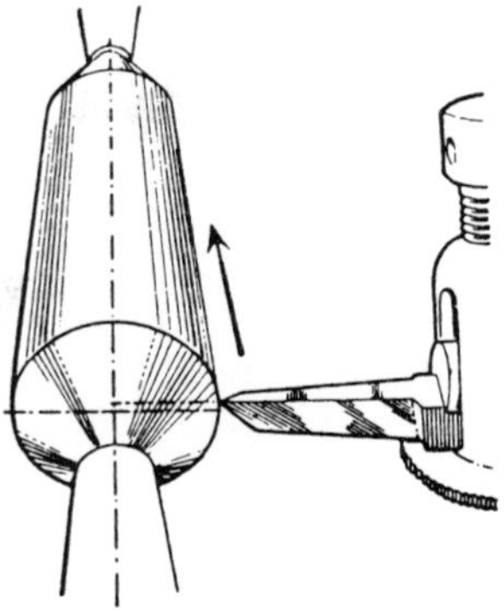

Fig. 140.—*Adjust cutter to cut just above line of centre.*

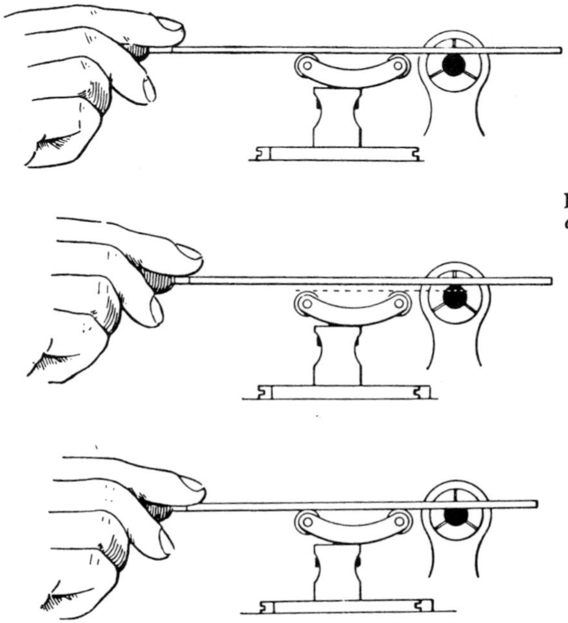

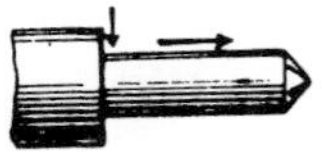

Fig. 141.—*Direction of cut to ensure a square shoulder.*

Fig. 143.—*Square filed, showing nick where square joins arbor.*

Fig. 142.—*Stages of filing a square with the aid of the double roller.*

the arbor (Fig. 141). That part of the arbor upon which a square is to be filed is nicked at the root so that a clean finish is given (Fig. 143).

When the arbor is cut almost to size, file the squares. To file a square accurately fit the arbor up in a chuck, lock the headstock with the index pin, remove the slide rest and fit in its place the double roller rest (Fig. 41). Bring up the roller rest close to the work, adjust the rollers so that if a file is placed upon the two rollers the end of the file will just touch the arbor upon which the square is to be filed. Then lower the double roller rest a little and proceed to file the arbor until the file touches the front roller, making sure the file contacts the back roller during the whole of the filing (Fig. 142), holding the file in the manner shown. Move the headstock round a quarter of a turn and lock again with the index pin. Proceed to file another flat, making sure not to move the double roller rest until all four flats have been filed. Examine the square and it may be that a full square has been formed or that a square with rounded corners is the result. To file a full square lower the roller rest a little more and proceed to file all flats again continuing thus until a full square is formed. The nick cut at the root of the square will have served its purpose and the part where the square joins the rest of the arbor will now be clean (Fig. 143). Reverse the arbor and file the square for the ratchet wheel.

Another method of producing a square is to use the circular saw with the Levin saw bed (Fig. 93). The procedure is to fit the arbor into the chuck of the chuck holder and the circular saw into the headstock. When the work has been set in the correct position hold the chuck holder firmly on to the part of the table and slide it forward on to the saw. The chuck is then turned a quarter of a turn, a cut made and so on. The illustration shows the square of a winding shaft being cut but the apparatus can be used for other purposes. A shorter square is filed on the other end of the arbor for the ratchet wheel. Next drill the hole in the arbor for the pin to hold the ratchet wheel. For this purpose fit the drill into a split chuck in the headstock and fit a V drilling block into the tailstock (Fig. 144). The arbor is first marked with a centring punch where the hole is to be drilled. Not only does this mark the position for the hole but also forms a lead for the drill.

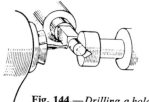

Fig. 144.—*Drilling a hole using the V-block runner.*

Fig. 145.—*Stages of filing the barrel arbor hook.*

The drill is made to rotate at moderate speed, the tailstock tightened on the bed at the correct position but the runner is left free so that it can be pressed on to the drill. Now file the hook ; the body of the arbor has been turned down so that metal is left in the centre the width of the hook. File as shown in Fig. 145.

The arbor is then hardened and tempered and is now ready for finishing. Fit up in the lathe as when first turning it. The various pivots can be polished by hand, using an iron polisher with oilstone-dust and oil and finishing with diamantine or they can be lapped with either of the lapping devices (Figs. 54, 55 or 56). Fit the iron lap, charged with oilstone-dust and oil, up on to the lapping spindle. Set the headstock and lapping device in motion, bring the lap up to the work carefully and when set at the correct depth run it along the pivot until the lap just touches the shoulder. The edge of the lap only is charged with the abrasive and sufficient will find its way to the end of the lap to grind the shoulder. Treat all the pivots in this manner, remove the arbor from the lathe and wash well in benzine to remove all traces of abrasive. Fit up again in the lathe and proceed in exactly the same manner, but using the bell metal lap charged with diamantine. The body of the arbor is ground with an iron polisher charged with oilstone-dust and oil and left grey from the grinding. The sides of the body, which were turned to a slight chamfer so as to reduce the area of the shoulder of the barrel pivots, are touched with the oilstone-dust and oil polisher, to clean, and left grey. The squares are polished next. If the between centres method has been used for turning, the carrier is removed and the arbor left perfectly free between the centres. With an iron polisher charged with oilstone-dust and oil, polish each of the four flats, a little to each at a time. Make the polisher rotate, tracing circles as it were, up and down the length of the square and at the same time employ some little downward pressure on the polisher. In this manner a perfectly flat surface will be maintained and no further finish will be necessary.

If the arbor was turned in the chuck, then remove the belt from the pulley and with the headstock free, the flats will find their own level when pressure is applied to the polisher.

If it is required to finish the end of the square dead flat, use the screw head tool (Fig. 64). The arbor is fitted into a split chuck in the screw head tool stock. The iron lap, charged with oilstone-dust and oil, is fitted up in the headstock. Allow the screw head tool to slide freely on its bed. Press the screw head stock up to the lap, which should rotate at a fair speed, and with the right hand make the stock rotate backward and forward with the palm of the hand, giving it a rolling action and at the same time pressing it up to the lap. When the end of the arbor is ground flat, clean off, and use the bell metal lap charged with diamantine and proceed to polish, imparting a high polish.

83

Using the Topping Tool

Having made the barrel it is found that when fitted into the mechanism the depth is not correct and it is necessary to use the topping tool (Figs. 59, 60 and 61). Assume that it is necessary to top the teeth of the barrel because the depth is too deep. Fit the barrel with its cover on to an arbor and fit up in the topping tool. Select a bed of a smaller diameter than the barrel so that when the cutter is in action the bed itself is not cut. Fit the barrel into the tool and adjust the runners so that the barrel actually touches and bears on to the bed. The top runner is made to bind the arbor and the object of this is to steady it; it should not be free. Before fitting the cutter into the headstock fit up a male centre in a split chuck and adjust the height of the barrel using the point as a guide. Adjust until the point touches the centre of the barrel teeth, similar to the method adopted when setting for cutting the teeth. Having selected the correct cutter fit it up in the headstock. Using the hook-shaped guide fitted to the topping tool, adjust the tool so that the guide is opposite the centre of the widest part of the cutter, this is to ensure that the teeth are cut upright. Adjust the stop controlling the depth the barrel teeth can intercept the cutter. The tool is now set ready for use. The headstock is made to rotate at a moderate speed.

In the foregoing the majority of the accessories have been employed and their application can be employed for numerous other jobs.

TURNING BALANCE STAFFS

There are at least four methods of turning a balance staff, or other small parts for that matter. They are: turning in the split chuck without removal; turning one end and then reversing and turning the other; between centres; using the split chuck and the wax chuck.

1. To deal with the turning in the split chuck without removal. Select a piece of blue steel the diameter of which is a little larger than the greatest diameter of the balance staff. Fit into a split chuck and allow it to project from the chuck a little more than the finished staff.

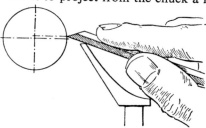

Fig. 146.—*Correct position to hold the graver.*

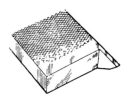

Fig. 147.—*Cutting tool for turning, made from an old file.*

84

Adjust the T-rest so that when the graver is resting upon it, its cutting edge contacts the work a shade above the line of centres (Fig. 146). Use an ordinary lozenge-shaped graver to turn the biggest part of the staff and the cutting tool (Fig. 147) to turn the shoulder at the back of the back slope and that part of the staff on to which the roller fits. Fig. 148 shows the various stages in turning. Each part is polished and finished immediately after turning.

2. Using the split chuck to turn one end of the staff and then reversing to turn the other end.* Care is always needed when selecting

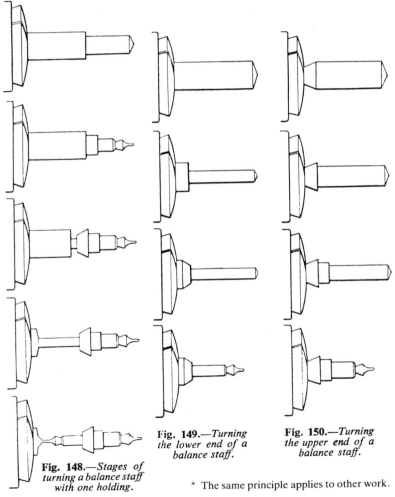

Fig. 148.—*Stages of turning a balance staff with one holding.*

Fig. 149.—*Turning the lower end of a balance staff.*

Fig. 150.—*Turning the upper end of a balance staff.*

* The same principle applies to other work.

85

the split chuck but particular care must be exercised now. A poor fit in the split chuck and the staff is almost sure to run out of true. Proceed to turn the staff as shown in Fig. 149. Now reverse and select another chuck smaller than the one just used and here be careful to select a chuck of the correct size. Turn the lower part of the staff as in Fig. 150.

3. Turning between centres. This form of turning is the oldest known and the only difference when employed in the lathe is the different method of rotating. The fit up is to use the safety pulley device (Fig. 151). The advantage of this system is that the power driving the work is controlled inasmuch as that if excessive pressure is applied to the work during turning the actual work stops rotating and damage thus avoided. The system is that the belt or line passes over one pulley and then a single line of the belt touches the pulley which directly drives the work. The extent the belt touches the pulley can be adjusted so that it can be hard or light. For turning balance staffs and other light pieces the safety pulley is the only system worth considering when turning between centres. Fig. 151 illustrates this

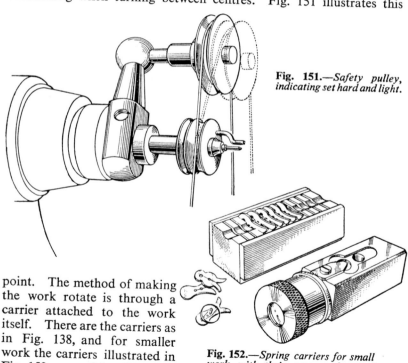

Fig. 151.—*Safety pulley, indicating set hard and light.*

point. The method of making the work rotate is through a carrier attached to the work itself. There are the carriers as in Fig. 138, and for smaller work the carriers illustrated in Fig. 152 are useful. The tool

Fig. 152.—*Spring carriers for small work, with their case, and a tool (right) for opening carriers.*

is to open the carrier, the work is inserted and the carrier allowed to spring on to and grip the work. This system is most efficient.

4. The other and last method of turning a staff in the lathe is to turn one part—usually the upper half—in the split chuck and instead of using another split chuck and fitting up to turn and finish the staff, a wax chuck is used to hold the work

The wax chuck is quite simple to make. Fit a piece of brass rod into a split chuck in the headstock (Fig. 153). Turn a V-shaped hollow into the end, sufficiently large and deep enough to hold the balance staff. " Catch " the centre (Fig. 153) and then turn the hollow with the lozenge graver as in Fig. 154. Make sure the bottom is clean with no " pip " (Fig. 155), then heat the chuck while still in the lathe and fill the hollow with shellac and while the shellac is soft place the staff into position as in Fig. 156. Cause the headstock to rotate at some speed and with the tip of the finger hold the staff as steady as possible (Fig. 157). As a rule the staff will run perfectly true by the time the shellac has set. Should it be found that the staff is not *perfectly* true, apply a little heat to make the shellac slightly soft, then hold a pointed peg-wood under the staff as in Fig. 158 and make

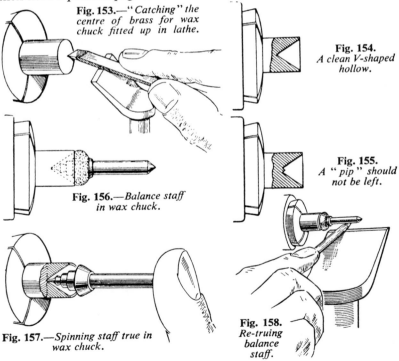

Fig. 153.—" *Catching* " *the centre of brass for wax chuck fitted up in lathe.*

Fig. 154. *A clean V-shaped hollow.*

Fig. 155. *A " pip " should not be left.*

Fig. 156.—*Balance staff in wax chuck.*

Fig. 157.—*Spinning staff true in wax chuck.*

Fig. 158. *Re-truing balance staff.*

the headstock rotate at a fairly high speed and at the same time just touch the staff with the peg ; by the time the shellac has set the staff will be running perfectly true.   Notes on staff fitting are given at some length in *Practical Watch Repairing*.

A good deal of debate has been used to discuss the pros and cons of a staff turned between centres and one turned in the split chuck. A staff turned between centres must be true, other things being equal. A staff turned at one holding of the split chuck must be true.   A staff turned in the split chuck by turning one end first and then reversing to turn the other end might be true, but so much depends upon the operator and the careful selection of the split chuck for the second operation.   A staff turned partly in the split chuck and then finished in the wax chuck must be true.

To sum up, the finest work is done between centres, and for good sound commercial work, turning the staff with one holding in the split chuck is the best.

Pivoting

While drilling for and fitting a new pivot is not considered good workmanship for the finer grades of work, there are occasions when it is commercially expedient to do it. It is for this reason that it is included in lathe work.

The word pivoting can mean turning train pinions and staffs, etc., and was the term employed by the old English watchmakers to define turning, e.g. " pivot a train in ", to turn the pinions of a watch train. The word pivoting now generally refers to fitting a new pivot.   For this purpose use the pivoting tool (Fig. 99) or the Jacot and pivoting tool (Fig. 100) for in either case the procedure is the same.   First, it is usually necessary to lower the temper of the part to be drilled and information about this is given fully in *Practical Watch Repairing*.   Select a drill a little larger than the diameter of the new pivot.   Then find a runner with a hole into which this drill will just fit.   The blade of the drill should fit the hole freely but without side-shake.   Fit the runner into the tool.   Fit the drill into the drill-stock

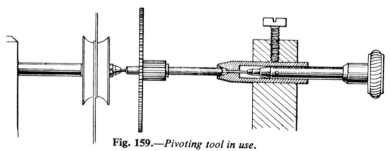

Fig. 159.—*Pivoting tool in use.*

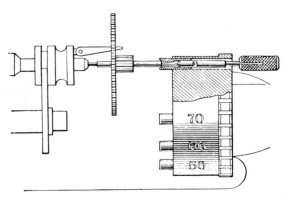

Fig. 160.—*Lerrac tool in use.*

and set the work up to be drilled in the tool. Apply oil to the cone side of the runner and also to the drill. Cause the work to rotate at a moderate speed and apply pressure to the drill, at the same time making the drill rotate a little, say half a turn one way and then half a turn back and be sure the drill is cutting all the time. Fig. 159 shows the pivoting tool in use and Fig. 160 the Lerrac tool in use.

More notes on pivoting and pivoting tools will be found in Chapter 6.

Chapter 9

CHOICE AND CARE OF THE MOTOR

The range of modern fractional h.p. motors provides a convenient means of driving a watch or clock lathe. They are reliable but it must be understood that these small motors cannot be applied indiscriminately. The suitability of any motor depends upon the operator's requirements so that it is not possible to particularise here, but it is probable that motors between $\frac{1}{16}$th and $\frac{1}{8}$th h.p. will meet all average demands in horological turning.

Allowance should be made for occasional jobs outside the general run of work and for future activities. To obtain maximum service the golden rule is to avoid underpowering.

Motors are obtainable from $\frac{1}{50}$th to $\frac{1}{3}$rd h.p. The latter is too powerful for normal requirements other than production work. A single power drive is often used for several machines in a workshop but modern practice favours individual drive, e.g. for the lathe, buffing spindle, drill, and of course the cleaning machine. This system is preferable.

The characteristics of motors also govern their application. For the specialised uses we are considering it is, therefore, as well to enquire from firms who handle watch and clockmakers' requirements or who are experienced in the supply and application of fractional h.p. motors particularly if voltage speed control is proposed.

In this regard it will be found that motor types, generally, fall into two classes, viz : " Variable speed " and " Constant speed ". It has to be understood that these terms refer to the motor's behaviour under load and not to its suitability to speed control. Unfortunately the term " variable speed motor " is used to denote motors especially constructed to provide two, four, or six operating speeds. It is as well, in making enquiries to appreciate the distinction that " variable speed " does not necessarily imply variable optional speed.

In general there are three classes of motor, running on direct current, on alternating current or on either. The first type, D.C., can be obtained in fractional horse-power sizes to run at minimum speed of about 2,000 r.p.m. The speeds of A.C. induction motors depend mainly on the frequency of the electricity supply which in Britain is 50* cycles per second and gives a choice of about 960, 1,440, and 2,800 r.p.m. With the 60 c/s. supply in the U.S.A., the choice is about 1150, 1730 and 3,460 r.p.m.

* 50 Hz.

Speeds of universal A.C./D.C. motors, one of the most popular types, vary considerably with the load, but the universal motor gives a good starting torque, and will work well over a wide range of voltage such as 200 to 250. Below 4,000 r.p.m., however, universal motors are not so " universal ", that is, there is a bigger difference between the speed on D.C. and that on A.C. for a given load.

Although not of quite so serious a consequence with small motors as with the larger machines it should be kept in mind that unlike other apparatus, the starting current taken by a motor is appreciably greater than its full load running current. In some instances as much as six times as great. This is referred to again.

In making an order or enquiry about a motor it is necessary to be precise and accurate. State the purpose of use and how it is proposed it shall be positioned. All motors are not made to run upside down, vertically or sideways. State the type of supply and voltage accurately : standard voltages in Great Britain are :—

Single phase 100/110, 200/210, 220/230, 240/250.

Three phase 230/250, 346/380, 400/440, 500/550.

D.C. 100/110, 200/220, 230/250.

Installation

The motor should be installed in a dry position with adequate ventilation and protected from dust, swarf, grit and sweepings. If a commutator type, arrange if possible that the brush gear is accessible. See that the driving pulleys are correctly aligned and that the motor itself is firmly clamped down either to a solid bed or a resilient mounting as the case may be. Do not use too tight a belt which may shrink and cause pronounced vibration and bearing wear or, in very bad cases, armature shaft deformation.

Wiring

It has been said that starting currents of motors are often much heavier than the full running load current. This must be allowed for in wiring the installation. Motors, fractional or otherwise, will not be satisfactory " hitched up " on bell wire. A long supply line of unsuitable gauge may curtail the motor's performance. No serious installation should be run off lighting points. Similarly it is inefficient, dangerous and foolish to use exposed leads, particularly single leads, draped around walls and benches. Such methods meet the instant condemnation of any inspecting official. See that power cable is employed properly and that it is sufficient to meet the change to a heavier motor if likely to be required. It will save time and expense. Ensure also, that plugs and sockets are of adequate rating.

Earthing lines and bonds should also be substantial and well connected and are a common sense protection. It is advisable to fuse the motor supply separately.

Faults and Maintenance

Failure to start

If the motor fails to start, or the fuses blow when switching on, it is important to locate the defect at once. When starting fails, lacking protective devices, the very heavy starting current continues to pass through the motor windings and severe damage is likely to result. Apart from the interruption of the work, repairs can be relatively costly. It is worth noting that if the current doubles, the heating effect increases fourfold. If trebled—ninefold, and so on.

Therefore, if the motor fails to start—switch off at once.

Similarly, act at once should the motor be accidentally stalled while the power is on ; either free the work instantly or switch off.

Although not critical, low mains voltage may cause starting failure and it will be aggravated by poor wiring.

If a voltage speed control is in use do not overlook resetting to its neutral position.

If the motor has been idle for a long period, the failure may be due to gummed or stiff bearings either of the motor or transmission. See that the latter are free and lubricate them before inspecting the motor. Unless grease packed and sealed, the motor bearings should be oiled or greased periodically *but very sparingly.*

On no account flood motor bearings or allow oil to contaminate the armature* and commutator assembly. A very slight oiliness may prevent rusting in the armature tunnel but a dry and damp-free motor is far better. A periodic run will off-set infrequent use.

The belt may have tightened by contraction, or drifting of one or more pulleys. When certain that belts and bearings are in order, give the motor a lead by hand and test the starting again.

A blown fuse may be the cause of starting failure or difficulties. In the case of three-phase motors there may be a buzzing noise on switching on. The motor may actually begin to run when assisted by hand but it must not be used until the supply has been properly restored otherwise serious trouble will result.

* Strictly, " armature " for D.C. machines. " Rotor " for A.C. machines.

A faulty switch may also cause starting failure. After switching off the main supply, examine the blades or contacts. See that they drop home correctly and that the spring mechanism operates each time and is not jammed or broken thus giving a false action. If pitted or dirty clean the blades with glass paper and wash out with a brush and carbon tetrachloride. A faulty or damaged switch is best replaced.

Brushes

Failing power and other defects may be caused by faulty brush action. The carbon brushes of a commutator or slip ring motor are deceptively simple-looking parts.

It is exceedingly important, in fact imperative, that only the correct design and grade of brush be used for a given motor. Both brush and commutator wear can be excessive if this warning is ignored.

Similarly, never mix carbon grades in a motor. If it is thought that brush wear is excessive do not experiment with harder grades. As a maxim, consult the makers or competent suppliers when replacing or ordering spare brushes and on no account depart from their recommendations.

When replacing brushes on larger machines it is necessary to pay particular attention to the face(s) which contact and bear upon the commutator and to " bed " these down. This practice is not always necessary with the smaller motors but it may be advisable to run the motor " light " after fitting. Follow the maker's instructions. Do not damage or destroy the finely grained surface of brushes in service. Also, they should not be changed about or reversed. The contact surfaces must be a precise " fit ". In the event of damage the cost of replacement renders futile the trouble and labour of attempting to face them up.

Examine for wear from time to time. This shows itself in the gradual shortening of the brush length and in an accumulation of carbon dust in the motor casing. Brush this away with a soft brush. The whole of the " business end " of a motor should be kept clean. Brushes should not be allowed to run too short.

The brushes should be free in their guides but without shake or chatter ; be held well forward by their springs and of such a length that the major portion of the brush remains nicely in the guide. Ensure that the springs work smoothly and hold the brush into firm, clean contact with the commutator or slip ring, and are not themselves deformed, squashed or twisted. In some instances coiled springs will bunch under compression in their guide or tunnel. Provided that they exert a steady pressure and hold the brush forward this is in order.

Commutators

No part of a motor is so likely to suffer from well meant attention than the commutator.

Beyond use of the soft brush and cleaning with a soft cloth moistened with carbon tetrachloride held in contact by a flat ended piece of wood or cut cork, it is best left alone.*

A commutator which shows a golden brown colour, a polished skin, and runs sparkless or with mere needle points of arcing beneath its brushes needs no interference whatsoever.

Assuming a clean motor, sparks carried round the commutator, flashing, and sputtering, are indication of possibly serious faults. If continuous, do not run the machine. Seek competent advice and service. Attempting to work the motor with faulty commutation brings its own reward.

The commutator segments are separated by mica strips usually sunk below the copper surface. If the spaces become choked with carbon dust and will not brush or wipe out, they may be cleaned very carefully with a pointed peg wood. It is very unwise to scrape or scratch about with metal.

Bright, thin lines, in the skin surface are an indication that grit or swarf has been caught in the brushes. If not scored, clean the surface thoroughly as above ; dismantle and thoroughly clean the brushes similarly ; reassemble and run " light " when all should bed down and be well. The only permissible lubricant is a single stroke of pure paraffin wax—not candle fat in any circumstances. If scoring has occurred it is unwise for any but experienced hands to attempt the rectification, if required.

At all times emery paper is *enemy* paper.

Overheating

Cooling is normally effected by a small fan, built in with the armature assembly, or by the mere rotation of the armature itself. Case openings must be kept free from fluff and dust. Swarf and particles allowed careless entry to the armature tunnel will cause heating—and other troubles.

A motor fitted too close to a radiator, hot pipe, oven, or in a confined space may overheat through inadequate ventilation. It has a running temperature of its own which may be quite high.

The most common cause of overheating is simply overloading.

* **Carbon tetrachloride is poisonous and should not be used. There are a number of safe alternatives readily available.**

If overheating occurs during quite normal working conditions, winding or insulation failure may be suspected. A voltage speed control incorrectly used or applied may cause overheating of pronounced character over part of the speed range.

This must be ascertained by consultation with the makers.

Overheating of a previously excellent commutator may be due to faulty spring action on the brushes gradually becoming apparent. Investigate without delay.

General

Oil transmission bearings, pulleys, etc., periodically. Oil or grease motor bearings very sparingly. Do not interfere with sealed bearings except under the manufacturer's instructions.

Keep the motor clean. If the motor fails to start, observe the warnings given and eliminate the simple and obvious causes such as main switches left open, a blown fuse, etc., before suspecting the motor. Dismantle the motor only as a last resort if assistance is not obtainable.

Although not in the least concerned with their operation it is a courtesy if not a necessity to fit a motor with interference suppression. Many are so equipped by the makers.

Speed Control

While power drive confers considerable advantages flexibility of control remains a very desirable feature in watch and clock turning. To this end speed control may be applied directly to the motor but some care and judgment are necessary to obtain acceptable results.

Attention has already been drawn to the use of the terms, " variable speed " and " constant speed " and a reminder is here given not to be confused by them.

Control is effected by varying the voltage fed to the motor windings and it is essential that the motor be of a suitable type. This must be ascertained from the manufacturers or suppliers.

Voltage control may be applied by means of a rheostat (variable resistance) arranged as a series resistance or as a potentiometer, or by a variable transformer.

The resistance may be used on both AC and DC supplies. The transformer can be used only on AC, but does not preclude the use of a DC motor for which a suitable rectifier unit can be incorporated.

Rheostat or resistance units provide a stepped or continuously variable control for hand or foot operation. They should be of robust construction, capable of passing the full load current at all settings, and well ventilated—particularly if much heat is dissipated. This heat loss is, electrically, wasteful. Such controls are widely available, e.g. the "Bercostat" range of rotary rheostats.

The "Regavolt" variable transformer offers similar facilities with the advantage of being more compact and efficient in terms of power loss. It is suitable for bench or panel mounting and lends itself to extensions of control requirements.

The new "Portavolt" portable variable range of transformers are designed for low-cost control and test of AC voltages. Ideal for appliance testing or where control of voltage dependent parameters such as current, power, temperature, light intensity and motor speed are required. Models are available at 4 amp or 10 amp, single phase output. The unit incorporates a "Regavolt" transformer housed in a sheet metal enclosure and comes complete with a mains input lead, output socket and meters for measuring the output voltage and current.

The availability of low-cost electronic speed controls in recent years has produced significant cost savings and improved control regulation.

"Bercostat", "Regavolt", "Portavolt" and "Regaspeed" are registered trade names of Claude Lyons Ltd., Brook Road, Waltham Cross, Herts EN8 7LR.

It must be appreciated that the simpler forms of control here mentioned do not compensate for certain motor characteristics and that some fluctuation of speed on and off load, and a limited range of control, may be experienced. Their success therefore largely depends upon requirements and if these are difficult to forecast, the best method of settling the question is to try it out.

All control units, connections, etc., should receive periodic inspection by a qualified electrician. If hand operated, their location well repays trial and error for convenience of working.

The foregoing notes are intended to render practical assistance within the scope of this book While much may be done without calling in the electrician, it is felt that in the unfortunate event of a serious motor failure, the best, safest and quickest course is to seek expert opinion from one of the many companies who offer a motor repair service.

Chapter 10
LATHES OF THE WORLD

Most of the lathes in this chapter, together with the equipment and accessories supplied as standard or available as optional extras, are long out of production. Likewise, many of the manufacturers either have ceased trading or changed their place of business. For-up-to-date information the reader is referred to the *Directory of Lathe Manufacturers*, page xiii. Lathes and accessories currently available are described and illustrated in the following chapter, *Lathes Today*, page 153.

STANDARD SET OF ACCESSORIES

Set of split chucks.
Set of step chucks.
Set of ring chucks.
Set of wax chucks.
Set of lantern chucks (large).
Set of lantern chucks (small).
Wood screw chucks.

Wood turning chucks.
T-rest.
Roller rest (single).
Universal chuck.
Runners for tailstock.
Drill holders.

LATHES OF THE WORLD
ARS *

Made by Atelier de Construction de Rennes, 22 Boulevard de la Tour-d'Anvergne, Rennes, France.

In design this lathe is reminiscent of the Lorch lathe. The bed is round with a flat at the back (Fig. 161). The spindle bore is for 8 mm.

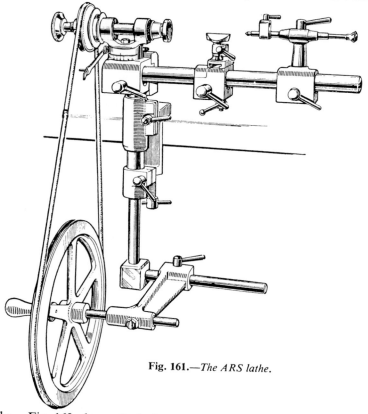

Fig. 161.—*The ARS lathe.*

chucks. Fig. 162 shows the lathe complete with accessories supplied by this maker ; it will be noted that the hand wheel is included in the cabinet.

* no longer made

98

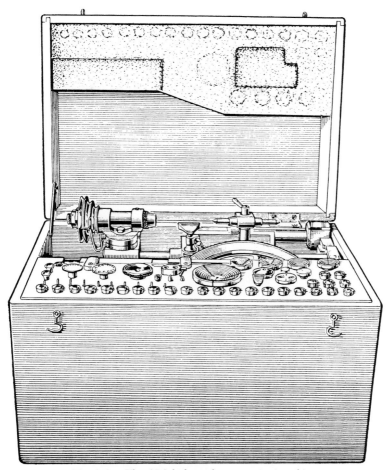

Fig. 162.—*The ARS lathe with accessories in cabinet.*

Specification

Model	A.R.S.
Bed	Round with flat.
Mounting	One foot with clamp.
Headstock	Double cone bearings.
Drive	Separate motor or hand wheel.
Tailstock	Solid runner.
General Finish	Nickel plated.
Dimensions	Spindle bore : 8 mm.
	Height of centres : 40 mm.
	Length of bed : 280 mm.

Equipment

The equipment for this lathe includes, in addition to the standard sets of accessories enumerated on page 98, the following:—

Self-centring drilling attachment.   Hand wheel.

BERGEON

(see also page 154)

Made by the machine tool manufacturers DIXI in Switzerland specially for and marketed by Bergeon & Co., of Le Locle, Switzerland. The bore of the spindle is 8 mm. The main parts of the lathe are enamelled a beige colour and the other parts are nickelled. The manufacturers claim that the advantage of this finish is that it is non-reflecting. They also say that the lathe is designed to take the majority of the accessories from other makers. Fig. 163 shows the Bergeon lathe. The bed is round with a flat ground at the back. A unique

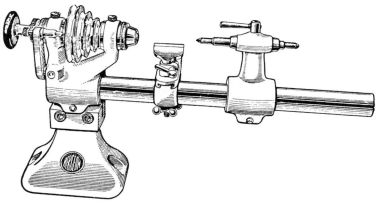

Fig. 163.—*The Bergeon lathe.*

feature is that a foot to support the tailstock end of the bed is obtainable separately. This converts the lathe into a heavy purpose machine and is useful when fitted up for wheel cutting or milling operations, as it gives the lathe added stability. Fig. 164 illustrates the Bergeon lathe with full complement of accessories.

Specification.

Model	" Bergeon ".
Bed	Round with flat.
Mounting	One or two feet with clamp.
Headstock	Cone bearings.
Drive	Either with separate motor or hand wheel.
Tailstock	Runner with chuck.
General Finish	Yellowish grey.
Dimensions	Spindle bore : 8 mm.
	Height of centres : 40 mm.
	Length of bed : 275 mm. and 325 mm.

100

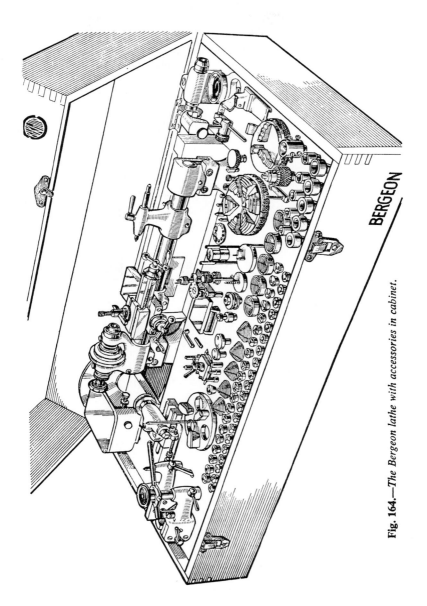

BERGEON

Fig. 164.—*The Bergeon lathe with accessories in cabinet.*

101

Equipment.

The equipment for this lathe includes, in addition to the standard set of accessories enumerated on page 98, the following :—

Drilling tailstock.
Fixed tailstock.
Swingover hand rest.
Gap bed lathe bar, length 275 mm.
Clamp to fix on the lathe bar.
Fixed foot.
Revolving foot.
Tightening key.
Cross slide.
Milling attachment.
Grinding attachment.
Dividing plate.
Mandrel face plate three jaws.
Screwed arbor.
Set of 10 recessed collets 5, 6 to 14 mm.
Box chuck with 8 clamping screws.
Grinding wheel holder.
Milling cutter holder.
Jacob style chuck holder.
Carrier chuck.
Complete universal runner.

Centring plate with 10 taper holes.
Pivot polishing accessory.
Runner combined with slide and pulleys.
Stake holder runner.
Set of 2 stake holders.
T rest roller.
Sawing table.
Revolving tool holder.
Set of 6 spare cutters.
Eye-glass stand with eye-glass.
Drilling attachment.
Countershaft.
Driving attachment for countershaft.
Hand fly-wheel.
Bergeon motor.
Hand resistance.
Bergeon motor three phase current.
Driving attachment for motor.
Foot-resistance with cord.
Transformer.

BOLEY

Made by G. Boley of Esslingen, Neckar, Germany. Obtainable through dealers in watchmakers' tools. The trade marks are " G. Boley ", " Boley ". Each tool is stamped with one of these

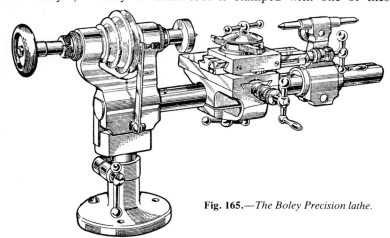

Fig. 165.—*The Boley Precision lathe.*

marks. The illustration, Fig. 165, shows a typical Boley lathe. In the catalogue it is stated :

The construction allows the lathe to be used with the headstock on the right or left of the operator, also the removal and replacing of the slide rest and hand rest (T-rest) transverse to the bar without removing the tailstock. The light yet strong construction of the lathe, coupled with the above advantage, makes this lathe the most perfect tool of its kind, for real precision work.

The round bar (bed) is flattened on the top for securely binding the movable parts.

The headstock has a hollow spindle and is arranged to take chucks, the spindle is hardened and ground, running in hardened bearings, which are adjustable. For simple dividing work the three step pulley cone is provided with four sets of divisions, viz. 4, 24, 28, 30, the headstock has fitted to it an index lever which can be placed either at the front or the rear of the headstock, and the point of this index engages in the holes of any of the division.

The guide of the runner in the tailstock is cut open underneath, being thus protected against dust. The lever screw for fixing the headstock and tailstock, also the clamping screw for the tailstock bar, can quickly and easily be reversed by means of the tapered screw (see Fig. 166) thereby transforming the lathe from a left-hand to a right-hand one.

The position of the lever of the clamping screws can be chosen as required.

The lathe frames are of best cast iron, the bearings and spindles are of cast steel ; all parts of the lathe are made to gauge and therefore interchangeable as far as the purpose of the fitting allows. The parts are ground and nickel plated. Upon request the parts can be supplied plain.

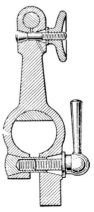

Fig. 166.
The lever screw for fixing head and tailstock of Boley lathe.

Specification

Model	" Boley " precision lathe.
Bed	Round with flat top.
Mounting	One foot and screws.
Headstock	Hardened and ground spindle with hardened and tapered adjustable bearings.
Drive	Separate shaft or hand wheel.
Tailstock	Hollow spindle to take runner collet.
General Finish	Nickel plated.
Dimensions	Spindle bore : 8 mm.
	Height of centres : 45 mm.
	Length of bed : 260 mm.

Accessories

The equipment for this lathe includes, in addition to the standard set of accessories enumerated on page 98, the following :—

Cutting sinkers.
Dividing or count plate for headstock.
Drilling device.
Drilling tailstock.
Drilling self-centring attachment.
Drilling self-centring discs.
Emery wheel.
Face plate.
Hand wheels.
Jacot drums.
Laps.

Mandrel headstock.
Pulley. Combination, large and small.
Pulley. Combination, safety.
Pivot, polishing device.
Pivot, polishing runners.
Saw table.
Slide rest, compound.
Transmission pulleys.
Tapping die.
Tapping tool attachment.
Wheel cutting attachment.

The firm of G. Boley also make two other lathes rather more robust than the one just described. The general design is reminiscent of the American Webster-Whitcomb and Moseley lathes. The bed is the hollow type with headstock, tailstock and T-rest fitting on to the flat and chamfered top of the bed, termed " prismatic bar ". These lathes are made with 8 mm. spindle bore and are supplied with a single or double support. The height of centre is 50 mm.

103

Figs. 167 and 168 show the Boley W.W. "America" lathe and the H.M.E. lathe with 400 mm. bed and two supports.

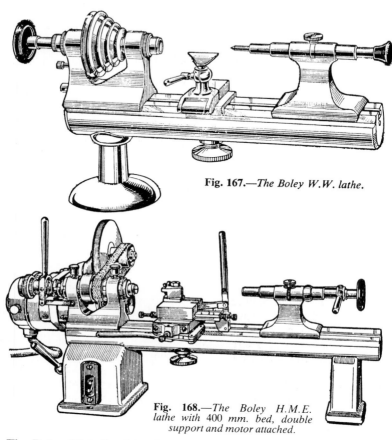

Fig. 167.—*The Boley W.W. lathe.*

Fig. 168.—*The Boley H.M.E. lathe with 400 mm. bed, double support and motor attached.*

The Boley High Precision F1 lathe is unique and requires a different technique in its use. It is illustrated in Figs. 169, 170 and 171. As will be seen from the last of these, it is used from the end, looking over the tail stock (21), when a hand tool is employed. This is a revolutionary break away from standard practice and may have considerable influence on future design. Note that the tool rest is on the right, looking from the end.

A rest (4) for the right hand, holding the tool, is part of the lathe and so is a mirror (10) to assist accurate turning, in fact, every possible aid is provided to enable the operator's skill to reach its highest level.

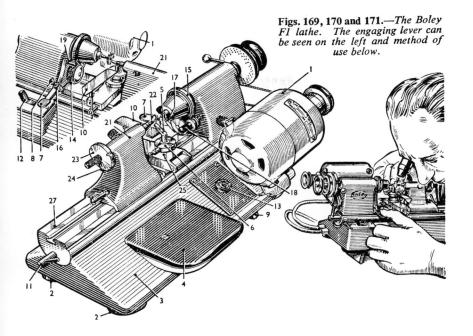

The belt from the built-in motor (1) can be fitted to either of three pulleys, one driving the spindle direct and the others through a lay shaft and friction pulley (14). When the lay shaft drive is being used, the watchmaker presses his left thumb on the lever (7), which causes the friction wheel to contact a disc (15) and rotate the spindle. As soon as pressure on the lever is released, the spindle is immediately brought to rest by the pin (19) on the lever. A stop (8) on the lever can be used to adjust the pressure exerted by the leather-covered friction wheel, so that the drive can be used in the same way as a safety pulley. Thus sensitive finger tip control of engagement is obtained, with sensitive adjustment to the maximum torque which is exerted by the spindle.

The motor is started and stopped by a switch on the left of the lathe. Another switch reverses the direction of rotation.

The unusual form of tool rest (5) with a tip-over arrangement (25), has a ring (6) at its base on which a finger can be rested to steady the tool. Longitudinal adjustment to the spindle for centre turning can be made by the knurled knob (18). There is a pin (17) for driving between centres. For eccentric turning, eccentric centres are provided in the runner (22), located by the slots in the disc (23) and the lock (24).

The prismatic bed (27) with its head and tailstocks and rest can be rotated axially through an angle of about 15 deg. on each side of the upright position to facilitate turning, being locked by the lever (11).

The lathe stands on three feet, two at the tail stock end (2), and one (9), which can be adjusted to alter the angle of the lathe, at the headstock end. The adjustable foot tilts the lathe towards the operator so that the best view of the workpiece can be obtained.

The basic specifications are : bed length 280 mm., centre height 50 mm., and spindle bore 8 mm.

A good range of accessories is available and includes slide rest, face plate, drilling attachment and a full range of split, wheel, wax and other chucks. The slide rest tool is of standard pattern and is fitted in the usual position. With it in use, the lathe is turned to the normal position in relation to the operator, otherwise operation of the slides would be left handed.

See also page 155 for details of model 1B.

BOLEY & LEINEN, see Leinen

THE C.L.H. 14

Made by C. Levitt & Son, Stockton-on-Forest, York, England. The maker claims that all headstocks and tailstocks are machined to standard gauges, with the round bed with flat at back. Fig. 172 shows the C.L.H. 14 standard lathe.

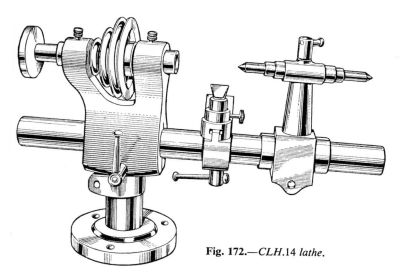

Fig. 172.—*CLH.14 lathe.*

Model	C.L.H. 14.
Bed	Round with one flat, adjustable and detachable.
Mounting	One foot with clamp.
Headstock	Parallel bearings with spindle adjustable. Cone bearings can be supplied if desired.
Drive	Separate motor or hand wheel. Integral motor supplied upon request.
Tailstock	Lever drilling stock for 8 mm. chucks.
General Finish	Plated.
Dimensions	Spindle bore : 8 mm.
	Height of centres : 40 mm.
	Length of bed : 180 mm.

Accessories

The equipment includes, in addition to the standard set of accessories enumerated on page 98, the following :—

Pivot steady, fits in place of T-rest.
Carrier plate.
Universal runner for tailstock with pulley and two loose centres and driver.
Lever drilling attachment, used in place of tailstock runner, for C.L.H. No. 12 and bench lathes.

Pivot runner used in place of centre runner for rolling pivots.
Separate lever drilling tailstock, for 8 mm. collets, etc.
Handwheel for driving lathes.
Boxes for lathe, collets, step chucks, etc., for C.L.H. 12 or 14.

Another lathe without tailstock is the C.L.H. 11 (Fig. 173). This is exactly similar to the C.L.H. 14 but with the bed fixed and no tailstock supplied or accommodation made for it.

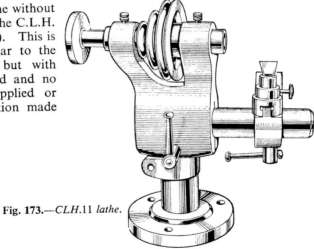

Fig. 173.—*CLH.*11 *lathe.*

Specification

Model	C.L.H. 11.
Bed	Round with one flat, not adjustable.
Mounting	One foot, a fixture.
Headstock	Parallel bearings.
Drive	Either by separate motor or hand wheel.
Tailstock	No tailstock.
General Finish	Plated.
Dimensions	Spindle bore : 8 mm.
	Height of centres : 40 mm.
	Length of bed : 90 mm.

Equipment

As for the C.L.H. 14 model.

Fig. 174 is C.L.H. 7 lathe for vice. A useful simple tool and as the maker says :

Diecast with an alloy as strong as steel. Can be used right or left hand. Hollow precision ground mandrel with draw in spindle for 8 mm. standard collets and step chucks. Adjustable bearings. Hardened T-rest. Ground runner with hollow and point centres. Fixed tailstock. Overall measurements : 8 in. × 3 in.

Fig. 174.—*CLH*.7 *lathe*.

Specification

Model	C.L.H. 7.
Bed	Flat bed.
Mounting	For use in vice : foot can be supplied with screw.
Headstock	Flat bearings.
Drive	By separate motor or hand wheel.
Tailstock	Drill spindle with 8 mm. check. Fixed tailstock.
General Finish	Polished and lacquered.
Dimensions	Spindle bore : 8 mm.
	Height of centres : 27 mm.
	Length of bed : 60 mm.

Equipment

As for the C.L.H. 14 model.

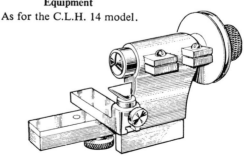

Another lathe by the same maker known as C.L.H. 8, Fig. 175, which is exactly similar to the C.L.H. 7 lathe but without tailstock. Overall measurement: 6 in. × 3 in.

Fig. 175.—*CLH*.8 *lathe*.

108

Specification

Model	C.L.H. 8.
Bed	Flat.
Mounting	For use in the vice : foot, with screw, can be supplied.
Headstock	Flat bearings.
Drive	By separate motor or hand wheel.
Tailstock	No tailstock.
General Finish	Polished and lacquered.
Dimensions	Spindle bore : 8 mm.
	Height of centres : 27 mm.
	Length of bed : 60 mm.

Equipment

As for the C.L.H. 14 model.

Both of these last mentioned lathes are useful tools and are considerably less expensive than a lathe with a movable tailstock. As the headstock is made to take all ordinary chucks such as split, wax, universal, many jobs can be done with this lathe equally as well as with the full standard lathe. Such jobs as turning balance staffs and pinions, turning out recesses with the aid of the wax chuck, and as the maker says, for watchmakers who " never use a tailstock ". All the C.L.H. lathes have a spindle bore of 8 mm.

CORONET

Production of the Coronet watchmaker's lathes ceased many years ago. This manufacturer made three sizes, the Ruby, Diamond and Jewel. The Ruby and Diamond were the two most likely to be of use to the watch and clock maker.

The Ruby, Fig. 176, can be converted into an upright drilling machine,

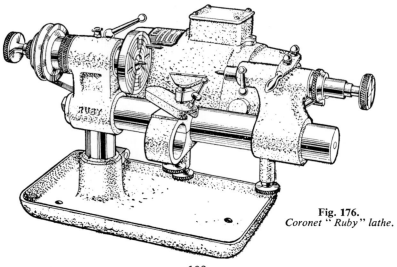

Fig. 176.
Coronet " Ruby " lathe.

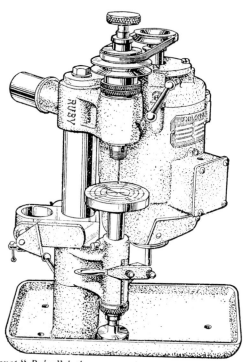

Fig. 177.—*Coronet " Ruby " lathe converted to use as upright drilling machine.*

as Fig. 177. As the makers say, the design covers the whole of the watch and clock makers' requirements. Provision is made for a slide rest, which when included with the lathe for turning purposes will also enable the operator to convert the lathe into a vertical milling machine. The motor shaft is double ended and can be supplied with adaptor for mounting a grinding wheel. This extension may also be used for the driving of flexible shaft equipment of any make. Spindle bore to take 8 mm. chucks.

Specification

Model	Ruby.
Bed	Round with flat.
Mounting	Round pillar swivelling on chip tray, with screws.
Headstock	Conical and ball bearings, adjustable.
Drive	Either by separate motor or with the motor as an integral part of the lathe.
Tailstock	Same as the headstock.
General Finish	Chrome and black, ripple.
Dimensions	Spindle bore : 8 mm.
	Height of centres : 38 mm.
	Length of bed : 279 mm.

Equipment

Slide rest.   Headstock made to take all standard 8 mm. chuck equipment.

The Diamond is a heavier duty and larger lathe, but is still precision made. Height of centres $2\frac{1}{4}$ in. and 15 in. bed (Fig. 178). The spindle is bored to take 8 mm. chucks. The headstock swivels to allow taper

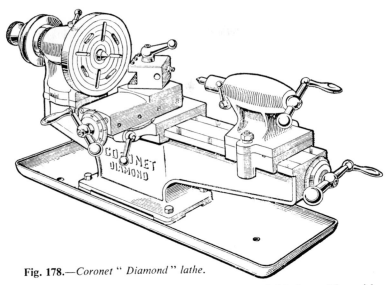

Fig. 178.—Coronet " Diamond " lathe.

turning and boring in the chuck and is graduated 10 deg. either side of zero line. The spindle can be released and removed instantaneously and replaced by the high speed unit for work requiring diamond or hard metal tipped tools. Both the Ruby and Diamond lathes are finished in black ripple enamel.

Specification

Model	Diamond.
Bed	Flat box type.
Mounting	Single base in one with bed.
Headstock	Conical and ball bearings.
Drive	By separate motor.
Tailstock	Hollow runner or runner for chuck required. Micro feed.
General Finish	Chrome and black ripple.
Dimensions	Spindle bore : 8 mm.
	Height of centres : 56 mm.
	Length of bed : 380 mm.

Equipment
As for model Ruby.

DERBYSHIRE

Made by F. W. Derbyshire, Inc., 265 Bear Hill Road, Waltham, Massachusetts, Mass. 02154 U.S.A.

111

Derbyshire make four types of lathes :

(1) Derbyshire Webster-Whitcomb and Derbyshire Large.

(2) Magnus.

(3) Elect.

(4) 750 and " A " (12·7 mm. max. collet capacity).

Equipment marked " Derbyshire " is interchangeable on the D.W.W., D. Large and Magnus models.

Equipment marked " Derbyshire Webster-Whitcomb " is used on this model only.

Equipment marked " Derbyshire Large " is used on this model only.

Equipment marked " Magnus " is for this model only.

Equipment marked " Elect " is for this model only.

Chucks marked " Magnus-Elect " are for either of the two models.

Equipment marked " D-E " or " Derby-Elect " can be used on any model.

The Webster-Whitcomb lathe, Fig. 179, is made with 12 in., 15 in. and 18 in. beds.

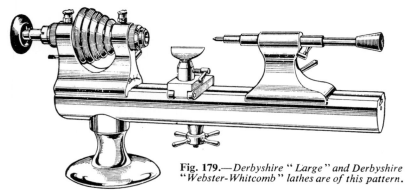

Fig. 179.—*Derbyshire " Large" and Derbyshire "Webster-Whitcomb" lathes are of this pattern.*

Specification

Model	D.W.W. and Derbyshire Large.
Bed	Prismatic.
Mounting	One foot, or two if required on the 18 in. bed, with screws.
Headstock	Hardened and ground spindle either with cone or ball bearings. Cone bearing is adjustable.
Drive	By separate motor or hand wheel.
Tailstock	Chuck holding tailstock is available. Micrometer feed with dial on screw tailstock.
General Finish	Machine tool grey.
Dimensions	Spindle bore : 8 mm.
	Height of centres : 50 mm.
	Length of bed : 12 in., 15 in. or 18 in.

112

Equipment

The equipment includes, in addition to the standard set of accessories enumerated on page 98, the following :—

Plain tailstock.
Closed tailstock.
Half-open tailstock.
Screw tailstock w/centre.
Plain chuck-holding tailstock.
Combination tailstock, rack and pinion feed, to take headstock chucks. (On above two items specify D.W.W. or D. Large.)
Plain lever tailstock.
Lever tailstock to take ⧻1A Jacobs chuck, less chuck.
Two-slided slide rest w/tool post, six square and two round tools, and round tool holder.
Three-slided slide rest w/tool post, set of tools, and round tool holder.
Double compound, rack and pinion, slide rest w/front tool post slide graduated to swivel 360°.
Two-slided slide rest w/lever action.
Three-slided slide rest w/lever action.
Forming slide rest w/rack and pinion cross slide, two tool posts, and two tool bits.
Tip-over hand rest.
Wheel cutter and milling attachment w/one cutter arbor (mounts on top slide of 2 or 3-slided S.R.).
Wheel cutter and milling tool w/one cutter arbor (fits directly to lathe bed). (Specify lathe model on above two items.)
Idler pulleys and stand (for driving pivot polisher or wheel cutter and milling attachment).
4 in. metal speed pulley. (With plain countershaft).
Pivot polisher w/cross-feed screw and one each boxwood and bellmetal laps.
Screw-cutting attachment w/15 gears to cut English threads.
Screw-cutting attachment w/15 gears to cut English and metric threads. (Above items require a slide rest.)
4-position, self-indexing, semi-automatic turret.
Back rest w/fixture bolt assembly.
Index plate, 8 in. dia., w/index pawl, 36 rows of holes, all numbers to 80 and even numbers to 100 ; also, 144-360-365 and 366.
Index latch and 7 plates ; ⧻3, 6, 7, 8, 48, 60

and 90 (to fit back end of headstock spindle).
Index latch and 6 plates ; ⧻30, 45, 60, 90, 180 and 360.
Index latch and 8 plates ; ⧻12, 50, 60, 80, 90, 100, 120 and 150.
72-tooth index and latch (for wheel cutters).
125-tooth index and latch.
Dog-face plate chuck with dog.
  Chuck only.
  Dog only.
Snyder-Bezel chuck, 2½ in. dia., O.D. mounted.
Snyder-Bezel chuck, not mounted.
Universal face plate, 3⅞ in. dia., with pump centre and draw-in rod, mounted.
Extension nose chucks, ·020 through ·054.
Buff chuck.
Flat face chucks, ⧻3 to 50 inclusive.
Jacobs No. 1A drill chuck, capacity 0 to ¼ in., mounted on chuck stem for combination tailstock.
Plain tailstock chuck holders.
Taper chuck.
Taper chuck with hard centre (for comb. tailst.).
Taper chuck for laps.
Taper reamer for laps on pivot polisher.
Saw arbor chuck.
Fly cutter arbor chuck.
Wheel cutter arbor chuck.
Grinding wheel arbor chuck.
Saw arbor chuck blank.
Jewelling chuck, soft sawed.
Balance chuck for pivot polisher.
Balance chuck for balance wheel.
Bracelet chuck, ⧻1 through 5.
Adaptor chuck.
Pivot polisher chuck for laps.
Set of cutting tools.
Foot pedal.
Drive plate.
Grinding wheel mount for pivot polisher
Cutter arbor.
Four-step cone pulley.
Motor cone pulley, 2½ in. diameter.
Countershaft pulley, 2¼ in. diameter.
Countershaft pulley, 3 in. diameter (standard).
Boxwood, bellmetal, steel, brass or iron laps.

The Elect lathe, Fig. 180, is made with 15 in. and 18 in. beds.

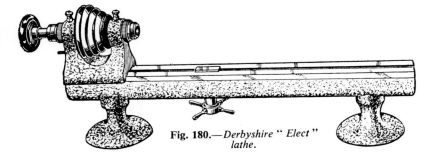

Fig. 180.—*Derbyshire " Elect "*
lathe.

113

Model	Elect.
Bed	Prismatic.
Mounting	One foot for 15 in. bed and two feet for 18 in. and 22 in. beds, with screws.
Headstock	Hardened and ground spindle, either cone or ball bearings. Cone bearing adjustable.
Drive	By separate motor.
Tailstock	Chuck holding tailstock is available. Micrometer feed with dial on screw tailstock.
General Finish	Machine tool grey.
Dimensions	Spindle bore : 10 mm. Height of centres : 60 mm. Length of bed : 15 in., 18 in. or 22 in.

Equipment

The equipment for this lathe is similar to that enumerated on page 113 for the D.W.W. and Derbyshire Large lathes.

The Derbyshire Magnus lathe (Fig. 181) is a heavier type of lathe and is made with 12 in., 15 in., and 18 in. beds.

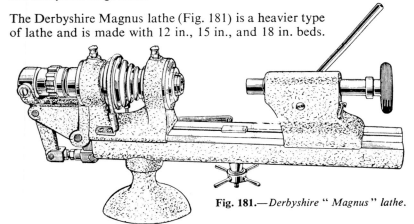

Fig. 181.—*Derbyshire " Magnus " lathe.*

Specification

Model	Magnus.
Bed	Prismatic.
Mounting	One foot, or two feet on the 18 in. bed, with screws.
Headstock	Hardened and ground spindle either cone or ball bearings. Cone bearing is adjustable.
Drive	By separate motor.
Tailstock	Chuck holding tailstock is available. Micrometer feed with dial on screw tailstock.
General Finish	Machine tool grey.
Dimensions	Spindle bore : 10 mm. Height of centres : 50 mm. Length of bed : 12 in., 15 in. or 18 in.

Equipment

The equipment for this lathe is similar to that enumerated on page 113 for the D.W.W. and Derbyshire Large lathes.

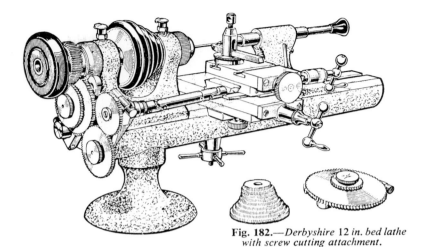

Fig. 182.—*Derbyshire* 12 *in. bed lathe
with screw cutting attachment.*

Fig. 182 is the Derbyshire 12 in. bed lathe, set up with screw cutting attachment of 14 gears, to cut both English and metric threads, mounted on the top slide rest ; plain tailstock.   A larger lathe made by Derbyshire is the Model No. 750 (Fig. 183).

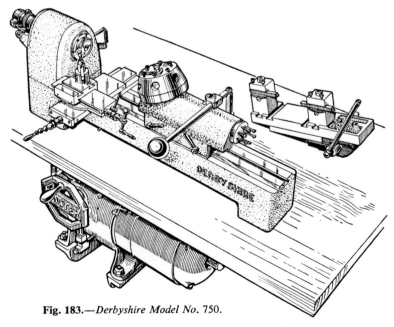

Fig. 183.—*Derbyshire Model No. 750.*

Specification

Model	No. 750.
Bed	Prismatic.
Mounting	Two pedestals, one piece casting with bed.
Headstock	Hardened and ground spindle either with cone or ball bearings. Cone bearing is adjustable.
Drive	By separate variable speed motor.
Tailstock	Chuck holding tailstock is available. Micrometer feed with dial on screw tailstock.
General Finish	Machine tool grey.
Dimensions	Spindle bore : 10 mm.
	Height of centres : 75 mm.
	Length of bed : 22 in.

Equipment

The equipment for this lathe is similar to that enumerated on page 113 for the D.W.W. and Derbyshire Large lathes.

Derbyshire make the most complete range of accessories it is possible to conceive and the general standard of craftsmanship is of the highest order.

FAVORITE

Made for Golay-Buchel & Cie, Lausanne, Switzerland. The lathe bed is round with a flat ground at the back. Fig. 184 shows the " Favorite

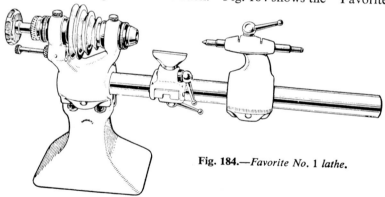

Fig. 184.—*Favorite No. 1 lathe.*

No. 1 " lathe and Fig. 185 the lathe complete with all accessories made by this firm. Golay-Buchel also supply a more robust lathe which they have named " Favorite 2 " (Fig. 186).* The bed is very substantial and of the flat type. A unique feature is that the outside diameter of the end of the spindle is cut with a thread. This, as the manufacturers say, allows the large types of chucks such as the universal, to be fitted on the outside of the spindle to avoid vibration. The lathe can be

* The Favorite No. 1 and 2 lathes are no longer made. See pages 157–8 for details of current models.

116

used for the light work of the watch repairer and also for small precision engineering work. The lathe is guaranteed to an accuracy of 1/100th part of a mm. Fig. 187 is the " Favorite No. 2 " lathe·fitted on to a board with motor and complete range of accessories.

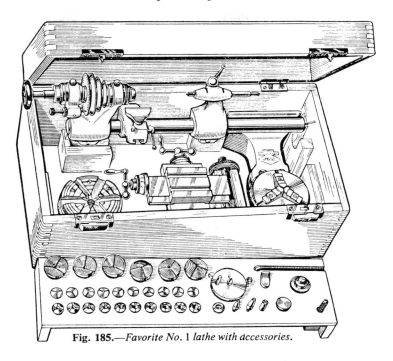

Fig. 185.—*Favorite No.* 1 *lathe with accessories.*

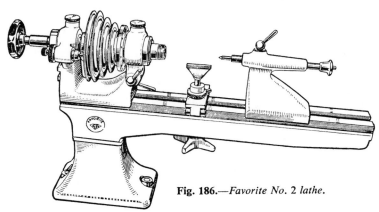

Fig. 186.—*Favorite No.* 2 *lathe.*

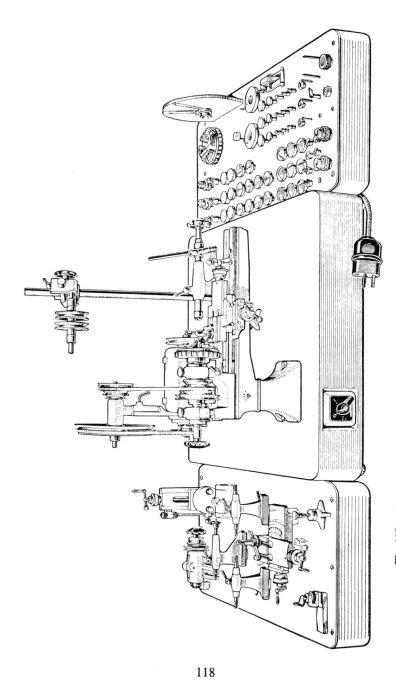

Fig. 187.—*Favorite No. 2 lathe fitted on to board with motor and complete range of accessories.*

Model	No. 1.
Bed	Round with flat side
Mounting	One foot with clamp.
Headstock	Bronze cone bearings.
Drive	Separate motor or hand wheel.
Tailstock	With chuck fitting and micrometer feed.
General Finish	Green enamel.
Dimensions	Spindle bore : 8 mm.
	Height of centres : 50 mm.
	Length of bed : 275 and 325 mm.

Equipment

The equipment for this lathe includes, in addition to the standard set of accessories enumerated on page 98, the following :—

Steadying device.	Slide Rest.	Lever drilling device.

Specification

Model	No. 2.
Bed	Cast steel, 33 mm. square section.
Mounting	One or two feet, solid with bed.
Headstock	Bronze cone bearings.
Drive	Separate motor.
Tailstock	With chuck fitting and micrometer feed.
General Finish	Green enamel.
Dimensions	Spindle bore : 8 mm.
	Height of centres : 50 mm.
	Length of bed : 300 or 400 mm.

Equipment

The equipment for this lathe includes, in addition to the standard set of accessories enumerated on page 98, the following :—

Drilling attachment.	Mandrel face plate.
Box chuck.	Saw table.
Jacots chuck.	Slide rest.
Jacot drum.	Wheel cutting attachment.

GAMMA*

Made by Elektroimpex, Budapest, Hungary ; the London agents are, English Exporters (London) Ltd., 9 and 10 Marble Arch, London, W.1.

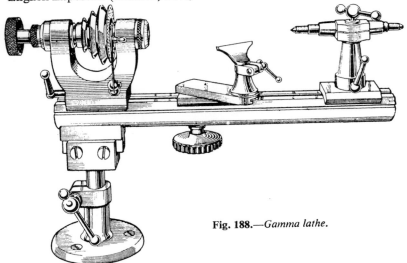

Fig. 188.—*Gamma lathe.*

* No longer in production.

This lathe (Fig. 188) has a flat top chamfered bed similar to the Webster-Whitcomb type of lathe.

The headstock is fitted with hardened and ground bronze conical bearings. Such bearings give good service and proof of this is the early Lorch lathes, still in use and giving good service.

Specification

Model	Gamma.
Bed	Prismatic 30 deg. to the two upper sides.
Mounting	One foot with screws.
Headstock	Cone bearing.
Drive	Either by separate motor or hand wheel.
Tailstock	Runner with chuck fitting and micro feed.
General Finish	Nickelled.
Dimensions	Spindle bore : 8 mm.
	Height of centres : 51 mm.
	Length of bed : 260 mm.

Equipment

The equipment for this lathe includes, in addition to the standard set of accessories enumerated on page 98, the following :—

Live face plate for tailstock with wire spanner and double pulley. Pulley ∅ 16·5 mm.
Change pulley for above 12 mm. ∅
Bell chuck.
Adaptor for connecting mandrels with bayonet lock.

Drill pump.
Wooden case fitted to accommodate all accessories of combination as above detailed.
Micrometric cross slide rest.

IME*

Made by Ideal Machine Tool & Engineering Co. Ltd., 282 Kingsland Road, London, E.8, England. The IME has several unique features. The bed is of the dovetail form (Fig. 189). Spring loaded fittings are provided for the retention of oil to lubricate the spindle bearings and oil retaining felts give protection to the bearings. The runner in the tailstock is secured by a 4-jaw chuck which grips the runner by slightly

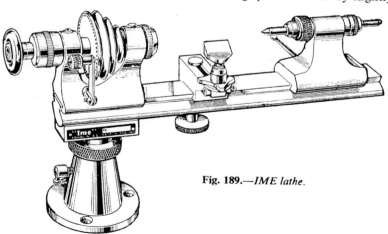

Fig. 189.—*IME lathe.*

* No longer in production.

turning the knurled cap. The T-rest itself is secured by a 4-jaw chuck in a similar manner to the tailstock runner.

This form of fixing is most convenient, a slight turn and the part is either fixed or released and it has the advantage, especially in the case of the runner, of securing with an even pressure to ensure truth. Another feature is that each lathe is supplied with a certificate of accuracy, the errors, if any, are tabulated (Fig. 190).

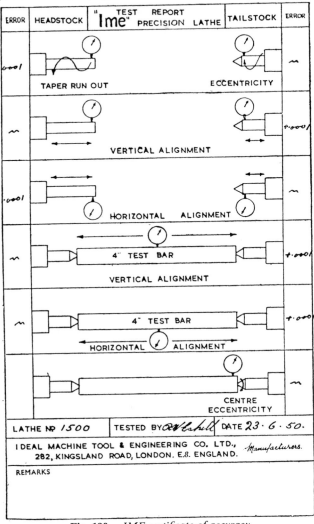

Fig. 190.—*IME certificate of accuracy.*

121

The bed is V-shaped which ensures absolute rigidity and prevents vibration. It is made of the best tool steel, precision ground and hand scraped. The bed is secured to an adjustable swivelling foot which gives a good clearance from the bench and allows ample room for the hand to adjust the T-rest.

The headstock and tailstock are line bored and ground in sets on a master bed in one operation. Both the headstock and tailstock are provided with a clamp which runs the full length of each part ; in this manner these parts can be made absolutely firm with the slightest touch of the tightening handle.

The conical bearings are hardened, ground and lapped and made of the finest quality high-carbon steel. Adjustment of spindle is effected by two nuts at the rear of the spindle. The hollow headstock spindle is made to take 8 mm. chucks.

The spindle is made of nickel chromium steel, hardened, ground and lapped. After assembling, the headstock spindle and the tailstock bushes are ground on a master bed to ensure perfect concentricity. The draw-in spindle of the headstock is provided with a hardened and ground revolvable conical seating. This fits into a corresponding cone at the rear end of the headstock ; side play is thus eliminated and the bearing will give good service for a great number of years.

The spindle is lubricated through special spring-loaded ball fittings, which are almost flush and quite unobtrusive. Dust covers are provided to protect front and rear bearings and two oil-retaining felt washers safeguard the bearings from within.

The three-speed pulley is made of duralumin and at one end a high-carbon steel plate with 60 holes for dividing purposes is attached. This may be replaced by another plate giving alternative division, should this be required. The pulley is indexed and secured by a spring-loaded pin, the tension of which is adjustable. These pulleys run perfectly true, both for concentricity and balance.

The runner, or centre of the tailstock is held in position by a form of collet or chuck. A slight turn of the knurled ring secures the runner firmly. Being gripped by an even pressure from four sides it is absolutely true.

Another feature of the tailstock is the renewable bush, which, should wear take place after long use, can be replaced in a few moments without affecting the alignment accuracy.

The tool rest is the tip-over style and here again a special feature is introduced. The actual T-rest is secured by a four-star piece which opens and closes a 4-jaw chuck, similar to the tailstock runner. The tool rest is adjustable for wear, being supported on screw adjustable balls.

Fig. 191.—*IME lathe with accessories and cabinet.*

Each lathe is tested at a speed of 5,000 r.p.m. for eight hours, after which it is dismantled, cleaned, re-assembled and rigorously inspected. A test sheet is supplied with each machine. The lathe and accessories are nickel plated and highly polished, and the wooden case provided is of polished mahogany. Fig. 191 shows the IME lathe with the full complement of accessories.

Specification

Model	W.B.3.
Bed	Double vee.
Mounting	One foot and screw.
Headstock	Double cone adjustable bearings.
Drive	By separate motor or hand wheel.
Tailstock	Hollow runner to take 8 mm. split chucks.
General Finish	Polished nickel.
Dimensions	Spindle bore : 8 mm.
	Height of centres : 40 mm.
	Length of bed : 254 mm., and 350 mm.

Equipment

The equipment for this lathe includes, in addition to the standard set of accessories enumerated on page 98, the following :—

Compound slide rest, for longitudinal and surface turning with square tool posts, collars graduated, fitted with ball thrust bearings, both slides operated from the front, nickel plated.

Vertical slide with graduated screw feed, complete with fixing clamp and tommy bar (used with compound slide rest).

Tailstock drilling attachment, consisting of runner, draw-in-bar to fit split chucks, inclusive 6 split chucks (0·4 ; 0·6 ; 0·8 ; 1·0 ; 1·2 ; 1·4 mm.).

Lever attachment for above.

Drilling (graduated screw feed) attachment, supplied with 3 chucks, 0·6 ; 0·8 ; 1·0 mm.

Self-centring drilling attachment, with centring pin, drill holder and centring plate with 15 holes from ·15 to 1·5 mm. and 8 female centres from 0·2 to 0·9 mm.

Safety friction pulley attachment for headstock, with female and male centre, collet-locked.

Carrier plate with male and female centre and draw-in-bar.

Mandril face-plate with 3 dogs and pump centre.

8-screw chuck (bell chuck).

Arbor for circular saws and milling cutters, $\frac{1}{4}$ in. diameter.

Arbor for circular saws and milling cutters, $\frac{3}{16}$ in. diameter.

LANCO*

Made by Lane Cove Engineering Co., 405 Pacific Highway, Lane Cove, N.S.W., Australia.

Lanco make two sizes of lathes, one with 6 mm. spindle bore and the other with 8 mm. Fig. 192 is the 6 mm. lathe and Fig. 193 the 8 mm.

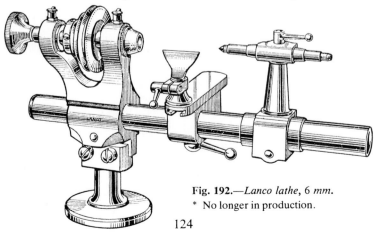

Fig. 192.—*Lanco lathe, 6 mm.*

* No longer in production.

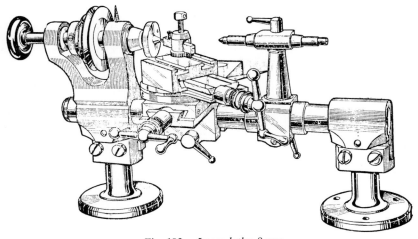

Fig. 193.—*Lanco lathe, 8 mm.*

Fig. 194 is the 8 mm. model complete with full equipment. Lanco term their lathes " Lorch type ".

Specification

Model	6 mm.
Bed	Round with a flat.
Mounting	One foot with screws.
Headstock	Cone bearings.
Drive	Either by separate motor or hand wheel.
Tailstock	Solid runner.
General Finish	Nickel plated.
Dimensions	Spindle bore : 6 mm.
	Height of centres : 39·687 mm.
	Length of bed : 8 in.

Model	8 mm.
Bed	Round with a flat.
Mounting	Two feet with screws.
Headstock	Cone bearings.
Drive	Either motor or hand wheel.
Tailstock	Solid runner.
General Finish	Nickel plated.
Dimensions	Spindle bore : 8 mm.
	Height of centres : 53·175 mm.

Equipment for the 6 mm. and 8 mm. models

The equipment for these lathes includes, in addition to the standard set of accessories, enumerated on page 98, the following :—

Compound slide rest.
Milling attachment.
Counter shaft.

Tailstock drill arbor with 0 to ⅛ in. Jacob chuck
2 in. grinding wheels.

125

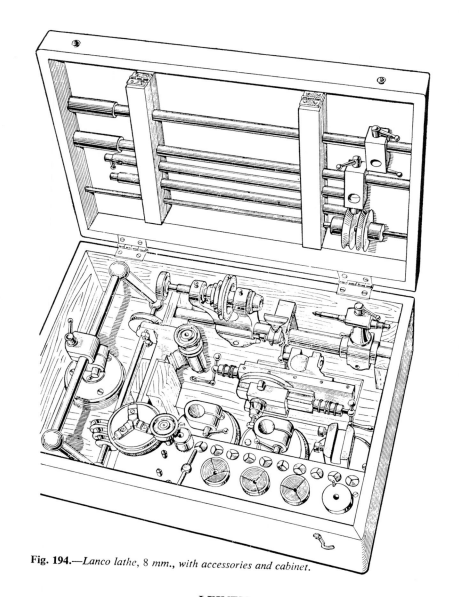

Fig. 194.—*Lanco lathe, 8 mm., with accessories and cabinet.*

LEINEN

Made by Boley & Leinen, Esslingen A.N., Germany. The lathes made by this firm bear the "Leinen" trademark. The illustration

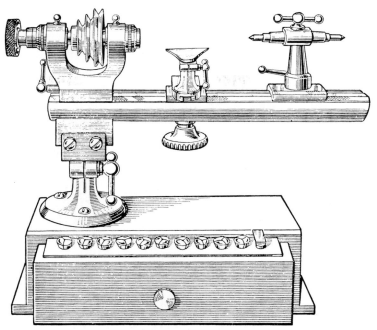

Fig. 195.—*Leinen Reform lathe.**

Fig. 195 shows the normal watchmakers' lathe, and the illustration Fig. 196 the W.W. Precision, with 400 mm. bed and two feet. See also pages 159–160.

The firm was established in 1905 by Josef Leinen and later Boley, a member of the family of G. Boley, joined the firm. Although the title of the firm is Boley & Leinen their lathes are known as Leinen. Fig. 197 shows the lathe with full complement of accessories.

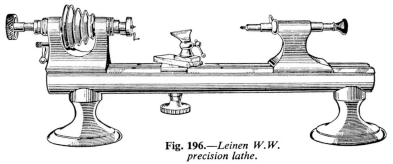

Fig. 196.—*Leinen W.W. precision lathe.*

* No longer made. A limited range of spares and accessories is still available however.

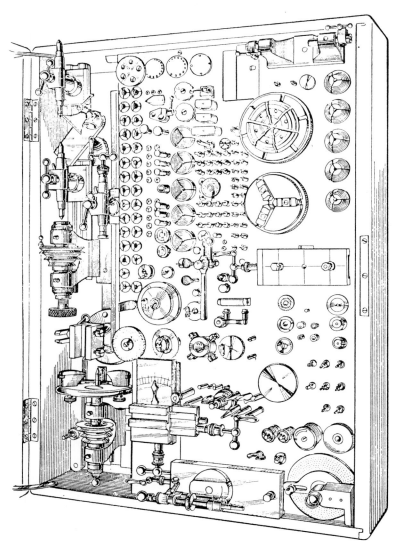

Fig. 197.—*Leinen lathe with accessories.*

The Leinen lathes are somewhat similar to the Boley lathes.

Specification

Model	Reform.
Bed	Prismatic.
Mounting	One foot and screws or two feet.
Headstock	Hardened steel spindle with double cone bearings.
Drive	Either by separate motor or hand wheel.
Tailstock	Hollow or solid runner.
General Finish	Nickel plated.
Dimensions	Spindle bore : 8 mm.
	Height of centres : 50 mm.
	Length of bed : 300 mm.

Equipment

The equipment for this lathe includes, in addition to the standard set of accessories enumerated on page 98, the following :—

Chucks, button.
Chucks, box.
Chucks, balance.
Chucks, carrier with male and female centres.
Dividing plates.
Drilling lever runner.
Drilling self-centring attachment.
Drilling self-centring plates.
Face plates.
Jacot drums.
Milling attachment.

Pulley, safety combination.
Rests, T tip over.
Rests, slide, compound.
Rests, double roller.
Rose cutters.
Runner, screw feed.
Saw tables.
Sinkers.
Topping tool attachment.
Wheel cutting attachment.

LEVIN

Made by Louis Levin & Son Inc., 3573 Hayden Avenue, Culver City, CA 90230, California, U.S.A.   See also pages 160–162.

Levin lathes are made with double cone bearings and also with ball bearings.   Fig. 198 is the cone bearing lathe and Fig. 199 the cone bearing assembly.

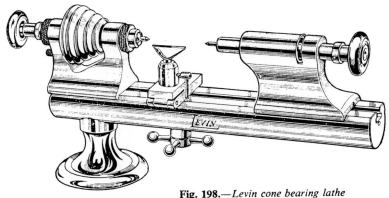

Fig. 198.—*Levin cone bearing lathe*

129

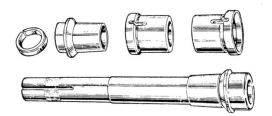

Fig. 199.—*Levin cone bearing assembly.*

Specification

Model	H.
Bed	Round with 60 deg. angular ways.
Mounting	One foot solid with bed.
Headstock	Hard steel spindle double cone bronze bearings.
Drive	Either with separate motor or hand wheel.
Tailstock	Runner with chuck.
General Finish	Chromium plate.
Dimensions	Spindle bore : 8 mm.
	Height of centres : 50 mm.
	Length of bed : 12 in.

Equipment

The equipment includes, in addition to the standard set of accessories enumerated on page 98, the following :—

Arbor, cutter, 4·4 mm.
Arbor, diamond wheel, ⅜ in.
Arbor, grinding wheel, ¼ in.
Arbor, saw, ¼ in.
Boring head.
Chucks, balance.
Chucks, crown, set of 13.
Chucks, vee centre.
Circular saw.
Cross slide.
Index plates, set of 40.

Pivot polisher and grinder.
Pivot straightener and polisher, less adaptor.
Screw cutting attachment.
Slide rest, 3 slide, plain.
Slide rest, 3 slide, lever feed.
Slide rest, 2 slide, plain.
Slide rest, 2 slide, lever feed.
Slide rest, lever feed attachment.
Slide rest, cutters, set of 6.
Wheel cutting and milling attachment.
Grinding attachment.

Fig. 200 is the pre-loaded ball bearing lathe and Fig. 201 the pre-loaded ball bearing assembly.

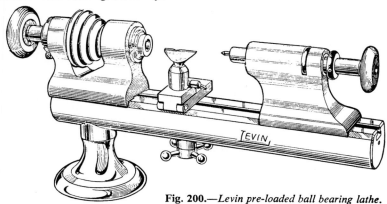

Fig. 200.—*Levin pre-loaded ball bearing lathe.*

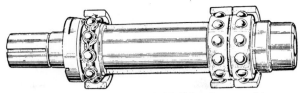

Fig. 201.—*Levin pre-loaded ball bearing assembly.*

Specification

Model	D.
Bed	Round with 60 deg. angular ways.
Mounting	One foot solid with bed.
Headstock	Hard steel spindle with pre-loaded ball bearings.
Drive	Either by separate motor or hand wheel.
Tailstock	Runner with chuck : rack and pinion feed.
General Finish	Chromium plate.
Dimensions	Spindle bore : 10 mm.
	Height of centres : 50 mm.
	Length of bed : 12 in.

Equipment

The equipment is similar to that enumerated on page 130 for H model.

LORCH*

Made by Lorch, Schmidt & Co., G.M.B.H. Frankfurt am Main, Ost 1, Germany. See also page 162 for later models.

The trade marks are " F. Lorch ", " L.S. & Co." and " Lorch, Schmidt & Co." each tool is marked with one of these marks.

The bores of the spindles are 6 and 8 mm. The lathes are made for right or left hand operation and the illustration, Fig. 202, shows the conventional Lorch right-hand lathe. It should be explained that left-hand lathes are not necessarily for left-handed people. Some craftsmen, especially continental, and more particularly the Germans,

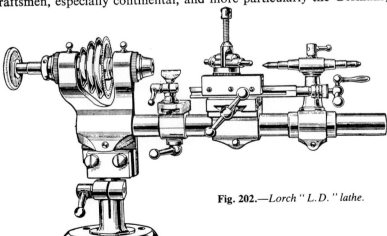

Fig. 202.—*Lorch " L.D. " lathe.*

* No longer in production.

131

prefer to work with the headstock on the right and therefore the work is on the left-hand side. Such craftsmen work with the graver in the right hand, it is just a matter of individual choice and use. One cannot say that work produced one way or the other is better. The bed of the Lorch lathe is round, with a flat surface on the side at the back. The majority of watchmakers' lathes are made with the spindle running in a double cone shaped bearing, so that any longitudinal thrust bears upon the cone shaped part of the bearing. The object of the cone shape is that by tightening the split nut the cones of the spindle are drawn closer to the cones of the sleeve in the headstock. In this manner both end shake and side play are eliminated. Adjustment and maintenance of the lathe have been dealt with in a previous chapter. The Lorch lathe manufacturers have introduced in recent years a ball thrust bearing model (Fig. 203). This means that the end

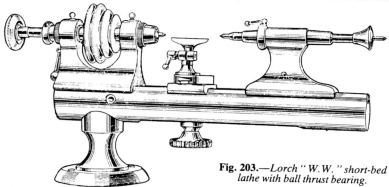

Fig. 203.—*Lorch " W.W. " short-bed lathe with ball thrust bearing.*

thrust due to work pressing longitudinally, as in the case when using the slide rest tool to make a countersink, is taken by the ball bearings and not the cone bearings. There are some objections voiced to ball bearings. It is argued that under a load the balls are flattened and this amount of flattening can and does affect a fine adjustment. If, for instance, the slide rest is set to cut into the metal say 0·25 mm. then the actual depth of the sink cut would be something less than 0·25 mm. due to the flattening of the balls. This objection could be overcome if the ball bearings are pre-loaded. It is well known among engineers that the flattening of ball bearings reaches a maximum under certain conditions, therefore, if the balls are loaded to their maximum capacity by screwing the races together, no further deformation will be experienced under a further load. It would appear that the ball bearings are acceptable in these circumstances. In more recent years the American lathe manufacturers have been giving their attention not only to a ball thrust bearing but also to ball bearings taking load and thrust combined. They stress that for a ball bearing to be

132

successful it must be loaded both for longitudinal thrust and lateral pressure. One might argue that the cone bearing has been in use satisfactorily for a great many years and the necessity for a ball bearing, thrust or otherwise, does not arise and we would be inclined to agree with this argument. The average watch repairer uses the lathe for comparatively light work, but when heavy face work has to be considered the loaded ball bearing has its advantages. The Lorch Co. make also a heavier type of lathe with what they term a prismatic guiding of the bed. As with the Boley lathe this is more of a precision tool and is made with a single and double support (Fig. 204). Fig. 205 shows lathe with full complement of accessories.

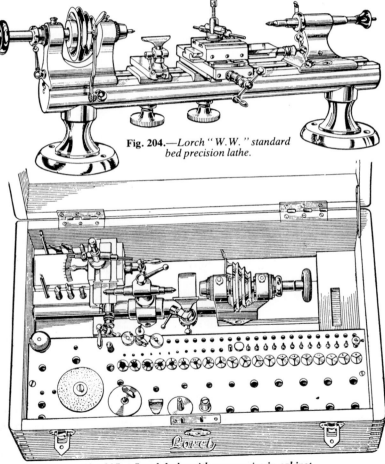

Fig. 204.—Lorch " W.W. " standard bed precision lathe.

Fig. 205.—Lorch lathe with accessories in cabinet.

Specification

Model	Precision lathe " L.D. ".
Bed	Round with a flat.
Mounting	One foot and screws.
Headstock	Adjustable hard bronze bearings.
Drive	By separate motor or hand wheel
Tailstock	Solid or hollow runners.
General Finish	Polished nickel.
Dimensions	Spindle bore : 8 mm.
	Height of centres ; 40 mm.
	Length of bed: 200 mm., 250 mm. or 300 mm.

Equipment

The equipment for this lathe includes, in addition to the standard set of accessories enumerated on page 98, the following :—

Carriers.
Chucks, box.
Dividing plates.
Emery wheels.
Face plate.
Hand wheels.
Jacot drums.
Milling attachment.
Mandrel.

Pivot polishing attachment.
Pulleys.
Roller rest, double.
Saw attachment.
Saw tables.
Self-centring drilling attachment.
Slide rest, compound.
Snailing attachment.

Specification

Model	Precision lathe " W.W. ".
Bed	Prismatic.
Mounting	One foot 280 mm. solid with bed. Two feet 400 mm. solid with bed.
Headstock	Hardened steel cone bearings.
Drive	By separate motor or hand wheel.
Tailstock	Hollow and solid runners.
General Finish	Polished nickel.
Dimensions	Spindle bore : 8 mm.
	Height of centres : 50 mm.
	Length of bed : 280 mm. and 400 mm.

Equipment

Same as for the Precision lathe " F. Lorch ".

MANHORA*

Made in Annecy (France) and the agent is A. Moynet, 26 Rue de Renard, Paris IV, France.

The bed is round with a flat ground at the back. The spindle is made to take 8 mm. chucks (Fig. 208). This manufacturer also

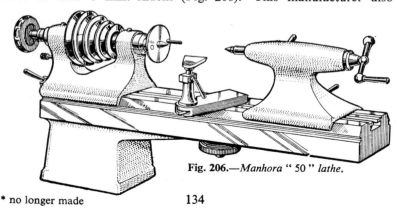

Fig. 206.—*Manhora " 50 " lathe.*

* no longer made

makes a heavy purpose lathe with spindle to take 8 mm. chucks (Fig. 57) known as the Manhora 189. The bed is rectangular and is supplied with or without the additional supporting foot. Fig. 208 shows the Manhora 40 with combination of accessories.

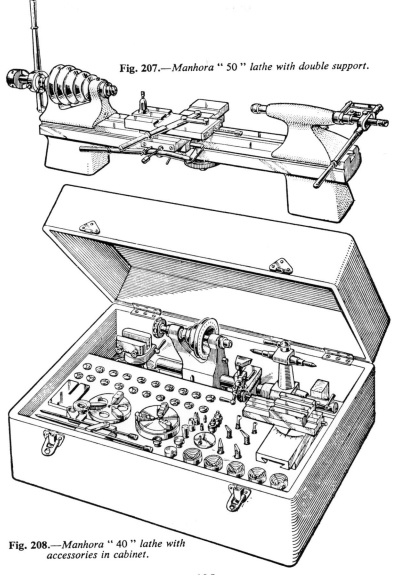

Fig. 207.—*Manhora " 50 " lathe with double support.*

Fig. 208.—*Manhora " 40 " lathe with accessories in cabinet.*

Model	Manhora 40.
Bed	Round with flat.
Mounting	One foot with screws.
Headstock	Steel spindle with manganese vanadium treatment. Double cone bearings, adjustable.
Drive	Separate motor.
Tailstock	Solid runner.
General Finish	Crackle.
Dimensions	Spindle bore : 8 mm.
	Height of centres : 40 mm.
	Length of bed : 250 mm.

Equipment

As for model 50.

Specification

Model	Manhora 50.
Bed	Rectangular section, prismatic top.
Mounting	One foot, solid casting with bed. Two feet with the 380 mm. and 400 mm. beds
Headstock	Steel spindle with manganese vanadium treatment. Double cone bearings, adjustable.
Drive	By separate motor.
Tailstock	Screw tailstock.
General Finish	Crackle.
Dimensions	Spindle bore : 8 mm.
	Height of centres : 50 mm.
	Length of bed : 280 mm., 380 mm. and 400 mm.

Equipment

The equipment for this lathe includes, in addition to the standard set of accessories enumerated on page 98, the following :—

Milling attachment.
Slide rest, compound.
Self-centring drilling attachment.

Saw table.
Face plate.

MARSHALL*

Made originally by C. & E. Marshall Co. of Chicago, Ill., U.S.A.

The specifications for the Marshall, Peerless and Moseley lathes is the same :—

Height of centres : 2 in.

Capacity of draw-in spindle : 0·1968 in. (6 mm.).

Body diameter of chuck : 0·3145 in.

Marshall lathe is a pre-loaded ball bearing lathe and the makers say this lathe is made of " the same high quality materials as the

* No longer in production.

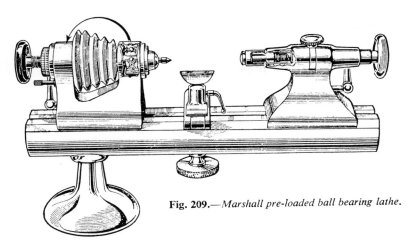

Fig. 209.—*Marshall pre-loaded ball bearing lathe.*

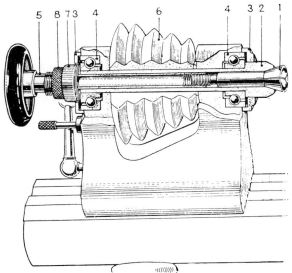

Fig. 210.—*Marshall pre-loaded ball bearing headstock.*
1. *Chuck.*   5. *Draw-in spindle.*
2. *Live spindle.*   6. *Pulley.*
3. *Dust shield.*   7. *Check nut.*
4. *Ball bearings.*   8. *Lock nut.*

Moseley and Peerless lathes ". Fig. 209 shows the Marshall lathe and Fig. 210 a cut-away section of the headstock.

Moseley. A similar lathe to the Marshall but with cone bearings (Fig. 211).

137

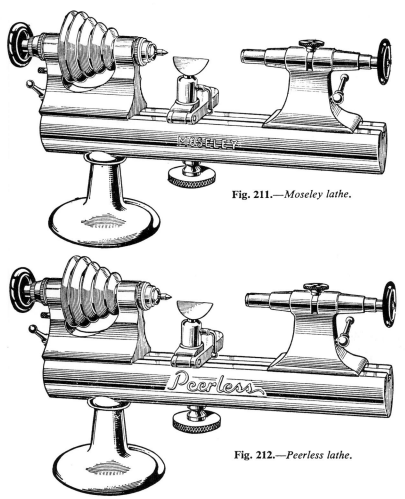

Fig. 211.—*Moseley lathe.*

Fig. 212.—*Peerless lathe.*

Peerless. Similar to the Marshall and Moseley lathes, with cone bearings. A little lower priced (Fig. 212).

MOSELEY, see Marshall*

PAULSON*

A German-made lathe manufactured to the specification and requirements of Henry Paulson & Co., 131 South Wabash Avenue, Chicago 3, Ill., U.S.A.

* No longer in production.
138

Five features are outlined by Paulson :—

1. Metric feed, tailstock thrust.
2. Improved grip on tailstock.
3. Tailstock spindle holds chuck.
4. Dust proof oil reservoirs.
5. Lathe head pulley has three rows of index holes.

The headstock has hardened steel cone bearings (see Fig. 213).

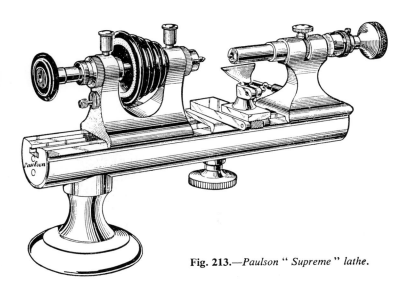

Fig. 213.—*Paulson " Supreme " lathe.*

Specification

Model	Supreme.
Bed	American bed, flat top with centre slot. Not adjustable.
Mounting	One foot with clamp.
Headstock	Double cone bearings of steel of extreme hardness.
Drive	Either by separate motor or hand wheel.
Tailstock	Chuck holding runner, with micro feed.
General Finish	Nickel.
Dimensions	Spindle bore : 8 mm. Height of centres : 50 mm. Length of bed : 11 in.

Equipment

The available equipment includes, in addition to the standard set of accessories enumerated on page 98, the following :—

Quick action draw-in attachment with hand lever.
Dividing head.
Roller rest, double.
Saw table with adjustable fence.
Hollow runner set of 12 sinkers.
Rose cutters.
Flat sinkers.
Jacot drum.
Disc.
Combined small pulley and runner.
Combined large pulley and runner.
Carrier collet.
8-screw collets.
Arbor with emery wheel.
Arbor for circular saws.
Arbor for wheels.
Arbor for balance.
Arbor with wooden or copper disc.

Mandrel face plate.
Drilling tailstock.
Universal crown collet.
Taps.
Compound slide rest.
Compound cross slide.
Turning tools and holder.
Vertical slide rest.
Dividing head.
Milling and grinding attachment.
Milling arbors.
Wheel rounding accessory.
Rounding cutters.
Wheel cutters for wheels.
Accessory with 8 polishing and grinding plates.
Universal bezel collet.
Universal drill collet with reversible jaws.
Transmission pulleys.

Fig. 214 is the Paulson lathe with plain tailstock.

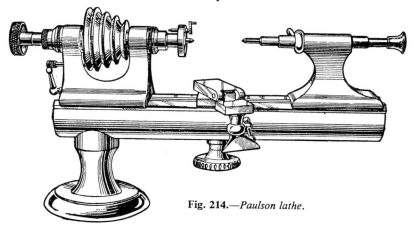

Fig. 214.—*Paulson lathe.*

Specification

Model	Superior.
Bed	American bed, flat top with centre slot. Not adjustable.
Mounting	One foot with clamp
Headstock	Double cone bearings of hardened steel.
Drive	Either by separate motor or hand wheel.
Tailstock	Simple runner type.
General Finish	Nickel.
Dimensions	Spindle bore : 8 mm. Height of centres : 50 mm. Length of bed : 11 in.

Equipment

Equipment is similar to that enumerated on page 139, for the Supreme lathe.

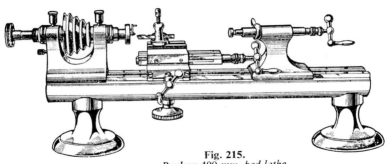

Fig. 215.
Paulson 400 mm. bed lathe.

Fig. 215 is the 400 mm. bed with two feet.

All the Paulson lathes are the W.W. style.

Specification

Model	Long bed.
Bed	American bed, flat on top with centre slot. Not adjustable.
Mounting	Two feet with clamp.
Headstock	Double cone bearings of hardened steel. Adjustable.
Drive	Either by separate motor or hand wheel.
Tailstock	Available with simple runner or with chuck holding micro feed and stop tailstock.
General Finish	Nickel.
Dimensions	Spindle bore : 8 mm. Height of centres : 50 mm. Length of bed : 18 in.

Equipment

The equipment for this lathe is similar to that enumerated on page 139, for the Supreme lathe.

PEERLESS, see Marshall*

* No longer in production.

PULTRA

The two lathes, Pultra 10 (Fig. 216) and the P.17 (Fig. 217) described on the following pages were originally made by Pultra Ltd., of Manchester. The former is no longer in production but an updated version of the latter, known as the Pultra Micro Series 1770, is now available from Bracehand Ltd., 86A Church Street, Langford, Biggleswade, Beds., SG18 9QA. See page 168 for details.

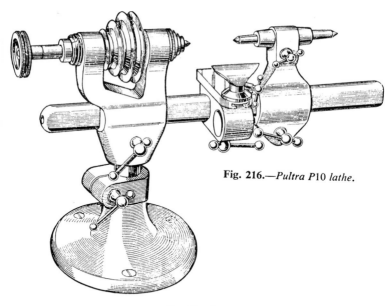

Fig. 216.—*Pultra* P10 *lathe.*

Specification

Model	P.10.
Bed	Round, with flat locating face, adjustable to height.
Mounting	One foot with clamp.
Headstock	Double cone bearing, hollow spindle, adjustable.
Drive	Either by separate motor or hand wheel.
Tailstock	Simple runner with clamp tailstock and chuck holding runner with lever attachment.
General Finish	Stove enamel.
Dimensions	Spindle bore : 8 mm.
	Height of centres : 50 mm.
	Length of bed : 10 in.

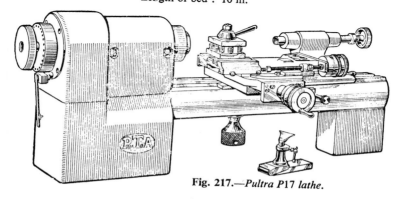

Fig. 217.—*Pultra* P17 *lathe.*

Equipment

The equipment includes, in addition to the standard set of accessories enumerated on page 98, the following :—

Compound slide rest.
Carrier plate complete with male and female centres.
Chuck bell, max. capacity 12½ mm.
Collet, taper bore, takes centres and shellac chucks.
Drive, hand, can be used from above or below the lathe.

Drive, universal motor with foot control, 1/12 h.p.
Faceplate 3½ in. diameter with dogs and pump centre.
Runner, combination pulley, with 2 centres.
Runner, hollow, complete with 2 chucks (1 mm., 1½ mm.) and ejector.

Specification

Model	P.17.
Bed	Prismatic, not adjustable.
Mounting	One or two feet models with screws.
Headstock	Hollow spindle, parallel bearings, adjustable.
Drive	Either by separate motor or with hand wheel.
Tailstock	Runner with chuck and micro feed.
General Finish	Cream, stove enamel.
Dimensions	Spindle bore : 10 mm.
	Height of centres : 50 mm.
	Length of bed : 12 or 16 in.

Equipment

Arbors and arbor blanks.
Arbor with ⅜ in. diameter shank to hold gear wheel, pinion and milling cutters.
Bar feed for production lathes.
Capstan box tool.
Capstan box tool with vee steady.
Capstan collet holder, 8 mm. bore.
Capstan Coventry diehead.
Capstan Coventry diehead with lifting device.
Capstan dieholder for dies ⅝ in. diameter.
Capstan Jacobs chuck, ⅛ in. with adaptor.
Capstan Jacobs chuck, ¼ in. with adaptor.
Capstan knee tool, radial
Capstan knee tool, tangential
Capstan sensitive drill holder
Capstan slide.
Capstan stop, adjustable.
Capstan tap holder, releasing.
Carrier plate.
Carriers, set of 7, capacity 13 mm.
Centre, male. No. 0 Morse
Centre, female.   No. 0 Morse.
Centre, male.   Taper 20 : 1.
Centre, female.   Taper 20 : 1.
Centre, male, half.   Taper 20 : 1.
Centre, female, half.   Taper 20 : 1.
Centre, male, large.   Taper 20 : 1.
Chip tray base plate.
Chuck, bell.
Chuck, 3-jaw.
Chuck, 4-jaw.
Chuck, Jacobs.   See Capstan.
Chuck, Jacobs ¼ in. with adaptor No. 0 Morse.
Chuck Jacobs ¼ in. with 10 mm. Spigot.
Chuck, disc and ring.
Chuck, shellac, set of 5.
Closing collar for large disc chucks.
Cutters, gear wheel and pinion, set of 8 to cover ·29, ·35, ·40, ·50 mm. Module.
Cutters, general purpose, milling, set of 5.
Diehead, Coventry for capstan.
Diehead, Coventry for lever tailstock.
Diehead, Coventry for screw tailstock.
Dividing attachment, universal, for headstock.

Dividing disc.
Dividing index with notchplate for headstock.
Dividing index with notchplate for quill-holder.
Drill pad, large, flat.
Drill pad, small, flat.
Drill pad, small, vee.
Driving attachment.
Driving units and starters.
Face plate.
Face plate.   Dogs only, set of 3.
Front plate for vertical slide.
File rest fits handrest.
Full gear cutting equipment.
Grinder bracket to hold quill for slide rest.
Grinding attachment.
Grinding and milling attachment.
Grinding wheels, mounted points, set of 6.
Grinding wheels 2½ in. diameter × ¼ in. thick, set of 3.
Handrest, tilting.
Handrest, fixed.
Handrest, Tee, wide.
Handrest, Tee, narrow.
Headstock lever attachment, fits on all head-stocks.
Raising block, 40 mm. high, for headstock.
Raising block, 40 mm. high, for tailstock.
Raising block, set of V 313, V 314 and Toolpost M 374.
Runner, combination pulley, with 2 centres.
Saw table, adjustable.
Saw, circular, set of 3, 0·01 in., 0·02 in., 0·032 in. thick.
Slide rests, compound slide, screw.
Slide rests, compound slide, lever.
Slide rests, compound slide, screw top, lever bottom.
Slide rests, compound slide, lever top, screw bottom.
Slide rests, cross slide, lever.
Slide rests, cross slide, screw.
Steady, fixed.
Steady, travelling.

SCOMEA*

Made by Société Commerciale d'Outillage et de Mécanique d'Aviation, 7 Rue Lauriston, Paris 16ᵉ, France.   A lathe of sturdy construction suitable for clock work and small scientific instruments.   The illustration (Fig. 218) shows the lathe fitted up with motor and the accessories.

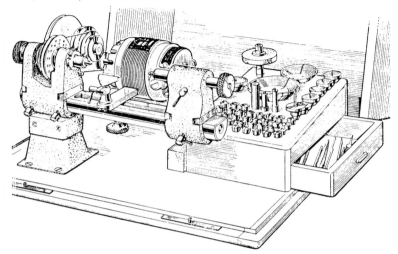

Fig. 218.—*Scomea lathe with motor and accessories.*

Specification

Model	Modern type lathe for clock making and small scientific instruments.
Bed	Round with flat top.
Mounting	One foot with screws.
Headstock	Cone bearings.
Drive	Motor is an integral part of the lathe.
Tailstock	Runner to take chucks.
General Finish	The cast portions are black finish and other parts are chrome plated.
Dimensions	Spindle bore : 8 mm.
	Height of centres : 50 mm.
	Length of bed : 300 mm.

Equipment

The equipment for this lathe includes, in addition to the standard set of accessories enumerated on page 98, the following :—

Bell-shaped small-scale holders, series of 5 pieces 1/2 mm. gauge.   Outside ⌀ 25 mm. No. 1, 2, 3. 4, and 5.

Bell-shaped large scale holders, series of 5 holders for ⌀ from 20 to 69 mm.

STAR

Made by R. Gentil & Co., La Brevine, Switzerland.

The bed is round with a flat ground at the back.

A useful feature of this lathe is the combinations in which they are available. Fig. 219 shows the lathe in its simple form. In addition

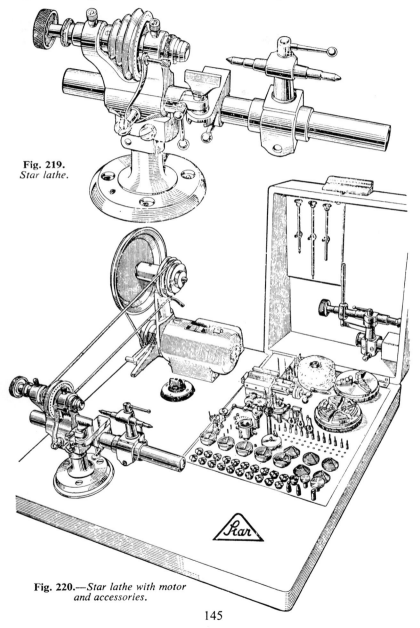

Fig. 219.
Star lathe.

Fig. 220.—*Star lathe with motor
and accessories.*

to the usual combination fitted into a box, it is supplied fixed on a table with motor complete as Fig. 220 with all accessories. It is also available fitted on to a bench complete with motor, and three drawers are fitted out with accessories to the lathe and two drawers with watchmakers' tools (Fig. 221).

Fig. 221.—*Star lathe and bench, with drawers fitted with accessories and tools.*

Specification

Models	No. 7, 6 mm., M7a, 8 mm. spindle bore.
Bed	Round with a flat.
Mounting	One foot with screws.
Headstock	Double cone bearings.
Drive	By separate variable speed motor or hand wheel.
Tailstock	Solid runner.
General Finish	Nickel plated.
Dimensions	Spindle bore : 6 mm. and 8 mm.
	Height of centres : 40 mm.
	Length of bed : 200 mm., 250 mm., 300 mm.
	or 400 mm.

The equipment includes in addition to the standard set of accessories enumerated on page 98, the following :—

Carriers.	Jacot drum.
Countersinkers.	Rose cutters.
Drilling, tailstock for chucks.	Safety pulley attachment.
Drilling, self-centring attachment.	Slide rest, compound.
Emery wheel.	Transmission pulleys.
Eccentric pulley chuck.	

STEINER*

Made by Y. Thiebaud, Bole, Neuchatel, Switzerland. This lathe is of unique design as the illustration Fig. 222 shows. The bed is round with a flat ground at the bottom. The bed is pierced at the position where

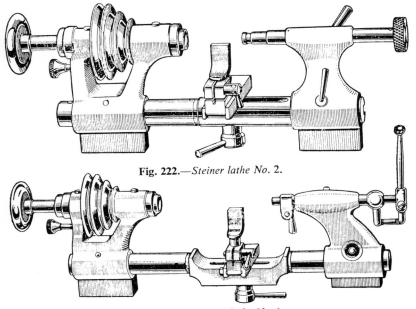

Fig. 222.—*Steiner lathe No. 2.*

Fig. 223.—*Steiner lathe No. 1.*

the T-rest is normally used and in one model, Fig. 223, this portion of the bed is ground to a special shape. The lathe generally is very neat, simple and well made. The model, Fig. 224, is especially made for pivoting, i.e. turning balance staffs, etc. It consists virtually of the bed and two tailstocks. Into one tailstock is fitted a runner with safety pulley device.

The lathes with headstocks are fitted with spindles to take 8 mm. chucks. Some of the accessories made by this manufacturer are unique and interesting and are described in Chapter 5 dealing with accessories.

* See also page 173.

Fig. 224.—
Steiner lathe No. 3.

Fig. 225.—*Steiner lathes and accessories
in cabinet.*

148

Fig. 225 shows the lathe combination complete.

Specification

Model	No. 1.
Bed	Round sectional with 3 flat grinding and resting surfaces.
Mounting	One foot with two screws.
Headstock	Cast steel spindle, hardened, ground and lapped. Phosphor bronze bearings.
Drive	Either by separate motor or hand wheel.
Tailstock	Spindle to take screw-in runner.
General Finish	Grey-green enamel. Machined parts nickel plated.
Dimensions	Spindle bore : 8 mm.
	Height of centres : 41 mm.
	Length of bed : 260 mm.

Equipment

Equipment includes, in addition to the standard set of accessories enumerated on page 98, the following :—

Jacot drums.	Slide rest.
Pivot drilling apparatus.	Mandrel face plate.
Slide centring runrer.	Hand wheels.

Specification

Model	No 2.
Bed	Round sectional with three flat guiding and resting surfaces.
Mounting	One foot with two screws.
Headstock	Cast steel spindle, hardened, ground and lapped. Phosphor bronze bearings.
Drive	Either by separate motor or hand wheel.
Tailstock	Spindle to take screw-in runner.
Dimensions	Spindle bore : 8 mm.
	Height of centres : 41 mm.
	Length of bed : 220 mm.

Equipment

As for lathe No. 1.

Specification

Model	No. 3.
Bed	Round sectional with three flat guiding and resting surfaces.
Mounting	One foot with two screws or can be clamped in the vice.
Headstock	Cast steel spindles with cast iron split bearings.
Drive	By separate motor, hand wheel or bow.
Tailstock	Spindle to take screw-in runner.
General Finish	Grey-green enamel. Machined parts nickel plated.
Dimensions	Height of centres : 41 mm.
	Length of bed : 220 mm.

Equipment

As for lathe No. 1.

WISKUM

Made by P. Wiskum, Julius Valentiners Vej 10, 2000 Copenhagen, Denmark.

The bed is round with a flat ground in the front (Fig. 226). It is claimed as a feature by the maker that the lathe is made to be interchangeable with the Lorch and similar lathes. The steel parts are made from Swedish steel. Fig. 227 shows the lathe complete with all accessories.

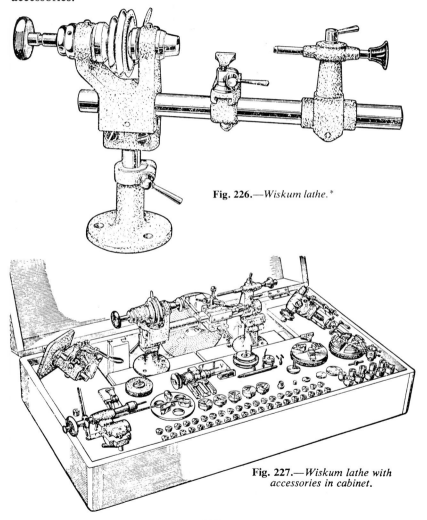

Fig. 226.—*Wiskum lathe.**

Fig. 227.—*Wiskum lathe with accessories in cabinet.*

Specification

Model	Wiskum, right or left hand.
Bed	Round with flat.
Mounting	One foot and screws.
Headstock	Cone bearings.
Drive	Either with separate motor or hand wheel.
Tailstock	Runner with micro feed.
General Finish	Black.
Dimensions	Spindle bore : 8 mm.
	Height of centres : 40 mm.
	Length of bed : 250 mm.

Equipment

The equipment includes, in addition to the standard set of accessories enumerated on page 98, the following :—

Driver chuck with carrier.
Slide rest assembly.
Wooden box.

WOLF, JAHN*

Made by Wolf, Jahn & Co., 418 Bergerstrasse, Frankfurt-on-Main, Germany.

Round head with feet at the back. This lathe is very similar to the Boley and Lorch lathes. Fig. 228 shows the lathe set up and Fig. 229 in its box with accessories.

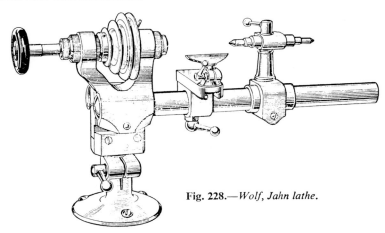

Fig. 228.—*Wolf, Jahn lathe.*

Specification

Model	" G ".
Bed	Round with flat.
Mounting	One foot with screws.
Headstock	Adjustable bearings, special steel, spindle hardened, ground and lapped.
Drive	By motor or hand wheel.
Tailstock	Spindle to take solid runners.
General Finish	Polished nickel.
Dimensions	Spindle bore : 8 mm.
	Height of centres : 45 mm.
	Length of bed : 250 mm.

* No longer in production. 151

Equipment

The equipment includes, in addition to the standard set accessories enumerated on page 98, the following :—

Box chuck.
Slide rest.
Saw table.
Mandrel face plate.

Index plate with 21 sets of holes.
Universal runner.
Rose cutters.
Carriers.

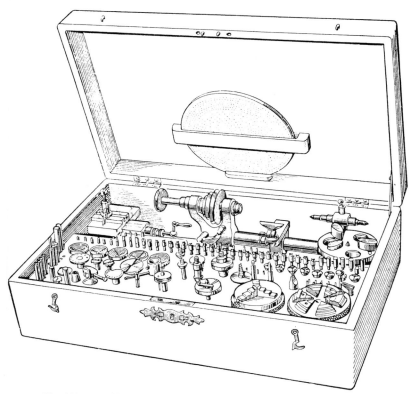

Fig. 229.—*Wolf, Jahn lathe in box with accessories.*

152

Chapter 11

LATHES TODAY

The proliferation of lathes manufactured in the Far East continues but, of late, with an important difference: the retailer or original manufacturer now exercises tight quality control so that the days of cheap, inferior machines are largely gone. Familiar and long-established names have moved to part or complete manufacture in China, Taiwan and Korea and, generally, make no secret of the source of origin. However, the buyer would be well advised to seek confirmation and request a test certificate, which reputable retailers are happy to offer.

There is a bewildering choice of lathes for the model engineer and it is essential to determine one's requirements at the outset. The two most important considerations are the centre height and the distance between centres, *not* the bed length, which govern the longest piece and diameter to be turned. The minimum for the model engineer is a centre height of 3" (76.2 mm) x 15" (381 mm) between centres.

Other features a beginner's lathe should have are a screw-cutting facility, backgear tumble reverse, 2MT tailstock, provision to fit a teeslotted cross slide and a set-over tailstock.

New or secondhand? In either case, is a guarantee offered? Is the range of accessories available adequate to cope with your immediate and future needs? And are spares available? Some manufacturers, Myfords, for example, offer a range of refurbished lathes with a one-year warranty and have spare parts available for machines thirty or more years after they were discontinued. There are companies – see the specialist magazines for details – who will make replacement parts for obsolete machines, but the cost is often prohibitive. Finally, in the case of a secondhand lathe, the electrics must be checked out by a competent electrician.

In complete contrast, whilst watchmaker's lathes are still available, the number of manufacturers continues to decline.

The inclusion of the BMT lathe for the first time in the last edition aroused so much interest it has been retained. Its survival, some sixty years after it was last made, says much for the quality of the lathe manufactured by British Machine Tools, who are reputed to have played a major role in the making of the code-breaking Enigma machine.

In this chapter, as in the previous one, the lathes are arranged alphabetically by maker's name, or by brand name where this is better known. All lathes are accompanied by a photograph with a description that has received the approval of the manufacturer or their agent. No attempt has been made at recommendation simply because the author has no knowledge of the purchaser's requirements.

The Axminster Sieg C2A mini lathe (Plate 1) is modestly priced and will appeal to the novice model maker. Constructed almost entirely of cast iron with ground and hardened bed ways. Fully featured saddle and carriage assembly. Powered leadscrew and cover. A special feature is the standard fitted digital read-out for easy and precise measuring of the tool post x and y travel. Supplied with an 80 mm 3-jaw chuck, 2MT centre, change wheel set, camlock tailstock, wrench set, oil tray and splash guard. The basic specifications are:

Distance between centres 300 mm
Centre height 90 mm
Cross slide travel 65 mm
Taper headstock 3MT
Taper tailstock 2MT
Spindle bore 20 mm
Power 250 watt 240 volt
Spindle speeds: 100–1100 rpm low range
                  200–2550 rpm high range

The range of accessories include a quick-change tool post, 110 mm face plate, lathe dog, C3 rocker tool post, travelling steady, fixed steady, clamping kit, choice of imperial or metric thread sets, 4-jaw independent chuck, vertical slide and ER32 collet holder.

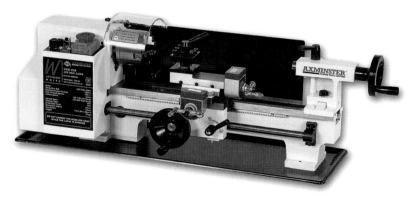

Plate 1   The Axminster Sieg C2A lathe

Manufactured by Shanghai Sieg Group and available in the UK from Axminster Power Tool Centre Ltd, Unit 10, Weycroft Avenue, Axminster, Devon EX13 5PH. In the USA this lathe is sold by Travers Tool Co. Inc. under their OTMT brand.

154

For the more ambitious modeller Axminster offer the larger and more powerful BV20 M2 (Plate 2) which is a vee-bedded lathe. The drive to the spindle is by means of gears rather than belts which allows for much easier speed changing. Reversing is achieved by motor reversal. The saddle can be manually or power fed. The lathe comes with a 4" 3-jaw self-centring chuck (including internal and external jaws) which is mounted to a back-plate integral with the spindle. The sliding tailstock has a calibrated feed and comes with a fixed centre. To complete the package, service tools, change wheels and chuck guard are included. Specifications are:

Distance between centres 350 mm
Centre height 110 mm
Cross slide travel 106 mm
Taper headstock 3MT
Leadscrew pitch 3 mm
Spindle bore 20 mm
Power: 375 watt 240 volt
Spindle speeds (6) 170–1950 rpm
Thread pitch metric 0.25–3.00 mm
            imperial 8–48 tpi

Accessories include: steel cabinet stand, 4-jaw 100 mm chuck, travelling steady, fixed steady, tailstock chuck with 2MT arbor and a 150 mm face plate. Available from Axminster Tool Centre.

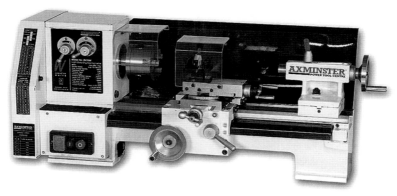

Plate 2   The Axminster BV20 M2 lathe

The Axminster Sieg C4 metal bench lathe (Plate 3) is of modern design and comes with many features not usually found at this price. Ideal for the enthusiastic model engineer or equally at home in a teaching environment.

155

The bed is a solid piece of cast iron heavily braced by cross ribs and ground slideways giving a high level of precision. Full electronic speed control comes as standard plus digital read-out of spindle speeds, a touch screen control panel, cross and longitudinal power feed and a quick lock tailstock. Both metric and imperial thread cutting capability. A powerful 1000 watt DC reversible motor with steel gears for thread cutting.

Distance between centres 410 mm
Centre height 109 mm
Cross slide travel 100 mm
Thread range metric 0.25–3.00 mm
                    imperial 8–24 tpi
Spindle speeds 150–2000 rpm
Spindle taper MT3
Taper tailstock MT2

Plate 3   The Axminster Sieg C4 lathe

There are many available options including a milling head to turn this into a capable machining centre, lockable floor stand, drip tray, face plate, clamping kit, fixed and travelling steadies and a 4-jaw independent chuck.

Manufactured by Shanghai Sieg Group and available in the UK from Axminster Tool Centre. In the USA this lathe is sold by Travers Tool Co. Inc., 128–15 26th Avenue, PO Box 541550, Flushing, NY 11354-0108, USA under their brand name OTMT.

For the professional watchmaker, clockmaker or toolmaker the Swiss-made Bergeon 50 offers outstanding quality. This precision lathe comes in a variety of packages and is also available in component form. Plate 4 shows the standard model fitted with the manually operated compound slide rest (supplied with one tool post and a turning tool), adjustable tailstock (spindle has male and female centres), and headstock. Also shown, but not fitted, is the tee rest which comes with two inserts of 12 and 25 mm in width.

Basic specifications: Centre height 50 mm, distance between centres 170 mm, chuck shank diameter 8 mm, bed length 325 mm and gap bed of 275 mm.

Plate 4   The Bergeon 50 standard model

An impressive range of accessories includes a drilling tailstock, rapid clamping device, lever type compound slide rest, milling attachment, 3-jaw face plate, rotating foot, drilling table, pivoting tools, specialist cutters for the cutting and milling of escape wheels, barrel ratchets, racks, locking plates, gear cutters for cutting teeth with either flat or round troughs and a grinding attachment. See pages 100–2 for earlier models.

Manufactured by Bergeon & Cie SA, 11 Avenue du Technicum, 2400 Le Loche, Switzerland.

Boley at one time made a range of small precision lathes, including those described on pages 102–6, but now their output is confined solely to the production of high precision CNC lathes with an industrial application.

The Boley model 1B (Plate 5) was among the last of their watchmaker's lathes made and was recommended for fine turning work requiring a high degree of accuracy. The headstock had diamond bored bearings and a two-stepped grooved pulley with a handwheel-operated collet attachment. The spindle was made from a special steel which had been hardened and ground.

A multi-purpose motor, giving variable speeds up to 4000 rpm, was available separately. The bed was machined all over and had a length of 400 mm with 200 mm between centres. Centre height 50 mm with a spindle bore of 8 mm. Full range of accessories.

Plate 5   Boley's small precision lathe, model 1B

The BTM watchmaker's lathe was a copy of a Boley lathe manufactured during the Second World War and 'extensively used in the watch trade and by the Navy, Army and Air Force depots for instrument repair work at home and overseas.' After the war hundreds of these precision-made lathes were sold on the secondhand market and are still in use today. Made by British Tabulating Machines and sold by E.H. Jones Ltd of North London, manufacture is thought to have continued through to the early 1950s. The lathe, complete with all the attachments shown in Plate 6 including a gap bed and case, cost £45 10s in December 1945. The most expensive component was the compound slide rest assembly which was priced at £25 3s 9d. Optional extras: stand, motor and lever-operated tailstock.

All the main castings, including the beds, were made of Meehanite. The hollow headstock spindle was carried in plain taper bearings with a running clearance of 0.00025". The headstock had an indexing device and the spindle drawbar came with a vulcanite handwheel. The basic specifications were:

Centre height 50 mm
Between centres 165 mm
Bed length 254 mm
Width of gap 50 mm
Centre of spindle to bottom of gap 70 mm
Bore through spindle 8 mm

Plate 6   BTM lathe: key to numbered parts. 1. Headstock, drawbar, tailstock with lug, tailstock without lug, straight bed and tailstock centres. 2. Gap bed. 3. Compound slide rest assembly. 4. Tee rest holder. 5. Tool rest wide. 6. Tool rest narrow. 7. 3-jaw chuck with backplate. 8. Bell chuck. 9. Driver plate assembly, carrier plate, centre and shank (male and female). 10. Pulley runner, pulley, carrier plate (long) and centres. 11. Driver pulley (small) and carrier plate (short). 12. Hollow centres small and large with glass containers. 13. Tommy bar (large). 14. Tommy bar (small). 15. Pulley runner ejector spindle. 16. Belt. 17. Step chucks nos. 1, 2, 3, 4 and 5. 18. Collets (wire). 19. Collets (sunk) 20. Box complete with locks, stay and hooks.

Chester have on offer in excess of thirty lathes ranging from those catering for the needs of the absolute beginner to advanced CNC models with an industrial application. The inexpensive Cobra lathe (Plate 7) is powered by a 150 watt motor with over-load protection and an interlocked chuck guard. Specifications are:

Distance between centres 250 mm (10")
Cross slide travel 60 mm (2¼")
Swing over bed 140 mm (5¾")
Spindle bore 9 mm (³/₈")
Spindle taper MT2
Tailstock taper MT1
Spindle speeds variable
Range of speeds 100–2000 rpm
Range of threads metric 0.5–1.25 mm in five steps
                  imperial 16–24 tpi in five steps

Plate 7   Chester's Cobra lathe

The lathe comes equipped with an 80 mm 3-jaw chuck, two-way tool post, MT1 dead centre, change gears, splash guard, tools and parts list. Optional accessories are available.

Available from Chester Machine Tools Ltd, Clwyd Close, Hawarden Industrial Park, Nr Chester, Flintshire CH5 3PZ.

The CL300M (Plate 8) is a competitively priced and robustly made lathe suited to the needs of the model engineer. It offers power feed, screw-cutting right and left hand threads, thread cutting indicator and fast carriage travel. It is supplied with a 4-way tool post, splash guard and drip tray, chuck guard, self centring 3-jaw 80 mm chuck and gear change set. Optional extras include 6-piece turning set, revolving centre MT2,

160

headstock centre MT3, tailstock chuck, fixed steady, travelling steady, 4-jaw 80 mm independent chuck, 160 mm face plate and a metric thread conversion kit.

Distance between centres 300 mm
Swing over bed 180 mm
Spindle taper MT3
Spindle bore 20 mm
Tailstock taper MT2
Spindle speeds (variable) 100–2500 rpm
Longitudinal feeds 0.1–0.2 mm
Imperial thread 18pcs 12–104 tpi
Power: 300 watt

Plate 8   The Clarke CL300M lathe

Marketed by Clarke International and available from stockists throughout the UK and the USA.

The Cowells 90CW (Plate 9), is a small compact lathe specifically designed for clock and watchmakers. Standard features include a headstock spindle and tailstock barrel which accept the universal horological 8 mm collets; headstock employs a hardened and ground spindle with phosphor bronze cone bearings; tailstock fitted with hardened and ground steel barrel, lever fed to ensure precision and may be offset for the turning of long and shallow tapers, long cross slide with three tee slots to permit the mounting of accessories; compound slide rest and single tool post. Mounted on a cast aluminium base which has a built-in tool tray. Basic specifications:

161

Centre height over bed 44.5 mm (1.75")
Distance between centres 203 mm (8")
Swing in gap 120 mm (4.7")
Swing over cross slide 47 mm (1.85")
Cross slide travel 89 mm (3.5")
Top slide travel 38 mm (1.5")

Motor: 220/240 volt DC single phase 4000 rpm continuously rated 125 watt output. Spindle speeds 0–4000 rpm by means of a thyristor variable speed drive.

The Cowells 90ME lathe (Plate 10) has the same dimensions as the 90CW but is powered by an AC 50Hz single phase 1425 rpm fwd/rev, continuously rated 90 watt motor. The drive is through steel gears for accuracy and longevity. It has an auto-traverse with adjustable trip to prevent accidental chuck collision. A range of screw-cutting gears (change wheels) is available giving pitches of between 0.312 mm and 3.2 mm. Backgearing for extra torque. Gap bed.

The Cowells Basic 90E is an economy version of the 90ME which may be supplemented to attain the full specification if desired at a later date.

Accessories include a wheel and pinion cutter, Jacot drum complete with cone plate unit, dividing head, tip-over tool rest and roller filing rest. All three lathes are individually built to an accuracy to within 0.005 mm (0.0002"), come with a tool kit, a five year guarantee and a test certificate. 110/115v DC electrics are available for the American market.

There have been many attempts over the years, some quite ingenious, to manufacture a vertical milling attachment to convert an existing lathe into a combination machine. But with few exceptions, most failed. Cowells resisted the temptation and produced an independent and portable vertical milling machine shown in Plate 11. This is of massive construction, capable of machining the toughest of materials to a high degree of accuracy. Spindle speeds 0–4000 rpm through thyristor variable drive from a 220/240 volt DC motor continuously rated 125 watt output (AC input). Table 203 x 50mm (8" x 2"), longitudinal travel 150 mm (6"), crossfeed travel 80 mm (3.1"), vertical travel 164 mm (6.5") and feedscrew pitches 1 mm. Used for flycutting, face milling, drilling, slitting, etc. Plate 12 shows the mill mounted with a tailstock from the 90 ME, a 3-jaw chuck and dividing head for the cutting of wheels and pinions.

Manufactured in the UK by Cowell Small Machine Tools, Tendring Road, Little Bentley, Colchester, Essex CO7 8SH.

Plate 9   The Cowells 90 CW lathe

Plate 10   The Cowells 90 ME lathe

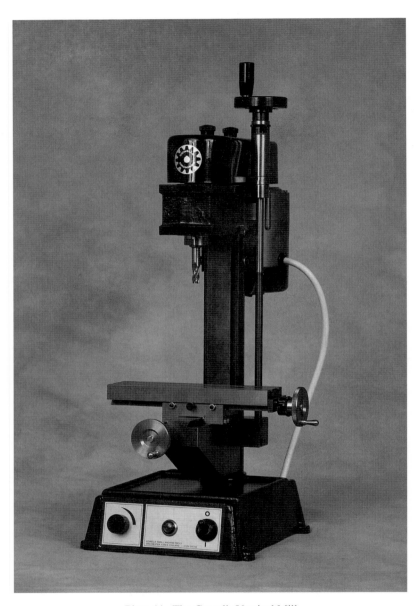

Plate 11   The Cowells Vertical Mill

164

Plate 12   Close up of the vertical mill set up for the cutting of pinions and wheels using a tailstock from 90ME lathe, 3-jaw chuck and dividing head.

F.W. Derbyshire Inc. has been manufacturing fine quality lathes since 1911 – see pages 111–16 for details of earlier models. Today production is concentrated on small manual instrument lathes and small computer numerical control (CNC) machines. The Derbyshire Type 460 lathe, available in two models, Model A (shown in Plate 13) and Model 750, is typical of the manual instrument. The primary difference in these units is the collet range and type used in the two models: both models are self-contained with motor and speed control mounted directly on the lathe. The bed length is 324 mm (12 ¾") with precision ball-bearing spindles. The bed is constructed of stress-relieved Meehanite. Collet types used on these lathes are 3C and the Derbyshire Magnus/Elect (also known as D or Derbyshire style) respectively. There is a comprehensive range of attachments and accessories available for these and all Derbyshire lathes.

F.W. Derbyshire Inc., 910 Boston Turnpike, Shrewsbury MA 01545, USA.

165

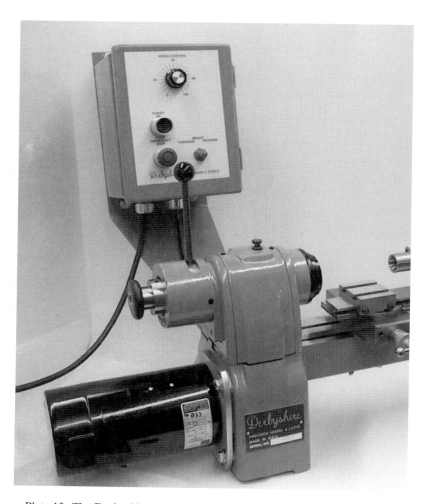

Plate 13 The Derbyshire Type 460 Model A lathe shown here with optional
lever collet closer, screw-feed two-sided slide rest and lever 3C tailstock

The Emco Unimat 3, a multi-purpose compact lathe (Plate 14) was discontinued in 1989, redesigned with additional safety features, and re-launched in 1997 as the Unimat 4 (Plate 15).

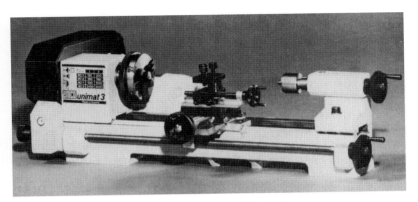

Plate 14 The Emco Unimat 3

Plate 15 The Emco Unimat 4 with vertical milling and drilling attachment

Basic specifications:
Distance between centres 200 mm
Centre height 46 mm
Swing over bed 92 mm
Turning diameter above cross slide 62 mm
Speed range (8 speeds) 130–4000 rpm

The lathe is supplied with machine bed, spindle head, tailstock, saddle and cross slide, 3-jaw rotary chuck, integrated permanent magnet 65/95 watt drive motor, tools and operating instructions.

Optional accessories include a machine mounting base complete with tool drawer, 3-jaw ring gear chuck, face plate, clamping plate, collet chuck holder, collets, live centre, quick-change tool holder, machine vice, thread cutting gear. The vertical milling and drilling attachment, requiring a separate drive unit and co-ordinate table, is an optional extra. Also fits the Compact 5.

The Emco Compact 5 (Plate 16) has many attributes that make it a very attractive lathe for the professional model engineer. It is larger than the Unimat 4, having a centre height of 65 mm and 350 mm between centres, and is more robustly constructed with a 16 mm bore spindle (standard MT2 hole taper) which runs in deep-grooved ball bearings that are sealed and lubricated for life.

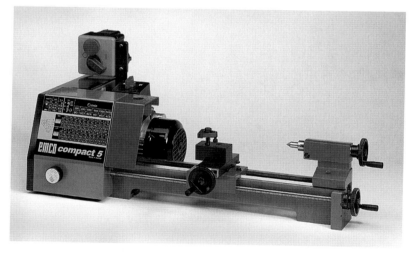

Plate 16   The Emco Compact 5

The lathe bed is constructed from high-grade, vibration absorbing grey cast iron and its sturdy ribs make it extremely resistant to twisting and torsion. The saddle and tailstock run in their own vee-ways. The Emco Compact lathe chuck (optional accessory) fits directly to the spindle without the need for a conventional backplate. The absence of a backplate, combined with its modern design, gives a reduction of approximately 25% in overall width and in weight.

A standard 500 watt continuously rated motor provides full power transmission by means of a vee-belt drive and at 50 cycles produces a six-speed range of 200–2400 rpm. There is a comprehensive range of accessories to choose from.

Larger, more robust and more powerful than the Compact 5, the Compact 8E has basic specifications of 450 mm between centres and a centre height of 105 mm. In addition to the usual lathe functions the Compact 8E allows for longitudinal turning, facing, external and internal turning, and automatic thread cutting of imperial, metric and module threads. European DIN 8606 inspection and accuracy standards.

The standard package consists of vee-bed, headstock, saddle, cross and top slide, tailstock, automatic power feed unit with six change gears, 4-way tool post, chuck guard, driving pin, lathe dog and ¾ hp single phase motor. The Compact V8 (Plate 17) is essentially a Compact 8 lathe fitted with a Varispeed drive system.

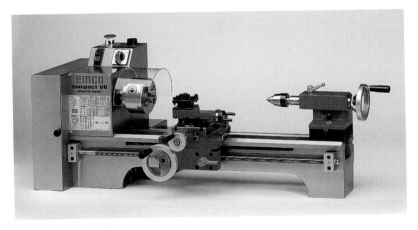

Plate 17   The Emco Compact V8 lathe

Originally manufactured in Austria, the smaller range of lathes are now being made in Taiwan to Emco's specifications. UK main agent: Pro Machine Tools Ltd, 17 Station Road Business Park, Stamford, Lincolnshire PE93 3DW. American agent: Blue Ridge Machinery Inc., PO Box 536, 2905 Putnam Avenue, Hurricane, WV 25526-0536, USA.

169

Golay Buchel & Cie of Lausanne, Switzerland, have ceased production of their Favorite range of precision lathes. Plate 18 shows the Favorite 3, which was available with or without a motor drive and had an impressive range of accessories, all of which were compatible with the Favorite 2 (see pages 116–19). The makers claimed perfect stability for their lathes, which were adaptable to meet a variety of uses, were made to Schlesinger standards and came with a control certificate. The basic specifications for the Favorite 3:

Height of centre 50 mm
Distance between centres 160 mm
Total bed length 350 mm
Spindle bore 8 mm

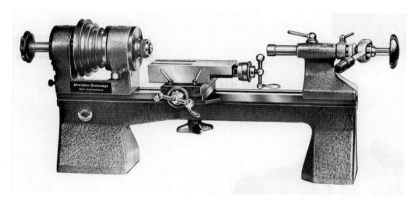

Plate 18   The Favorite 3 lathe

Grizzly provide a unique service for potential customers: simply call them (in the US the number is toll-free and is 800-523-4777; if you are outside the US the number is 1-360-647-0801), identify a specific Grizzly lathe and you will be put in contact with a customer who has purchased the lathe you are interested in, allowing you to obtain at first hand an unbiased report.

Grizzly stock a large range of lathes and combinations which are available from three strategically placed showrooms – Washington, Missouri and Pennsylvania. The Grizzly 7" x 12" mini lathe (Plate 19) is a great starter machine and is reasonably priced. Powered by a 3/4 hp motor 110 volt single phase and features variable speeds, 16 tpi reversible leadscrew, forward and reverse at all speeds, chip tray and splashback guard, threading dial indicator plus imperial and metric graduations. Specifications:

Distance between centres 12"
Swing over bed 7"
Spindle bore 20 mm
Spindle nose taper MT3
Tailstock taper MT2
Tailstock travel 2 ½"
Cross slide travel 2 ¾"
Speed range low 0–1100 rpm
            high 0–2500 rpm
Range of threads 12–52 tpi
Number of thread pitches 18

Plate 19　The Grizzly 7" x 12" mini lathe

The lathe comes equipped with a 3" 3-jaw chuck with external jaws, 6 ¼" face plate, steady rest, four position turret post, complete set of change gears, MT2 dead centre and wrenches. A stand is an optional extra.

Available from Grizzly Industrial, Inc., 1821 Valencia Street, Bellingham, WA 98229, USA.

For over thirty years Hemingway have been supplying kits specifically designed for the model engineer and today the range extends to over 100. Some of these kits are aimed at the Myford owner and require a minimum centre height of 3" and 13" between centres.

Here is a selection of the many available kits: versatile dividing head (Plate 20), floating reamer holder (Plate 21), gear and retracting top slide attachment for the Super 7, sensitive knurling tool (Plate 22), travelling and fixed steadies for the Myford series 7 and centring microscope. Kits come complete with detailed instructions, drawings, photographs and notes on construction.

171

In addition to kits, Hemingway offer a substantial range of internal combustion and stationary steam engines.

Hemingway Kits, 126 Dunval Road, Bridgnorth, Shropshire WV16 4LZ.

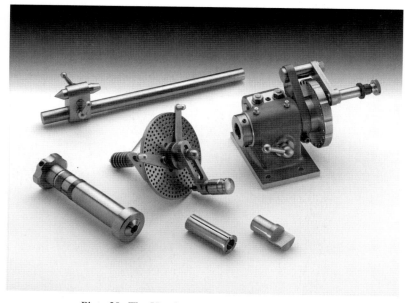

Plate 20   The Hemingway versatile dividing head

Plate 21   The Hemingway floating reamer holder

Plate 22   The Hemingway sensitive knurling tool

The Hobbymat MD65 (Plate 23) was originally manufactured in what was then East Germany and exported in large quantities. However, production ceased in the latter part of 1966. Since that date the rights have been owned by two different companies but currently the lathe is made by Unitech-Maschinen GmbH, Clemens-Winkler-Strasse 6, 09116 Chemnitz, Germany. It is described as a screw-cutting centre lathe with machining

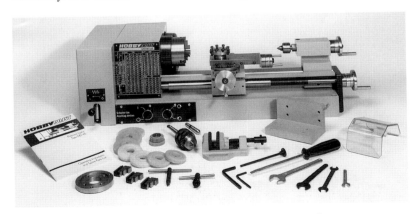

Plate 23   The Hobbymat MD65 with accessories

173

capability and ideally suited to the needs of the model engineer. As Plate 23 shows, the lathe and its 0.33 hp motor drive form a self-contained unit. A wide range of accessories is supplied as standard and a motorised milling/drilling attachment is available as an optional extra.

The machine bed is continuously cast and is ground. Adjustable precision taper roller bearings carry the headstock spindle. There is an auto-traverse feature, controlled by a lever to the left of the switch panel, and a reversing facility. Sets of change wheels, supplied as standard, allow for metric or imperial pitches and a choice of feed rates.

> Distance between centres 300 mm
> Centre height 65 mm
> Spindle capacity 12 mm
> Spindle speeds 250/500/1000/ 2000 rpm

A limited range of accessories and spare parts is available from Essel Engineering, Maesiocyn, Tylwch, Llanidoes, Powys SY18 6WD who also stock the lathe.

The German made Leinen precision lathe has been known for decades as an instrument of quality. See pages 126–9 for details of the early machines. The lathes, shown in Plates 24 and 25, were robustly made and should ideally be mounted on a heavy cast iron base which is vibration free. The wide prismatic bed ensured a secure and exact slide for all accessories and attachments making faulty alignment practically impossible. Versatile and eminently suitable for watchmakers, clockmakers and instrument makers.

Plate 24 shows the WW80 which has a distance of 80 mm between centres and a bed length of 280 mm: consisting of bed (single foot), headstock, carrier plate, tip over hand rest, tee rest and tailstock.

Plate 24   The Leinen WW80 lathe

174

Plate 25 shows the WW81aaa version which had 200 mm between centres and a bed length of 400 mm. This was made up from a double footed bed, headstock, carrier plate, tip over hand rest, tee rest, compound slide rest and a screw-fed tailstock.

Plate 25 The Leinen WW81aaa lathe

Model WW82, shown in Plate 26, was mounted on a heavy cast iron base with swivel-mounted flange plus drive and counter-shaft. The centre height was 50 mm, distance between centres 105 mm, bed length 305 mm,

Plate 26 The Leinen WW82 lathe

spindle bore 8 mm and swing over slide rest 58 mm. A choice of motor drives, all with infinitely variable speeds in both directions and single or three phase feeds. The range of accessories was most impressive.

The new generation of Leinen lathes were introduced in 1985, CNC versions in 2008, and are still made in Germany. The current WW80 (Plate 27) is still single footed and the WW81 (Plate 28) double footed. Both have 8 mm spindle bore, centre height of 50 mm, but 105 mm between centres for the WW80 and 200 mm for the WW81.

Plate 27   The current Leinen WW80 lathe

Plate 28   The current Leinen WW81 lathe

The latest WW81aaa , not shown here, has the same basic specifications as the WW81 save for the tailstock, which has a screw-feed attachment and a compound slide rest.

176

Manufactured by Pratecma, Inh Thomas Schafer, Gunther-Irmscher-Strasse 10, 73630 Remshalden-Grünbach, Germany.

The founder of Louis Levin Inc. of California and his son, Samuel, specialised in the design and manufacture of high-quality equipment for the watchmaker. They also published the monthly magazine, *Horology*, for the Horological Institute of America. Louis and Samuel were the authors of *Practical Benchwork for the Horologist* (1938), which is still considered to be an invaluable work of reference and much sought after to this day.

Levin lathes are highly regarded by clock and watchmakers alike, but today the company no longer produces the horological hand tools for which they once had a reputation second to none. Levin now concentrates on making extremely accurate instrument lathes for the machining of miniature and micro-miniature parts.

The Levin 13" instrument lathe, shown in Plate 29, which has a maximum between centres of 3 ½", can be equipped with any model compound slide rest, double tool cross slide, milling or grinding attachment and all style D collets, chucks, arbors and tool holders.

The headstock is fully enclosed with special precision pre-loaded angular contact ball bearings. The front bearings consist of a pre-loaded pair of angular contact bearings with a single radial bearing in the rear. The spindle is fully hardened from end to end. On headstocks using type 3C collets (clear through capacity ½" or 13 mm), the headstock is furnished with a special adaptor and drawbar assembly which permits the use of the more accurate and sensitive type D collets (clear through capacity $5/16$" or 8 mm) for holding work under 8.0 mm diameter.

The tailstock is lever operated through a sensitive rack and pinion feed system. The spindle is hardened throughout its length and accepts all type D collets. A camlock device on the tailstock permits locking the spindle rigidly in any selected position. The lathe bed is cast from Meehanite and has fully ground precision ways. It has an overall length of 13" and is furnished complete with a tee bolt, nut and collar assembly for the attachment of tooling. The pedestal is cast integral with the bed and a tee slot is provided throughout the length of the bed ways. It may be bolted to any flat surface or a choice of two benches.

The motor drive unit of 1/8 hp permanent magnet motor, variable speed control and cast iron chip tray are included with some models of this lathe. The unit provides infinitely variable spindle speeds from 0–5000 rpm with dynamic braking. Electrics: 115 volt, 60 Hz, single phase AC only. A coolant system and a foot switch control are optional extras.

See pages 129–30 for details of earlier models.

Manufactured by Louis Levin & Son Inc., 13550 Larwin Circle, Santa Fe Springs, CA 90670, USA.

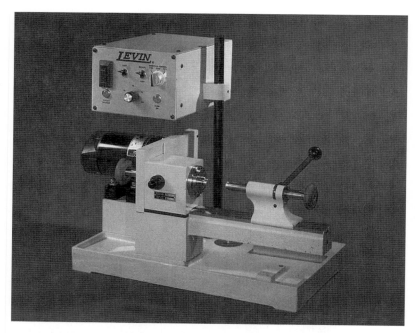

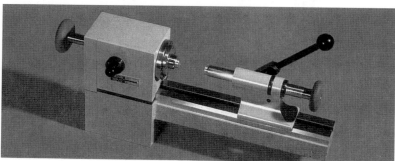

Plate 29 The Levin 13" instrument lathe. Top picture shows lathe fitted with 1/8 hp motor drive and variable speed control unit. Mounted on a cast iron chip tray. Lower, the basic machine. Both illustrations show the lathe fitted with the rack and pinion lever-operated tailstock

The production of Lorch lathes ceased in 1976, but the sheer quality of these German-made lathes is demonstrated by the fact they are still being employed today. The KD50 (Plate 30) was a larger machine recommended

178

for the finest turning with maximum accuracy in engineering, clock and watchmaking and instrument manufacture. The 400 mm prismatic bed was made of a special alloy steel with wear-resistant properties and had vee guideways. The motor reversing switch was housed in the machine base below the headstock. Drive was provided through vee-belts from a two-stage motor belt pulley to the transmission and from there to the triple-stepped pulley of the headstock.

A compound slide rest for the cutting of parallel and tapered threads, drilling tailstock with lever, quick-action ball pressure chuck, hand lever rest, and a milling unit were just some of the accessories available for this model. Distance between centres 180 mm, centre height 50 mm and a spindle bore of 8 mm. See pages 131–4 for earlier models.

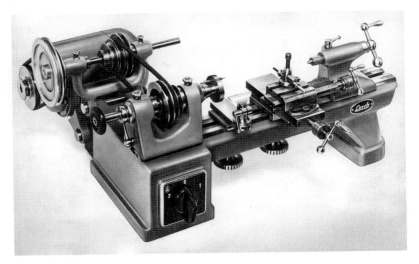

Plate 30 The Lorch KD50 precision lathe

International collaboration between the late C.H. Smith (UK) and A.J. Lofquist (USA) resulted in the development of several purpose-made accessories which considerably extend the versatility of the South Bend 9" and 10K lathes. These accessories, most of which are illustrated on pages 180–1, can also be adapted for fitting to similar makes of lathe such as the Boxford, Atlas and Blomquist, etc.

The tee slot cross slide shown in Plate 31 permits a wide range of boring and milling operations, whilst the reversible milling base (Plate 32) allows the original South Bend vertical slide to be set up on the cross slide in a greater range of positions.

An improved vertical slide (Plate 33), a 8 ½" face plate (Plate 34) for fitting to a 1½" x 8 tpi mounting, and a rear tool post (Plate 35) are also available. The range has been extended and now includes a Loop collet chuck, filing machine, boring and facing head, indicator/saddle stop, steady rest, boring and ball turning tool post, quick-change tool post, work post and a quick retracting tool post. All supplied in high-grade 35–40,000 lb tensile grey castings with full size drawings giving details of the required machining dimensions.

Available from Metal Lathe Accessories, PO Box 88, Pine Grove Mills, PA 16868, USA

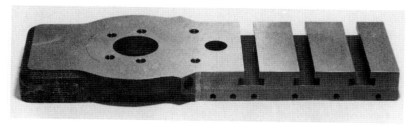

Plate 31   Tee slot cross slide

Plate 32   Reversible milling base

Plate 34   A 8½" diameter faceplate

Plate 33   An improved vertical slide

180

Plate 35   Rear toolpost fitted to the new cross slide

At first sight Micro-Mark's Microlux (82710) mini 7" x 14" lathe (Plate 36) looks very like many other small Chinese lathes, but there are several important differences. It is at least 2" longer than most and 6" longer than another popular brand and is made to Micro-Mark's own specifications. The Microlux has a lever-lock tailstock instead of a nut that requires tightening. The cross slide and compound rest dials both advance 0.050" per revolution against 1 mm for most of the other lathes. Its motor is also more powerful at 350 watts compared with 250 watts for most mini lathes.

The rigid, heat-treated cast-iron bed has precision ground vee-ways and the hardened and accurately finished main spindle is supported by ball bearings with metal gears. Spindle bore 0.787", taper MT3, and tailstock taper MT2. Spindle speeds 100–3000 rpm, with built-in tachometer. Thread cutting (18) from 12–52 tpi. It comes complete with a splash guard and chip pan, tool set, instruction/parts diagram and 3-jaw self-centring chuck.

Plate 36   Micro-Mark's Microlux 7 x 14 lathe

Optional extras: 6 ¼" face plate, steady rest, 4-jaw independent chuck, quick-change tool post, tailstock chuck MT2, live centre chuck MT2, self-centring 3- and 4-jaw chuck plus lathe stand.

Available exclusively from www.micromark.com.

For 75 years Myford have served the needs of the model engineer, first with the ML1, ML2, ML3 and ML4 range of lathes, all of which have been long discontinued.

The ever popular ML7 was launched as long ago as 1946, followed by the Super 7 (Plate 37) in 1953. Both lathes had a swing over bed of 7" (178 mm) and 19" (483 mm) between centres. Unlike the ML7, which had plain white metal bearings, the Super 7 spindle runs in a tapered bronze bush at the chuck end and a pair of angular ball bearings at the rear. The ball races are housed between screwed rings, which are used by moving the spindle backwards and forwards to provide a precise method of adjusting the front bearing clearance. The spindle is immensely rigid and known for its long, trouble-free life: the backgear assembly was similarly reinforced by the use of stronger gears and is fitted with a very handy flick over quick-release mechanism.

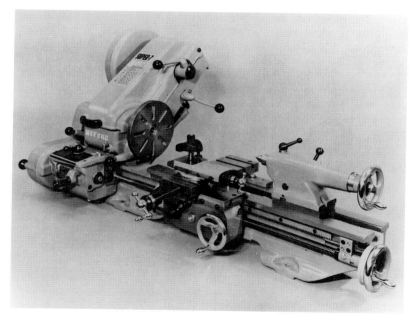

Plate 37   The Myford Super 7 lathe

182

The Super 7 Plus, which was introduced in 2001, has a spindle bore able to pass a 1" diameter bar, a MT42.5 x 2 mm pitch nose and a MT4 taper socket. The headstock and its bearings are arranged exactly as before but with spindle gears and backgears enlarged and modified. The motor drive to the countershaft is now by a Poly vee-belt with two-step pulleys, as previously, which has made a significant improvement to smooth running at top speed.

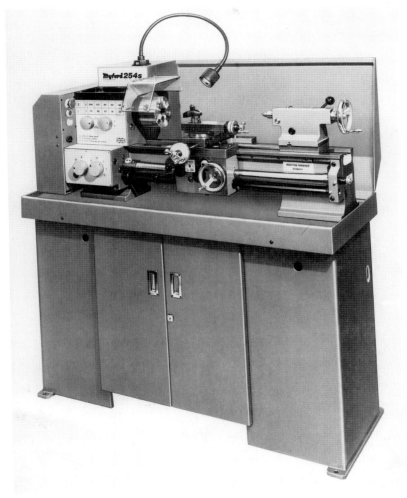

Plate 38   The Myford 254S lathe

183

Myford introduced the 254S high speed centre lathe (Plate 38) in 1984, and following a capacity increase in 1989, the name was changed to 254 Plus. Compared to the Series 7 lathe, the manufacturer claimed the 254S and 254 Plus had greater capacity and capability without any proportional increase in physical size. It was available in either metric or imperial versions with a choice of either single or three-phase electrics and powered by a 0.75 Kw (1 hp) motor. The direct belt drive ensured quiet operation at high speeds, whilst the reduction gearing in the low range gave the low speed torque essential for heavy work. There was also a vari-speed version, the 254V Plus, which featured an electronically controlled variable speed inverter control and a powerful 1.5 Kw (2 hp) motor. It had two infinitely variable speed ranges giving 250–2000 rpm in direct drive and 30–275 rpm in backgeared drive. The 254 series is no longer in production.

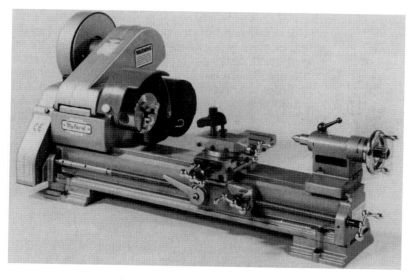

Plate 39   Myford's Diamond 10 lathe

The Diamond 10 (Plate 39) was launched by Myford to mark their sixtieth anniversary. This was a small precision lathe backed up with the most comprehensive range of readily available attachments and accessories. The two-speed countershaft produced ten spindle speeds ranging from 48–2000 rpm; the slower speed allowing for screw-cutting or the facing of large components.

MYFORD LATHES

Standard Specifications	Super 7 Sigma Plus (entry level)	Super 7 Plus (standard machine)	Super 7 Connoisseur
14 speeds 27–2105 (50Hz)	✓	✓	−
Variable speeds (within 3 speed ranges) 26–3000 rpm	✗	✗	✓
3.5" x 18.75" gap-bed	✓	✓	✓
Long bed 31" between centres option	✓	✓	✓
Backgeared and screw-cutting	✓	✓	✓
Screw-cutting gearbox	optional	optional	✓
Metric screw-cutting on inch machines and inch screw-cutting on metric	Imperial leadscrews on all lathes. Conversion sets available for both change wheel and gearbox models.	Imperial leadscrews on all lathes. Conversion sets available for both change wheel and gearbox models.	Imperial leadscrews on all lathes. Conversion sets available for both change wheel and gearbox models.
Power cross feed	✗	✓	✓
Hardened bed	optional	optional	✓
Countershaft clutch	✓	✓	✓
Poly-V countershaft	✓	✓	✓
Poly-V headstock drive – countershaft and headstock	✗	✗	✓
Big bore (25.4 mm) spindle	✓	✓	✓
Motor and EC safety switch gear	✓	✓	✓ + Vari-speed with tachometer
Spindle nose safety reverse feature	✓	✓	✓
Friction micrometer dial on tailstock handwheel	✗	✗	✓
Safety locking belt guards	✓	✓	✓
Coolant equipment	optional	optional	optional
Light unit	optional	optional	optional
Headstock spindle indexing	✓	✓	✓
Thread-dial indicator	Optional on change wheel model. Standard on gearbox models.	Optional on change wheel model. Standard on gearbox models.	✓
Needle roller thrust bearing to cross-slide feed screw	✗	✗	✓
Motor feed	0.55Kw (3/4hp) single-phase	0.55Kw (3/4hp) single-phase	0.75Kw (1hp) single-phase to 3-phase variable-speed inverter

The five change wheels fitted to the lathe were pre-set to provide a fine longitudinal feed. Optional sets of change wheels completed the screw-cutting range and feeds permitting conversion from metric to imperial or vice versa.

The lathe bed was a one-piece high quality grey iron casting. Both the top of the bed and the dovetail shears were precision ground. A substantial spindle was fitted to a rigid headstock casting and mounted in large taper roller bearings. A quality 100 mm (4") 3-jaw geared scroll chuck with threaded body was provided as standard. The Diamond 10 converted into a compact but capable milling machine with the VMD milling and drilling attachment. The basic specifications were:

Centre height 84 mm (3 $^3/_{16}$")
Distance between centres 460 mm (18")
Headstock spindle nose thread 1 $^1/_8$" 12 tpi
Spindle nose register 1 ¼"
Spindle nose bored 2MT
Carriage swing over cross slide 98 mm (3 $^7/_8$")
Swing over saddle 149 mm (5 $^7/_8$")

As part of a rationalization programme, production of the Diamond 10 has now ceased.

The current range consists of the Super 7 Sigma Plus, the Super 7 Plus and the Super 7 Connoisseur. The basic specification of all three lathes is given below – see the comparison table on page 185 for differences:

Bed cast in grade 240 iron.
Belt driven, 14 speeds (27–2105 rpm on 50 Hz machines) achieved by a two-speed drive from motor to countershaft, a four-speed drive from countershaft to headstock spindle and a backgear reduction on both the Sigma and Super 7. The Connoisseur has variable spindle speeds of 26–3000 rpm achieved in three distinct speed ranges by means of a two-speed drive from countershaft to headstock spindle and a backgear reduction. Both primary and secondary drives are fitted with poly vee-belts.
Centre height 89 mm (3 ½")
Distance between centres 475 mm (18 ¾") or 780 mm (30 ¾")
Headstock spindle bored 26 mm to clear 25.4 mm (1") and incorporating a safe reversing feature. The spindle nose is precision bored and ground 4MT. Imperial model with 10 tpi cross slide and top slide feedscrews and nuts: inch graduations on the tailstock barrel and leadscrew handwheel. Metric model with 2.0 mm pitch.

186

Plate 40 Long bed Super 7B Connoisseur lathe mounted on a long industrial stand and fitted with a Rishton VMA attachment with a tee slotted boring table fitted to the cross slide.

The Connoisseur carriage features power cross feed (facing), a tee slotted cross slide and the top slide swivels 360°. Both cross slide and top slide feedscrews are fitted with adjustable micrometer dials. The cross slide feedscrew is fitted with a needle thrust bearing to increase sensitivity.

The tailstock is a self-ejecting type and the barrel feedscrew has a three start thread to give rapid movement. The tailstock handwheel is

187

fitted with an adjustable friction dial having 60 divisions reading 0.005" per division. A metric version is not available but the equivalent per division is 0.127 mm. The barrel is precision bored 2MT. The tailstock body can be set over on its base in either direction to turn long shallow tapers.

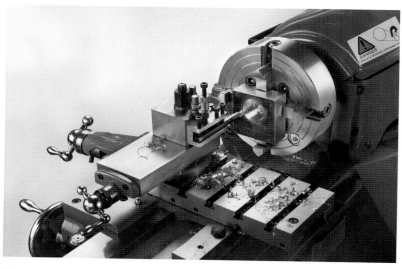

Plate 41   Myford Super 7 lathe fitted with a 160 mm 4-jaw independent chuck and an interchangeable tooling set. The block mounted in the chuck is being bored out.

Lathes can be supplied as either a change wheel model or fitted with a quick-change gearbox. Machines are fitted with a countershaft clutch unit. A plain taper front headstock bearing supports the spindle in radial loading while a pair of angular contact ball races at the rear provides support for axial loads.

For motor drive details see comparison table on page 185. Supply control units for single phase 110 volt 50/60Hz are available.

Lathes can be supplied for bench mounting, fitted to either a tray top cabinet stand or a heavy duty industrial stand.

Myfords now have a substantial business in the refurbishment of pre-owned lathes. Approximately 95% are dismantled so that the beds can be reground along with both cross slide and top slide. Alignments are checked after re-assembly to ensure they are the same as a new machine. Lathes are often fitted with a new motor and switch gear and always supplied with a new chuck. The machines come with a one year warranty.

Innovative design and continuously improved engineering standards have maintained Myfords as the foremost British manufacturer of quality lathes and the availability of spares for lathes discontinued up to thirty years ago reflects the high value of their secondhand machines.

Myford Ltd, Wilmot Lane, Chilwell Road, Beeston, Nottingham NG9 1ER.

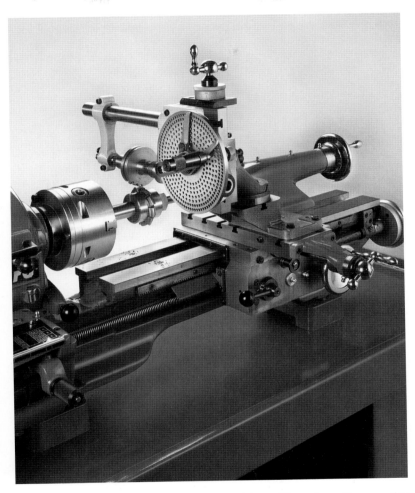

Plate 42   Super 7B Connoisseur lathe fitted with a milling arbor with a sprocket cutter which is supported between the 125 mm 3-jaw GS Pratt Burnerd Griptru and the tailstock. The duplex sprocket blank is supported between centres on the Myford dividing head which is mounted on the cross slide to provide additional capacity.

Plate 43 Close up of a Super 7 Sigma lathe with a standard 125 mm 3-jaw GS chuck and an optional rack operated attachment fitted to the tailstock. An optional interchangeable tooling set is mounted on the top slide as is an interchangeable rear tool post mounted to the rear of the cross slide.

The American-made Peatol Micro II lathe (sold in the US under the maker's name of Taig), Plate 44, is described as a full-size lathe in miniature, capable of producing quality work with a wide range of applications. Ideal for the novice, but equally at home in the industrial workshop. Reliability is assured by the use of large oversize spindle ball bearings and the fabrication of all stressed components in heat-treated steel alloys.

The lathe is available in kit form or ready assembled. The basic price includes a choice of a 3- or 4-jaw chuck – the latter being independently adjustable, but not a tailstock. Basic specifications:

> Centre height 2 ¼"
> Distance between centres 9 ¾"
> Swing over bed 4 ½"
> Maximum collet diameter $^9/_{32}$"

190

Plate 44   The Peatol Micro II lathe

Accessories include a drilling tailstock, compound top slide which allows for the cutting of tapers and angles, milling attachment, vertical slide, rotating centre, face plate and lifting blocks which raise the centre height from 2 ¼" to 3".

A suitable ¼ hp motor with an 11 mm shaft and a six-speed pulley set is available from the UK agents, Peatol Machine Tools, 19 Knightlow Road, Harbone, Birmingham B17 BPS. American manufacturer: Taig Tools, 12419 East Nightingale Lane, Chandler, AZ 85286, USA.

The German company Unitech-Maschinen manufacture a whole range of lathes, but there are two models which will appeal to the model engineer. First, the Prazi MD 200, a well designed and accurate lathe with a comprehensive range of accessories. Available in metric or imperial. The precision spindle has the capability to accept various watchmaker turning accessories, WW and Boley collets. The basic specifications are:

> Distance between centres 7.87" (200 mm)
> Centre height 2.05" (52 mm)
> Swing over bed 3.94" (100 mm)
> Swing over cross slide 1.57" (40 mm)
> Cross slide travel 2.16" (55 mm)
> Leadscrew diameter .465" (11.8 mm)
> Spindle accuracy .0002" (.005 mm)
> Spindle taper MT2
> Spindle speeds (3) 690, 1200, and 2240 rpm
> Tailstock travel 1.60" (40 mm)
> Tailstock taper MT1
> Motor: 1/6 hp (120 watts 110 volts)

191

The lathe comes with a 2.60" 3-jaw precision chuck with external and internal jaws, 4-way turret tool post, tool bit, dead centre, tool kit, instruction and parts manual. A new deluxe version MD200+ with optional MT1 spindle is available.

The Prazi SD 300 (Plate 45) is a more robust machine than its smaller companion and has a headstock with adjustable spindle tapered roller bearings with an accuracy of .0002" which provides close tolerances on turning, facing and boring operations. The bed is precision ground with a heavy-duty headstock construction which assures rigidity, high resistance to twisting and quality work finishes. Both cross slide and top slide have fully adjustable gibs for maintaining consistent accuracy. Taper turning is performed with a standard moveable top slide. An impressive range of accessories is available for turning, milling, drilling, boring and gear cutting. The optional spindle belt drive powermill attachment can easily be mounted to the lathe to create a powerful mill combination. The heavy-duty mill head swivels 360°. Optional spindle speeds are available and there is a choice of imperial or metric versions. Also sold under the Unitech brand name.

The basic specifications are:
Distance between centres 11.81" (300 mm)
Centre height 2.56" (65 mm)
Swing over bed 5.12" (130 mm)
Swing over cross slide 2.44" (62 mm)
Cross slide travel 3.15" (80 mm)
Top slide travel 2.17" (55 mm)
Leadscrew diameter .750" (19 mm)
Spindle accuracy .0002" (.005 mm)
Spindle nose chuck flange
Spindle taper MT2
Spindle bore .472" (12 mm)
Spindle speeds (4) 300, 600, 1200, and 2400 rpm
Tailstock quill diameter .866" (22mm)
Tailstock taper MT1
Tailstock travel 1.50" (38 mm)
Threads imperial 18: 8–64 tpi
metric 18: 0.2–3.00 mm
Motor: 1/3 hp (250 watts 110 volts)

The lathe is supplied with a motor, 3" 3-jaw chuck with internal and external jaws, compound swivel top slide, 4-way turret tool post, tool bits, dead centre, nine piece change gear set, imperial/metric threads, power

Plate 45   The Prazi SD lathe fitted with a milling machine attachment

longitudinal feed, tool kit, operations and parts manual and emergency stop.

Manufactured by Unitech-Maschinen GmbH, Clemens-Winkler-Strasse 6, 09116 Chemnitz, Germany.

Proxxon have a worldwide reputation for machine power tools and manufacture a number of lathes which are of interest to the model engineer. A first choice would be the PD 230/E shown in Plate 46. The specifications are:

Distance between centres 230 mm
Swing 52 mm
Height over cross slide 28 mm
Cross slide travel 60 mm and top slide 45 mm
Steel tool holder accepts 8 x 8 mm cutters
The MT1 (short) spindle has a 10.5 mm bore, runs in precision ball bearings giving an accuracy of 0.01 mm without chuck, and 30 mm travel
The thread cutting capability covers the most important pitches of 0.5, 0.625, 0.7, 0.75, 0.8, 1.0, 1.2 and 1.5 mm

Spindle speeds are changed by means of a belt and provides 300, 900 and 3000 rpm. The electronic speed controller further extends the speed range down from 100 rpm and up to 3000 rpm. The automatic feed offers 0.05 or 0.1 mm per revolution.

Plate 46   The Proxxon PD 230/E lathe

The quiet running 220–240 volt 50Hz, 140 watt motor is fitted with a forward/reverse switch. The 3-jaw chuck has a capacity of 2–35mm with internal jaws and 24–68 mm with external jaws. The handwheels are fitted with zero adjustable scales with one revolution equalling 1mm feed (40 divisions) and hence 0.025 mm/division. The top slide, used for taper turning, and a tool holder are included along with a MT1 live centre.

Among a host of optional extras are a splash guard and chip collecting tray, dividing attachment, a milling/drilling attachment, collet set, 4-jaw independent chuck, centre turning attachment, gear chuck, fixed steady and a quick-change tool post.

194

Manufactured by Proxxon GmbH, Im Spanischen 18–24, D-54518, Niersbach, Germany. Available from a number of UK retailers including Metal Smith, Rejon Machine Tools and Proxxon-Direct.Com.

The Pultra Micro Series 1770 (Plate 47) are built in modular form and then assembled according to customer's personal requirements. Available in both imperial and metric. The basic machine comprises of bed, tool posts, bed bolt, chip tray, operator's manual and comes with an outfit of spanners. There is a choice of headstock, both ball and roller bearing, of either handwheel or lever-operated drawbar. Likewise two tailstocks and compound slides as well as a lever cut off slide and a capstan slide.

The bench drive unit is powered by a ½ hp motor which gives nine spindle speeds of 240–6000 rpm. Alternatively, the lathe assembly can be supplied mounted on a rigidly constructed welded steel cabinet, in which case the motor drive and spindle speeds are similar to the bench version.

The basic specifications are centre height 70 mm (2 ¾"), collet shanks 10 mm (25/64"), between centres 177 mm (7") and a swing over bed of 95 mm (3 ¾").

A wide range of accessories is available including a variety of chucks, coolant feed, lighting unit, radius turning slide, bar feeds, fixed or travelling steady, quick-change tool post, collets for use with headstocks and lever-operated tailstocks, carrier and face plate, centre adaptors, milling and grinding attachments.

The Pultra lathe is manufactured by Bracehand Ltd who also make the larger Smart & Brown lathes.

Plate 47   The Pultra Micro Series 1770 lathe

195

The name of Schaublin is synonymous throughout the world with their precision made lathes, tools and accessories, which are unsurpassed. Schaublin offer a range of CNC industrial lathes as well as manual models and of the latter model 70 CF is ideally suited to the needs of the watch and clockmaker and the precision engineer. The version shown in Plate 48 is cast iron mounted, but the basic lathe is available free standing with or without the digital electronic programmable control unit or foot control. The latter operates the spindle brake.

The basic specifications are:
Maximum swing over bed 130 mm
Height of centres 70 mm
Maximum distance between centres 275 mm
Headstock spindle bore to accept Schaublin W12 collets.

The 70MI has the same specifications, but the motor drive is integrated into the headstock unit and has the advantage of operating on a single phase supply, whereas the 70 CF is three phase.

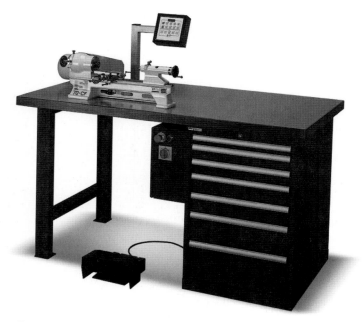

Plate 48   The Schaublin model 70 CF lathe which has the motor drive, pulley-operated, fitted behind the headstock. Three phase supply

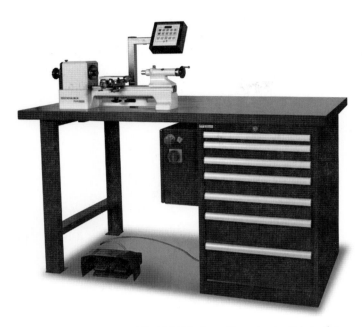

Plate 49 The Schaublin 70 MI lathe with motor built into the
headstock. Single phase supply

In addition to being made to a fine degree of accuracy, the sheer variety
of mountings, drives and accessories means that every conceivable job can
be undertaken with absolute confidence.

Manufactured by Schaublin Machines SA, Rue Principale 4, 2735
Bevilard, Switzerland and available from their agents in the UK and USA.

The Sherline lathe has a dedicated following on both sides of the Atlantic
and will be of interest to the first-time buyer, though it is interesting to
note the manufacturer claims nearly half of all sales have an industrial
application. Plate 50 shows model 4000 (imperial) which also has a metric
equivalent, model 4100. The basic specifications are:

> Distance between centres 8.00" (200 mm)
> Swing over bed 3.5" (90 mm)
> Travel of cross slide 4.25" (110 mm)
> Headstock: hole through spindle 0.405" (10 mm)
> spindle nose ¾"–16 tpi
> spindle nose taper 1MT
> spindle speeds 70–2800 rpm without belt changes,

There is a second pulley position available that offers extra torque at lower rpm if required.

Plate 50   The Sherline 4000 (imperial) lathe

Powered by a built-in high torque 90 volt DC motor with a variable speed control, which, it is claimed, will operate on any power supply throughout the world with a supply range of 100–240 volts 50 or 60Hz, without any change of controller or the need for a transformer.

Supplied as standard: 2.75" (70 mm) x 6" (152 mm) cross slide, standard 1 5/8" (41 mm) laser engraved aluminium handwheels, pulleys, belt, face plate, lathe dog, two dead centres, three hexagonal keys, tool post, high-speed cutting tool, and instructional booklet. A comprehensive range of accessories, including a vertical milling attachment is available for both the model engineer and clockmaker.

Manufactured in the USA by Sherline Products Inc, 3235 Executive Ridge, Vista, CA 92081-8527, USA. UK agents Millhill Supplies Ltd, Unit 37, Broton Drive, Broton Trading Estate, Halstead, Essex CO9 1HB.

The Smart & Brown 'L' series lathe (Plate 51 shows model L2PLH/1) is presented in a range of five basic models with a choice of two lever-operated headstocks:

LCC has a six-station capstan slide and lever-operated cut off slide.

LCP lever-operated tailstock and lever-operated compound slide.

LCL screw-operated tailstock and screw-operated compound slide.

All the above models are supplied mounted on a cast iron bed and a fabricated steel cabinet containing a 4:1 reduction drive from a two-speed demag motor/brake unit with thermistor protection producing 12 spindle speeds of 150–3000 rpm.

Whereas the two remaining models, which are also supplied mounted, are powered by a two-speed direct drive unit, again with thermistor protection, producing six spindle speeds of 416–2518 rpm.

LCO lever-operated cut off slide only.

LCS lever-operated compound slide only.

The basic specifications, common throughout the range, are:

Centre height 100 mm (4")
Distance between centres (tailstock models) 343 mm (13 ½")
Swing over bed 203 mm (8")
Maximum collet bore 25 mm (1")
Maximum diameter through spindle 31 mm (1 ¼")

There is an impressive range of accessories available from the manufacturers, Bracehand Ltd, Unit 1, Stanford Bury, Shefford, Bedfordshire SG17 5NS.

Plate 51   The Smart & Brown model L2PHL/1 lathe, one of
several available formats

Founded in 1987 Smithy has established a reputation for robust combination machines. The MI 1220 XL (Plate 52), the smallest in the range, is a complete package for the model engineer – lathe, mill and drill at an attractive price. The basic specifications are:

Distance between centres 20" (working capacity 18 ½")
Swing over bed 12", 6 ¾" over work table
Speed ranges lathe (6) 160–1600 rpm
           mill (12) 125–1600 rpm
Taper heads MT4
      tails MT3
Spindle bore 1.03"
Powered by a ¾ hp motor

Plate 52 The Smithy MI 1220 XL combination lathe

    The CZ 239 (Plate 53) is a more powerful machine with larger capacity but the same three-in-one versatility. The distance between centres is increased to 36", has a spindle which accepts bar stock up to 1½" diameter and is powered by a 1½ hp motor.

    Both lathes are available in metric and imperial versions, are sold with a two-year extended warranty, come with a premium tool pack, a thirty-day money-back guarantee, a toll-free helpline, operator's manual, plus a comprehensive DVD.

    Smithy Company, PO Box 1517, Ann Arbor, MI 48106-1517, USA

Plate 53   The Smithy CZ 239 combination lathe

The South Bend 9" lathe (Plate 54) is a firm favourite with model engineers in the USA and has a following in this country and, whilst production ceased some years ago, spares are still available. Its principal features were the robust hardened and accurately machined bed with unique three vee-ways, as shown in Plate 55, which ensured precise alignment of headstock, tailstock and carriage. Subsequently superseded by the slightly larger 10K model (Plate 56), this retained the best characteristics of the 9" and had the following basic specifications:

> Bed length: a choice of 42" or 54"
> Distance between centres 22" (559 mm) or 34" (864 mm)
> Swing over cross slide 6 ¼" (159 mm)
> Headstock
>   capacity through spindle $^{27}/_{32}$" (21 mm)
>   size of centre, MT2
> Tailstock
>   size of centre, MT2
>   spindle travel 2 $^{1}/_{8}$" (54 mm)

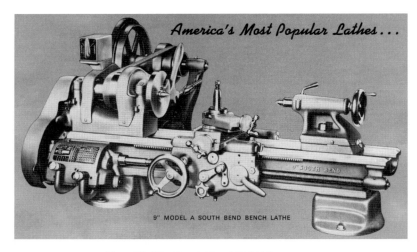

Plate 54   The South Bend 9" (4 ½" centres)

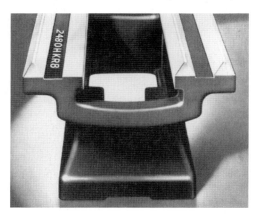

Plate 55   A close-up showing the unique vee-ways
of the South Bend lathe bed

The 10K was available for bench fitting or for mounting on a steel cabinet which had three useful drawers, a built-in chip pan top and a safety drive interlock device. Both versions had a quick-change gear box and a unique worm drive apron with friction clutch that provided a wide range of thread cutting pitches, cross and longitudinal power feeds. Whilst the horizontal 1/2 hp motor drive (bench model only) offered a choice between a 12-speed flat belt or a 16-speed vee-belt drive.

The Precision 10" South Bend lathe (Plate 57) which replaced the 10K

Plate 56   The South Bend 10K lathe

Plate 57   The South Bend Precision 10" lathe

had 33" centres and a bed length of 54". It was available in two versions, engine or toolroom models, and both had flame hardened bed ways. They were claimed to be fast with high spindle speeds, extremely accurate in operation and ideally suited for screw-cutting to the exacting tolerances needed for precision thread gauges, taps, dies, etc.

The Precision 10" was in turn replaced by the larger G-26-T bench lathe (Plate 58). The South Bend G-26-T bench lathe had additional power, a larger spindle hole and overall increased capacity. This had hardened and ground gears in a high-speed headstock, geometrically provisioned 12 spindle speeds (54–2000 rpm), spindle mounted with tapered roller bearings, enclosed gear box, 36" centres and 13" swing. There was a choice of motor drives and a wide range of optional equipment. The G-26-T lathe has now been superseded by the GS26LT cabinet lathe.

Plate 58   The South Bend G-26-T bench lathe

Production at South Bend, Indiana ceased in 2007 and the right to market South Bend lathes was acquired by LeBlond Ltd, then transferred to South Bend Lathe Co. in March 2009.

The Star lathe (see pages 144–7) is one of the few precision watchmaker's lathes to have survived virtually unchanged since the first publication of this work in 1952. It is still available with the same specifications: 40 mm centre height, a choice of bed length – 200, 250, 300 or 400 mm, headstock with either 6 or 8 mm boring, fixed and adjustable tailstock and hand rest, all of which can be purchased separately or in boxed combination sets with a variety of accessories, plus a mounted version complete with motor drive.

Manufactured by M. Gentil & Co., Village 156, 2406 La Brevine, Switzerland. Available from a number of UK stockists including Cousins, Henri Picard & Frere and Walsh.

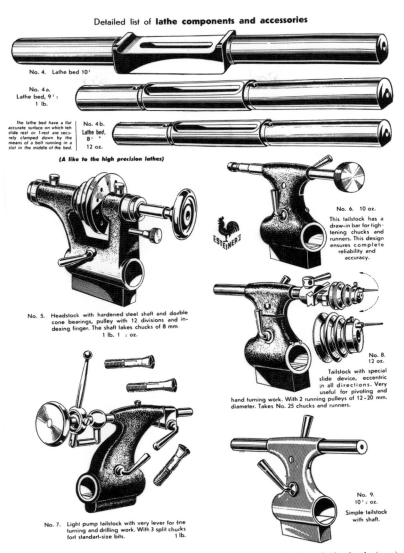

No. 4. Lathe bed 10¹

No. 4 a.
Lathe bed, 9¹⁄₂
1 lb.

The lathe bed have a flat
accurate surface on which teh
slide rest or 1-rest are securely clamped down by the
means of a bolt running in a
slot in the middle of the bed.

No. 4 b.
Lathe bed,
8⁵ "
12 oz.

(A like to the high precision lathes)

No. 5. Headstock with hardened steel shaft and double
cone bearings, pulley with 12 divisions and indexing finger. The shaft takes chucks of 8 mm.
1 lb. 1 ⁻ oz.

ESTEINER.T

No. 6.   10 oz.
This tailstock has a
draw-in bar for tigh-
tening chucks and
runners. This design
ensures complete
reliability and
accuracy.

No. 8.
12 oz.
Tailstock with special
slide device, eccentric
in all directions. Very
useful for pivoting and
hand turning work. With 2 running pulleys of 12 - 20 mm.
diameter. Takes No. 25 chucks and runners.

No. 7. Light pump tailstock with very lever for fine
turning and drilling work. With 3 split chucks
fort standart-size bits.   1 lb.

No. 9.
10¹⁄₂ oz.
Simple tailstock
with shaft.

Plate 59   An illustration showing the unique design of Steiner lathe beds (*top*),
basic headstock (*centre left*) and a choice of four tailstocks

The Steiner brand, made by Horia SA, 23 Rue de l'Avenir, 2852
Courtételle, Switzerland, is a symbol of precision and quality recognised
world-wide. As previously explained (see page 147) their lathe beds are

of unique design for, in addition to being half-round with a flat ground bottom, they are slotted to facilitate secure clamping of the tee rest and/or slide rest. Plate 59 shows the basic headstock (number 5) with a choice of four tailstocks (numbers 6, 7, 8 and 9). Lathe bed number 4, at the top of the illustration, is only available in a length of 260 mm (10 ¼"), whilst the alternative design comes in a choice of 260 mm (10 ¼") and 220 mm (8 ⁵/₈"). All their lathe components, accessories and tools are available separately or in a variety of boxed sets, one of which is shown in Plate 60.

Plate 60   Just one of the many Steiner boxed combination sets – shown here is Set M

The Stevens milling machine is only 25 cm high but is very versatile and accepts 8 mm horological collets. It lends itself to a wide variety of uses in the watchmaking, clockmaking and small instrument fields. The top cross slide is provided with two 6 mm tee slots for work holding. The pulley accepts the readily available 4 mm lathe belting and is driven by a fractional hp motor – not provided. The headstock can be universally positioned allowing the machine to be used as a lathe.

The 8 mm headstock is available separately and can be used for a number of operations such as grinding, milling or gear cutting.

Manufactured and available from Stevens Machine Tools, 51 Cowley Road, Uxbridge, Middlesex UB8 2AE.

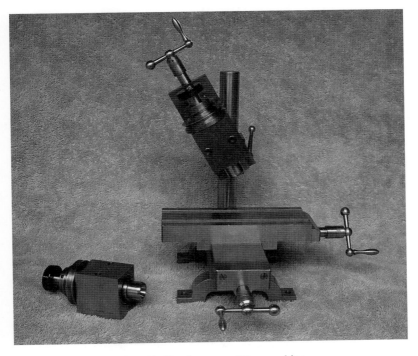

Plate 61   The Stevens milling machine

The compact Toyo lathe was originally manufactured by Sakai of Japan and marketed under a variety of names worldwide including Sakai, Record, and Toyo Record. It is now made in Korea by Woo Sung E. & I. Co. Ltd, South Korea, who sell under their own brand name, Manix, as well as Toyo Record, and Sakai in the USA. The smaller version, ML-1 shown in Plate 62 with automatic feed gear mounted on the left of the motor housing, is no longer available. This lathe had a centre height of 50 mm and a distance between centres of 250 mm.

Plate 62 The discontinued Toyo ML-1 shown with automatic feed gear
mounted left of the motor housing

There are now two larger models: the Manix ML-210 (Plate 63) and the
Manix ML-360 Plate 64).

Plate 63 The Manix mini lathe ML-210 shown here with the
optional extra back plate and drip tray

208

Both have a vee-guided bed which is hardened and precision ground to ensure strength and rigidity. The capacitor start motor drive provides a range of six speeds and can be run clockwise and anti-clockwise. The hardened and accurately finished main spindle is supported with precision taper roller bearings. There are many accessories to choose from including a milling attachment for each lathe. The basic specifications are:

	ML-210	ML-360
Centre height	52 mm	75 mm
Distance between centres	210 mm	360 mm
Swing over carriage	58 mm	96 mm
Carriage cross travel	60 mm	85 mm
Main spindle centre	MT1	MT2
Main spindle speeds	280, 540, 780, 910, 1710 and 2500 rpm	230, 450, 740, 850, 1630 and 2500 rpm
Motor	condenser single phase 110, 115, 220, 240 volt. Input 130 watt, output 70 watt	condenser single phase 100, 115, 220, 240 volt. Input 470 watt, output 300 watt

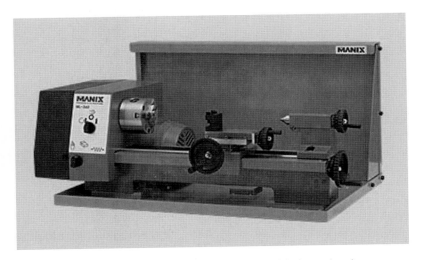

Plate 64 The Manix mini lathe ML-360 with the optional
extra back plate and drip tray

209

UK agent: Rejon Machine Tools, Mumby Lodge, Mumby's Drove, Three Holes, Wisbech, Cambridgeshire PE14 9JT. American agent: Progress Machine & Tool Corp., 645 South Olive Street, Los Angeles, CA 90014, USA.

There are a number of overhead drives for the small lathe on the market, but that shown in Plate 65 deserves consideration because of its availability either as a set of aluminium alloy castings or in complete kit form requiring only straightforward machining on a 3 ½" lathe. Recommended drive is a ¹/₈ hp Parvalux SD13 motor with a 6mfd capacitor.

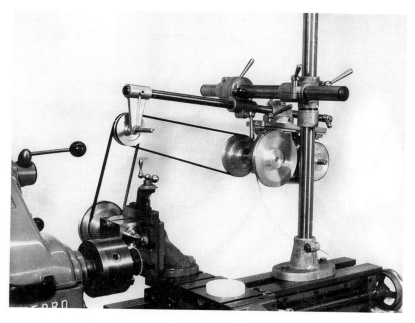

Plate 65   An overhead drive for the small lathe

The wide range of speeds (150–4000 rpm) makes this unit ideal for the cutting of clock wheels and pinions. Available direct from the manufacturer, J.M.W. (Clocks), 12 Norton Green Close, Sheffield S8 8BP, who also offer division plates for use with their overhead drive unit (Plate 65), the milling and drilling spindle shown in Plate 66, a versatile lathe filing rest suitable for lathes with 3" centres upwards (Plate 67), a pivoting and Jacot tool which is supplied complete with a Jacot drum (Plate 68), and a fusee cutting tool, which is mounted on the lathe cross slide, shown in Plate 69. Plus a range of cutters for clock wheels and many other tools for the clock and watch repairer and model engineer.

Plate 66   Milling and driving spindle

Plate 67   Lathe filing rest

Plate 68   Close-up showing pivoting tool set up for burnishing a pivot

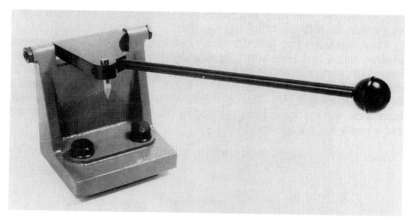

Plate 69   Fusee cutting tool

The German company Walter Blombach GmbH, established in 1885, has an international reputation for the quality of their machine tools and a range of conventional and CNC lathes sold under the Wabeco brand name. Wabeco lathes are sold with a five-year warranty and are supplied with a test report.

The lathe range comprises the D2000E (Plate 70), D2400E (Plate 71) and the D3000E, all with twin-bar beds, plus the D4000E (Plate 72) and the D6000E with the more conventional prismatic cast iron bed with inverted vee-ways. All lathes are fitted with taper-roller bearing headstock spindles bored 20 mm to take a MT3 taper centre with an optional 30 mm bore and have an electronically infinitely variable drive giving speeds of 30–2300 rpm from a 1.4 Kw, 230 volt 50 Hz single phase motor. Also available in 110 volt 60 Hz and imperial models. Other features are the leading spindle drive with gear change quadrant for thread cutting plus automatic longitudinal feed, on the D3000E only, from a separate motor drive which is usually found only on the more expensive lathe. Optional gear sets for metric (0.4–4.00 mm) and imperial (10–32 tpi).

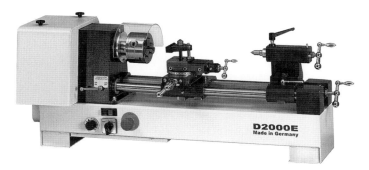

Plate 70   The Wabeco D2000E lathe

The D2000E has 350 mm between centres whilst the D2400E and the D3000E have 500 mm and all with a centre height of 110 mm. The D4000E has 350 mm between centres and a centre height of 100 mm. The more robust D6000E has 600 mm between centres and a centre height of 135 mm. There is a high speed version of the D6000E with a 2.0 Kw motor drive producing spindle speeds of 100–5000 rpm.

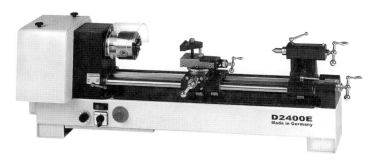

Plate 71   The Wabeco D2400E lathe

213

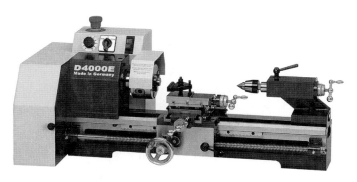

Plate 72   The Wabeco D4000E lathe

Sole UK importer: Pro Machine Tools Ltd, 17 Station Road Business Park, Barnack, Stamford, Lincolnshire PE93 3DW. American importer: MDA Precision, 3290 Hecker Pass Highway, Gilroy, CA 95020, USA.

The Warco mini lathe (Plate 73) has much to offer the model engineer and is competitively priced. This lathe has quality printed circuit boards for long term reliability, is given a thorough check prior to dispatch, and comes with an individual accuracy test report. Supplied with a range of standard accessories including a 80 mm 3-jaw chuck with inside/outside jaws, face plate, 4-way tool post, threading facility, swarf tray and rear splashback and thread dial indicator. Available in metric or imperial. Conversion kits are an optional extra. Specifications:

> Distance between centres 300 mm (12")
> Centre height 90 mm (3 ½")
> Spindle bore 20 mm ($^3/_4$")
> Headstock taper 3MT
> Tailstock taper 2MT
> Speeds 50–2900 rpm infinitely variable
> Range of metric threads 0.5–2.5 mm
> Range of imperial threads 12–52 tpi
> Motor ¾ hp single phase

Plate 73   The Warco mini lathe

Impressive range of additional accessories. Marketed by Warren Machine Tools (Guildford) Ltd, Warco House, Fisher Lane, Godalming, Surrey GU8 4TD.

LATHE, TOOL AND MATERIAL STOCKISTS

The following listings are provided for the reader's benefit and does not claim to be exhaustive. Neither can the publisher guarantee the accuracy of the services offered, although they were correct at the time of preparation. For further information readers are recommended to refer to current issues of the relevant specialist magazines. In the UK: *Engineering in Miniature* (www.teepublishing.co.uk/eim.php), *The Horological Journal* (www.bhi.co.uk), *Clocks* (www.clocksmagazine.com), and *Model Engineer* (www.model-engineer.co.uk) and *Model Engineers' Workshop*. In the USA: *The Mart*, published by the National Association of Watch and Clock Collectors (www.nawcc.org), *Watch & Clock Review, Horological Times* (www.awci.com), *Model Engine Builder* (www.modelenginebuilder.com) and *The Home Shop Machinist* (www.homeshopmachinist.net).

Most of the suppliers included here have very informative websites, downloadable catalogues and may be contacted by telephone, fax or email. In terms of archive data, the website www.lathes.co.uk can have few equals for information on lathes, accessories, part lists, instruction booklets and machine tools. Another site of interest is that of www.littlemachineshop.com which has a useful mini lathe comparison page.

UNITED KINGDOM

Arrand Engineering
The Forge, Knossington, Nr Oakham, Leicestershire LE15 8LN
Tel/fax: 01664 454 566
British manufacturer of quality taper tooling, engineer's small tools and machine tool accessories. Material stockist.

Axminster Power Tool Centre Ltd
Head Office
Unit 10, Weycroft Avenue, Axminster, Devon EX13 5PH
Tel: 0800 371 822

South West
Trafalgar Way, Axminster, Devon EX13 5PB
Tel: 01297 35058

South Central
Cressex Business Park, Lincoln Road, High Wycombe, Buckinghamshire HP12 3HZ
Tel: 01494 885 480

South East
Sheppey Way, Bobbing, Sittingbourne, Kent ME9 8QP
Tel: 01795 437 143
Web: www.axminster.co.uk
Impressive range of machine tools and lathe accessories. Mammoth illustrated catalogue.
Stockist of Axminster BV20M2 and Axminster Sieg C2A, Axminster Sieg C4 and a range of larger lathes.

Beatson Fans & Motors Ltd
16 Newhall Road, Sheffield S9 2QL
Tel: 0114 244 9955
Fax: 0114 244 9956
Web: www.beatson.co.uk
Major stockist and repairer of electric motors. New and secondhand.

Chester Machine Tools Ltd
Head Office
Clwyd Close, Hawarden Industrial Park, Nr Chester, Flintshire CH5 3PZ
Tel: 01244 531631
Fax: 01244 531331

Midlands Showroom
Unit 4, Plant Lane Business Park, Burntwood, Staffordshire WS7 3GN
Tel: 01543 448 940
Web: www.chesteruk.net
Machine tools plus a large range of lathes.

Chronos Ltd
Unit 14, Dukeminster Estate, Church Street, Dunstable LU5 4HU
Tel: 01582 471 900
Fax: 01582 471 920
Web: www.chronos.ltd.uk
Suppliers of machine tools, accessories, measuring equipment, books and materials.
Stockist of Clarke, Wabeco, Unimat 4 and Compact 5 lathes plus accessories.

College Engineering Supply, The
2 Sandy Lane, Codsall, Wolverhampton WV8 1EJ
Tel: 0845 166 2184
Fax: 01902 842 284
Web: www.collegeengineering.co.uk
Materials and machine tool castings stockist.

Cowells Small Machine Tools Ltd
Tendring Road, Little Bentley, Colchester, Essex CO7 8SH
Tel/fax: 01206 251 792
Web: www.cowells.com
Manufacturer of the Cowells lathe, vertical milling machine and a
comprehensive range of machine tools and accessories for the small
lathe.

Clarke International
Hemnall Street, Epping, Essex CM16 4LG
Tel: 01992 565 333
Fax: 01992 561 562
Web: www.clarkeinternational.com
Machine tools and own brand lathes

Cousins Material House Ltd
Head Office
Unit J, Chesham Close, Romford, Essex RM7 7PJ
Tel: 01708 757 800
Fax: 0800 731 1095

Birmingham Showroom
41 Warstone Lane, Hockley, Birmingham B18 6JJ
Web: www.cousinsuk.com
Material stockist. Agent for Bergeon and Star lathes. Also sell books.

The Engineers Emporium
L.A. Services Ltd, Bramcote Fields Farm, Bramcote, Warwickshire
CV11 6QL
Tel: 01455 220 340
Web: www.theengineersemporium.co.uk
Secondhand machine tools, attachments, accessories, lathe and mill spares.
Replacement parts made to order. Manuals and handbooks.

Essel Engineering
Maesiocyn, Tylwch, Llanidloes, Powys SY18 6JJ
Tel: 01686 412 040
Web: www.esselengineering.co.uk
Manufacturers and suppliers of accessories and a limited range of spare
parts for the Hobbymat MD65 lathe, which they also sell. Secondhand
lathes.

Folkestone Engineering Supplies
62 Canterbury Road, Hawkinge, Kent CT18 7BP
Tel: 01303 894 611
Fax: 0870 762 5556
Web: www.metal2models.btinternet.co.uk
Material stockist.

G.L.R. Distributors Ltd
Unit 3, Gresley Close, Drayton Fields Industrial Estate, Daventry,
Northamptonshire NN11 8RZ
Tel: 01327 878 988
Fax: 01327 876 396
Web: www.modelmakingsupplies.co.uk
Stockist of materials and machine tools for the model engineer.

G. and M. Tools
The Mill, Mill Lane, Ashington, West Sussex RH20 3BX
Tel: 01903 892 510
Fax: 01903 892 221
Web: www.gandmtools.co.uk
Large selection of quality used machine tools, milling machines, workshop
equipment, lathes and lathe accessories.

Griffiths Engineering
Wardlow, Tideswell, Buxton, Derbyshire SK17 8RP
Tel: 01298 871 633
Fax: 01928 872 874
Web: www.lathes.co.uk
World's largest machine tool reference archive. Vast collection of techni-
cal literature and specialist books. Short-run accessories and parts for
older lathes and millers. Flat, round and link belts from stock or made to
order. Pages of advertising for machine tools – for sale or wanted.

G.K. Hadfield
Old Post Office, Great Salkeld, Penrith, Cumbria CA11 9LW
Tel: 01768 870 111
Web: www.gkhadfield-tilly.co.uk
Specialist horological bookseller.

Hemingway Kits
126 Dunval Road, Bridgnorth, Shropshire WV16 4LZ
Tel/fax: 01746 767 739
Web: www.hemingwaykits.com

Specialist supplier of kits and materials for the model engineer.
Downloadable illustrated catalogue.

Home & Workshop Machinery
144 Maidstone Road, Foots Cray, Sidcup, Kent DA14 5HS
Tel: 020 8300 9070
Fax: 020 8309 6311
Web: www.homeandworkshop.co.uk
Extensive range of used workshop machinery including Boxford, Myford,
etc. lathes.

'Items' Mail Order Ltd
Mayfield, Marsh Lane, Saundby, near Retford, Nottinghamshire DN22 9ES
Tel/fax: 01427 848 880
Materials, machine tools, taps and dies and specialist supplier of BA
screws, brass and steel.

Claude Lyons Ltd
Brook Road, Waltham Cross, Hertfordshire EN8 7LR
Tel: 01992 768888
Fax: 01992 788000
Web: www.claudelyons.co.uk
Manufacturers of power and voltage control equipment. See page 96.

Maidstone Engineering Supplies
10–11 Larkstore Park, Lodge Road, Staplehurst, Kent TN12 0QY
Tel: 01580 890 066
Fax: 01580 891 505
Web: www.maidstone-engineering.co.uk
Material stockist.

Meadows & Passmore Ltd
1 Ellen Street, Portslade, Brighton, East Sussex BN41 1EU
Tel: 01273 421 321
Fax: 01273 421 322
Web: www.m-p.co.uk
Materials, tools and specialist books for the clockmaker and repairer.
Stockist of the Emco Unimat 4 lathe and accessories for same. Useful
catalogue.

Metal Smith Ltd

Department W, Enterprise Close, Telford Way Industrial Estate, Kettering NN16 8NS
Tel/fax: 01536 410 536
Web: www.metalsmith.co.uk
Stockist of traditional machine tools and large stocks of brass and nickel silver sheet and sections. Offers a specialist tooling service and the Proxxon range of power tools including the PD 230/E lathe.

Millhill Supplies Ltd

Unit 37, Broton Drive, Broton Trading Estate, Halstead, Essex CO9 1HB
Tel: 01787 472 236
Fax: 01787 477 797
Web: www.millhillsupplies.co.uk
Sole UK agent for Sherline miniature lathes and milling machines, together with accessories. Stockist of a wide range of machines and tools for the model engineer.

MJ Engineering

The Forge, Cricket Hill Lane, Yateley, Hampshire GU46 6BB
Tel: 01252 890 777
Web: www.mjeng.co.uk
Material stockist.

Peatol Machine Tools

19 Knightlow Road, Harborne, Birmingham B17 8PS
Tel/fax: 0121 429 1015
Web: www.peatol.com
Peatol lathe, mill, and accessories.

Henri Picard & Frere Ltd

8 Pixholme Court, Pixham Lane, Dorking, Surrey RH4 1PG
Tel/fax: 020 8949 3142
Web: www.picard.co.uk
Agent for Star lathes. Supplier of horological tools and materials.

Pro Machine Tools Ltd

17 Station Road Business Park, Barnack, Stamford, Lincolnshire PE93 3DW
Tel: 01780 740 956
Fax: 01780 740 957
Web: www.emcomachinetools.co.uk
Exclusive importers of Emco Hobby Machines: Unimat 3, Unimat Basic, Unimat 4, Compact 5 and Compact 8 lathes, plus accessories. Also sole importer of Wabeco machine tools and lathes.

RDG Tools
Grosvenor House, Caldene Business Park, Burnley Road, Mytholmroyd,
Nr Hebden Bridge, West Yorkshire HX7 5QJ
Tel: 01422 885 069
Fax: 01422 884 917
Web: www.rgdtools.co.uk
Machine tools plus lathe spares and accessories, in particular for Myford
and Boxford.

Reeves 2000
Appleby Hill, Austrey, Warwickshire CV9 3ER
Tel: 01827 830 894
Fax: 01827 830 631
Web: www.ajreeves.com
Claims to be the world's largest stockist of model engineering supplies,
including castings, taps, dies, endmills, drill bits, slot drills, fastenings
etc.

Rejon Machine Tools
Mumby Lodge, Mumby's Drove, Three Holes, Wisbech, Cambridgeshire
PE14 9JT
Tel: 01945 774 020
Fax: 01945 773 993
Web: www.rejon.co.uk
Specialist stockist of Emco Unimat, Proxxon, Manix and Toyo Record
lathes, together with a wide range of accessories and machine tools.

Shentonbooks
La Rochelle, Venns Gate, Cheddar, Somerset BS27 3BY
Tel: 0845 838 5523
Fax: 0845 838 5532
Web: www.shentonbooks.com
Specialist horological bookseller.

Stevens Machine Tools
51 Cowley Road, Uxbridge, Middlesex UB8 2AE
Tel: 01895 251 995
Manufacturer of the Stevens Milling machine. John Stevens is an independent instrument maker specialising in machines for the watch and
clock maker.

TEE Publishing

The Fosse, Fosse Way, Radford, Semele, Leamington Spa, Warwickshire CV31 1XN
Tel: 01926 614 101
Fax: 01926 614 293
Web: www.teepublishing.co.uk
Specialist technical publisher and retailer of rare and out of print titles devoted to horology and model engineering.

P.P. Thornton (Successors) Ltd

The Old Bakehouse, Upper Tysoe, Warwickshire CV35 0TR
Tel: 01295 680 454
Fax: 01295 680 067
Web: www.ppthornton.com
Manufacturers of cutters for clock wheels, pinions and dead beat scape wheels, musical box worm wheels and ratchets.

Toolco

Unit 4, Ebley Industrial Park, Westward Road, Ebley, Stroud, Gloucestershire GL5 4SP
Tel 01452 770 550
Fax: 01452 770 771
Web: www.toolco.co.uk
Machine tools. New and secondhand lathes.

J.M.W. (Clocks)

12 Norton Green Close, Sheffield S8 8BP
Tel: 0114 274 5693
Fax: 0114 274 0295
Web: www.j-m-w.co.uk
In addition to the accessories described on pages 210–212, this firm manufactures clockmakers' depthing tools and supplies all types of specialist tools, parts and materials for the clockmaker, watchmaker and model engineer. A useful catalogue is available.

H.S. Walsh & Sons Ltd

Head Office and Kent Showroom
243 Beckenham Road, Beckenham, Kent BR3 4TS
Tel: 020 8778 7061
Fax: 020 8676 8669

London Showroom
44 Hatton Garden, London EC1N 8ER
Tel: 020 7242 3711
Fax: 020 7242 3712

Birmingham Showroom
1–2 Warstone Mews, Warstone Lane, Hockley, Birmingham B18 6JB
Tel: 0121 236 9346
Fax: 0121 236 9355
Web: www.hswalsh.com
Stockist of Star, Emco, Unimat 4 and Compact 5 and Vector lathes, together with accessories. Vast range of tools and equipment. Mammoth illustrated catalogue.

Warren Machine Tools (Guildford) Ltd
Warco House, Fisher Lane, Chiddingfold, Surrey GU8 4TD
Tel: 01428 682 929
Fax: 01428 685 870
Web: www.warco.co.uk
Stockist of a range of lathes including the Warco Mini, milling machines, drill presses, metal forming machines and a range of machine tools.

USA

Alley Supply Company
PO Box 848, Gardnerville, NV 89410
Tel: 775-782-3800
Fax: 775-782-3757
Web: www.alleysupplyco.com
Lathes, milling machines, tools and cutters

Alro Metals Plus (formerly ASAP Source)
2466 South Industrial Highway, Ann Arbor, MI 48104
Tel: 734-213-2727
Fax: 734-747-7139
Web: www.asapsource.com
Material stockist.

Antique Clockworks Ltd
160 Loretto Street, PO Box 21, Loretto, MN 55357-0201
Tel: 763-479-1935
Web: www.antiqueclockworksltd.com
Stockist of Sherline lathes plus accessories, replacement parts, tooling and cutting tools and Starrett collets.

Bay-Com Enterprises Inc.
4439 Lake Avenue, Interlochen, MI 49643
Tel: 888-452-6947
Fax: 231-276-7194
Web: www.bay-com.com
Instructional videos and DVDs. Stockist of the Diamond Toolholder.

Blue Ridge Machinery and Tools
PO Box 536, 2905 Putnam Avenue, Hurricane, WV 25526-0536
Tel: 800-872-6500
Fax: 304-562-5311
Web: www.blueridgemachinery.com
Machine shop suppliers. Stockist of Myford, Sherline, Emco Unimat and Jet lathes. Accessories for Atlas, Sherline, Unimat and Jet lathes. Instructional books and DVDs.

Jules Borel & Company
1110 Grand Boulevard, Kansas City, MO 64106
Tel: 800-776-6858
Fax: 800-776-6862
Web: www.julesborel.com
Stockist of Bergeon lathes and accessories.

Campbell Tools Co.
Springfield, OH 45504
Tel: 937-882-6716
Fax: 937-882-6648
Web: www.campbelltools.com
Stockist of Jet, Sherline, Smithy, Prazi, Emco and Maier lathes and accessories, plus accessories for Unimat SL and older Atlas lathes.

CDCO Machinery Corp.
1129 Tower Road, Schaumburg, IL 60173
Tel: 800-417-2305
Fax: 888-731-8949
Web: www.cdcotools.com
Measuring, cutting and machine tools.

discountcampus
Tel: 800-621-8334
Web: www.dicountcampus.com
Online dealer of Sherline lathes and accessories.

emachinetool
268 Route 206, Flanders, NJ 07836
Tel: 888-808-0850
Fax: 888-808-0861
Web: www.emachinetool.com
Machine tools and lathes including Proxxon.

Enco Manufacturing Company
400 Nevada Pacific Highway, Fernley, NV 89408
Tel: 800-873-3626
Fax: 800-965-5857
Web: www.use-enco.com
Stockist of Sherline, Delta and own-brand lathes as well as machine tools.

Otto Frei & Jules Borel Inc.
PO Box 796, 126 Second Street, Oakland, CA 94604
Tel: 510-832-0355
Fax: 800-900-3734
Web: www.ofrei.com
Bergeon agent. Watchmakers' tools.

Grizzly Industrial, Inc.
Washington Showroom
1821 Valencia Street, Bellingham, WA 98229

Missouri Showroom
1815 West Battlefield, Springfield, MO 65807

Pennsylvania Showroom
1203 Lycoming Mall Circle, Muncy, PA 17756
Tel: 800-523-4777
Fax: 800-438-5901
Web: www.grizzly.com
Machine tools and lathe accessories. Wide range of own-brand lathes and combinations. Impressive 700 page catalogue.

Hobby Metal Kits, LLC
PMB 173–1660 South Church Street, Watertown, WI 53094
Tel: 608-345-2617
Fax: 920-390-2166
Web: www.hobbymetalkits.com
Material stockist.

International Sales & Marketing Group
1685 Algonquin Street, Unit 420, Huntington Beach, CA 92649
Tel/fax: 714-846-2700
Web: www.ismg4tools.com
Stockist of Prazi, Apollo, Wabeco, Promaster and Sakai lathes, plus accessories, as well as machine tools.

KRF Company
7080 Meadowbrook Road, Benton Harbour, MI 49022
Tel: 800-857-6664
Web: www.krfcompany.com
Supplier of the Omni-Post quick change tool post system.

Louis Levin & Son Inc.
13550 Larwin Circle, Santa Fe Springs, CA 90670
Tel: 562-802-8066
Fax: 562-802-3778
Web: www:levinlathe.com
Manufacturers of precision lathes for production of miniature and micro-miniature parts.

LittleMachineShop
396 West Washington Boulevard #500, Pasadena, CA 91103
Tel: 800-981-9963
Fax: 626-797-7934
Web: www.littlemachineshop.com
Tooling, parts and accessories for bench top lathes.

MDA Precision
3290 Hecker Pass Highway, Gilroy, CA 95020
Tel: 408-847-7796
Web: www.mdaprecision.com
Stockist of Wabeco and Prazi lathes.

Metal Lathe Accessories
PO Box 88, Pine Grove Mills, PA 16868
Tel: 814-234-3543
Web: www.statecollegecentral.com/metallathe
Specialist kits for South Bend, Atlas, Boxford and similar lathes.

New England Brass & Tool Inc.
75 Pond Street, Winchester, MA 01890
Tel: 800-781-8907
Fax: 781-729-4490
Web: www.brassandtool.com
Specialist supplier of materials for the clockmaker and model engineer.

Progress Machine & Tool Corp.
645 South Olive Street, Los Angles, CA 90014
Tel: 800-841-8665
Fax: 213-489-2140
Web: www.progresstool.com
Stockist of machine tools and Proxxon and Manix lathes plus accessories.

Sherline Products Inc.
3235 Executive Ridge, Vista, CA 92081-8527
Tel: 800-541-0735
Fax: 760-727-7857
Web: www.sherline.com
Manufacturer of Sherline lathes, mills and accessories. Useful instruction
guide and illustrated catalogue.

Smithy Company
PO Box 1517, Ann Arbor, MI 48106-1517
Tel: 800-476-4849
Fax: 800-431-8892
Web: www:smithy.com
Machine tools, own-brand lathes – manual and CNC, and accessories.

Speedy Metals
2505 South 162nd Street, New Berlin, WI 53151-2807
Tel: 866-938-6061
Fax: 262-754-4428
Web: www.speedymetals.com
Materials stockist.

Taig Tools
12419 East Nightingale Lane, Chandler, AZ 85286
Tel: 480-895-6978
Fax: 480-895-9648
Web: www.taigtools.com
Manufacturers of mini lathes and milling machines.

Travers Tool Co. Inc
128–15 26th Avenue, PO Box 541550, Flushing, NY 11354-0108
Tel: 800-211-0270
Fax: 800-722-0703
Web: www.travers.com
Technical support: 718-661-5637 or www.tech@travers.com
Metalworking tools and stockists of the OTMT (Sieg) range of lathes plus accessories. Illustrated catalogue with lots of useful technical data.
Branches in: Duncan, South Carolina; Chatsworth, California; Quebec, Canada; Queretaro and Monterrey, Mexico; and France.

Victor Machinery Exchange, Inc
56 Bogart Street, Brooklyn, NY 11206-3817
Tel: 1-800-723-5359
Fax: 718-366-7026
Web: www.victornet.com
Specialist in machine shop supplies, metal-cutting tools and precision measuring instruments.

Index

INDEX

A

accessories, 19–56
  standard set, 98
accuracy, certificate of, 121
alignment, checking, 17
Alley Supply Company, 225
Alro Metal Plus, 225
American Watch Tool Co., 1
Antique Clockworks Ltd, 225
Arrand Engineering, 217
ARS lathe, 98
Axminster lathes,
  BV20 M2, 155
  Sieg C2A, 154
  Sieg C4, 156
Axminster Power Tool Centre
  Ltd, 217–8

B

back centre, or runner definition, 3
lash, to reduce when indexing, 78
balance pivoting tool, 54
  staffs, turning, 84
Ballow, G.F., 2
Ballow, Whitcomb & Co., 2
barrel arbor,
  making, 79
  turning, 70
batch production equipment, 44
Bay-Com Enterprises Inc., 226
bearing spindle,
  adjustment, 11
  ball bearing, 12
  checking endplay, 18
  cone assembly, 10
  lubrication, 11
Beatson Fans & Motors Ltd, 218

bed, definition, 3
belts,
  jointing plastic, 47
  tension, 7, 92
  types and advantages, 6
"Bercostat" rheostats, 96
Bergeon lathes, 100–2, 156–7
Blombach GmbH, Walter, 212–14
Blue Ridge Machinery and Tools,
  226
Boley lathes, 102– 6, 157–8
Boley & Leinen lathes, *see* Leinen
Borel & Co., Jules, 226
boring, chuck for, 54
Boston Watch Co., 1
Boxford Ltd., 5
Bracehand Ltd., *see* Pultra *and*
  Smart & Brown lathes
BTM lathe, 153, 158–9
burnishing, *see also* pivot polish-
  ing
  Lerrac tool, 59

C

Campbell Tools Co., 226
carrier, 80, 86
  pulley, 79
CDCO Machinery Corp., 226
centres,
  definition, 4
  runner for filing, 35
  turner between, 80, 86
Chester lathes, 160
Chester Machine Tools Ltd, 218
Chronos Ltd, 218
chucks (or collets),
  arbor for turning, 31
  automatic closers, 44

balance, 30
boring, 54
box, 25
brass split, 27
button or crown, 28
carrier, 30
circular saw, 30
definition, 4
drill, Jacobs, 30
emery wheel, 2
flat face, 21
identification, 21
interchangeability, 8
lantern, 28, 58
ordering, 21
ring step, 27
sizes, chart for different lathes,
   20
sizes and equivalents, table, 23
split, 19, 22
step or disk, 26
tightening, 16
universal (3- and 4-jaw), 27, 70
wax, 24, 70
   centring on, 25, 74, 87
   making, 87
   removing from, 75
wear, 9
wheel, 28
wood screw, 29
wood turning, 29
circular saw, 30
CL300M lathe, 160–1
clamping nuts, design of, 15
Clarke lathe, 161
cleaning lathes, 17
C.H.L. lathes, 106
Cobra lathe, 160
College Engineering Supply, 218
collets, see chucks
Coronet lathes, 109
cover for lathe, 6
Cowells lathes,
   90CW, 161–3

90ME, 162–3
Basic 90E, 162
Cowells Vertical Mill, 164–5
Crawfords, 19
cutters, hand,
   fine cuts, 69
   grinding, 69
   handle, 69
   holding, 67, 72, 84
   sharpening, 67
   slide rest, angles, 64
      design, 63
      fixing, 66
      making, 84
      position and use, 71, 81
      sharpening, 64
      types, 64
   square nose tool, 69
   testing for sharpness, 68
   types, 64
cylinders, runner for turning, 36

D

Dale chucks, 21
dead centre lathes, 57
   converting a lathe, 58
F.W. Derbyshire, 2
Derbyshire lathes, 111–16, 165–6
diamantine, 65
dimensions of lathes, 4
   W.W. standards, 9
discountcampus, 226
dividing plates, 75
drill stocks, 36
drilling,
   tailstock device, 46
   V-block runner, 82
drives, see also transmission
   foot wheel, 53
   hand wheel, 5, 52
   motors, electric, 51, 90–6
   overhead, 48–50, 210

E

emachinetool, 227
Emco lathes,
   Compact 5, 168–9
   Compact 8E, 169
   Compact V8, 16
   Unimat 3, 166–7
   Unimat 4, 167–8
Enco Manufacturing Co., 227
Essel Engineering, 219
eye glass for lathe, 54

F

face plates, 4, 40
Favorite lathes, 116–19, 170
filing with roller rest, 32, 81, 211
fine cuts, 69, 73
Folkestone Engineering Supplies,
   220
Otto Frei & Jules Borel Inc., 227
fusee cutting tool, 212

G

G. & M. Tools, 220
G.L.R. Distributors Ltd, 220
Gamma lathes, 119
Gentil, *see* Star
Golay Buchel, *see* Favorite
gravers, *see* cutters, hand
Griffiths Engineering, 220
Grizzly International, Inc., 227
Grizzly lathe, 170–1

H

Hadfield, G.K., 220
headstock definition, 3
Hemingway Kits, 171–3

Hobbymat MD65 lathe, 173–4
Hobby Metal Kits, LLC, 227
Home & Workshop Machinery,
   221
Horia, S.A., *see* Steiner

I

IME lathes, 120–4
indexing for wheel cutting, 75
interchangeabilty, 8
International Sales & Marketing
   Corp., 228
'Items' Mail Order Ltd, 221

J

Jacobs chuck, 30
Jacot drum, 37, 58, 59, 210–12
   tool, 62, 88, 174, 210–12
J.M.W. (Clocks), 210–12, 224

K

KRF Company, 228

L

Lanco lathes, 124–6
lapping attachment, 38
   screw head tool, 44, 83
   snailing, 78
laps,
   bell metal, 38, 83
   box wood, 39
   copper, 78
   iron, 39, 83
   making, 78
Leinen lathes, 126–29, 174–6
Levin lathes, 129–31, 177–8

light for turning, 5, 55
Lorch lathes, 131–4, 178–9
Lyons Ltd., Claude, 96, 221

M

Maidstone Engineering Supplies, 221
mandrel, *see* spindle
Manhora lathes, 134–6
Manix lathes, *see* Toyo
Marshall lathes, 136–8
Meadows & Passmore Ltd, 221
Metal Lathe Accessories, 179–80
Metal Smith, 222
Micro-Mark, 181–2
Microlux lathe, 181–2
Millhill Supplies Ltd., 222
milling and driving spindle, 210–11
milling machine, 164–5, 206–7
M J Engineering, 22
Moseley, C.S., 1
Moseley, lathes, *see* Marshall
motors, electric,
  advantages of, 46
  brushes, 93
  commutators, 94
  controllers, 95
  faults and maintenance, 92
  foot switches, 48
  hand switches, 50
  horsepower, 47, 90
  installation, 91
  overheating, 94
  speed control, 95
  speeds, 90
  wiring, 91
mounting, 5
Myford lathes,
  254 Plus, 183, 184
  254S, 184
  254V Plus, 184
  Diamond 10, 184, 186

M series, 182
Super 7, 182
Super 7 Connoisseur, 185–9
Super 7 Plus, 183, 185, 186
Super Sigma 7 Plus, 185, 190

O

oiling, 18
overhead drive, 48–50, 210

P

Paulson lathes, 138–41
Peatol lathe, 190–1
Peatol Machine Tools, 222
Peerless lathes, *see* Marshall
Pickard & Frere Ltd, Henri, 222
pinions, runner for turning, 36
pivot polishing,
  balance pivot tool, 54
  by hand, 83
  Jacot drum, 37, 58, 59
  Jacot tool, 62, 210–11
  pivoting tools, 38, 54, 59, 210–11
pivoting (fitting a new pivot), 61, 88
pivots, runner for turning, 35
plated finish, 15
"Portavolt" transformer, 96
Pratecma lathes, *see* Leinen
Prazi lathes,
  MD 200, 191–2
  SD 300, 192–3
pre-loaded ball bearings, 12
Progress Machine Ltd, 222
Proxxon PD 230/E lathe, 194–5
pulley groove angles, 11
pulley transmission, 48–50
Pultra lathe, 141–3, 195
pump centre, 40

R

RDG Tools, 223
Record lathes, *see* Toyo
Reeves 2000, 223
Reform lathes, *see* Leinen
"Regavolt" transformer, 96
Rejon Machine Tools, 223
rests, tool,
    definition, 3
    double roller, 32
    dressing tee, 31
    roller, 32
    slide, controlled action, 46
    tip over tee, 31
    types, 33
right-hand lathes, 5
rose cutters, 37
    tailstock device for, 46
rounding-up tool, *see* topping tool
runners,
    for filing centres, 35
    slide runner, 58
    for turning cylinders, 36
    types, 35

S

safety pulley, 86
Sakai lathes, *see* Toyo
sawing,
    circular saws, 30
    squares, 56, 82
    table, 35
Schaublin lathes,
    70CF, 196
    70MI, 196–7
Scomea lathes, 144
screw cutting attachment, 43, 155
    head tool, 43, 83
shentonbooks, 223
Sherline lathes, 197–8
Sieg lathes,

2CA, 154
C4, 156
sinking tools, 37
slide rests, *see* rests
    runner, 58
slipping tool on slide rest, 31
Small Machine Tools, *see* Cowells
Smithy lathes,
    CZ 239, 201
    MI 1220 XL, 199–200
snailing, 78
South Bend Lathes,
    9", 201–2
    10K, 202
    G-26-T, 204
    GS26LT, 204
    Precision 10", 202–3
speed,
    control, 95–6
simple calculation, 52
    for turning, table, 72
spindle or mandrel, bearings, 10
    definitions, 39
    design, 9
    history, 1
spool propulsion for Jacot tool, 61
squares,
    filing, 32, 81
    sawing, 56, 82
Star lathes, 144–7, 204
Steiner lathes, 147–9, 205–6
Stevens Machine Tools, 223
Stevens milling machine, 207

T

Taig lathe, *see* Peatol
tailstock,
    definition, 3
    design, 14
    drilling device, 46
    feeds and stops, 15
    runner, 36

taps, 37
Tee Publishing, 224
tee rests, *see* rests
testing after damage, 17
Thornton (Successors) Ltd., P.P., 224
Toolco, 224
topping tool, 40, 84
Toyo lathes,
    ML-1, 207–8
    ML-210, 208–9
    ML-360, 209
transmission, 6, 46–8, 52
Travers Tool Co. Inc., 230
turning, *see also* cutters
    arbor, 31
    balance staffs, 84
    between centres, 80, 86
    facing cuts, 73
    merits of different methods, 58, 88
    speeds, table, 72

U

under-cutting with graver, 68
Unimat, *see* Emco
Unitech-Maschinen lathes, *see* Prazi

utility set, 55

V

Victor Machinery Exchange Inc., 230

W

Wabeco lathes,
    D2000E, 213
    D2400E, 213–4
    D4000E, 213, 214
    D6000 E, 213
Walsh & Sons Ltd, H.S., 224
Warco mini lathe, 214–5
Warren Machine Tools (Guildford) Ltd., 225
wax brass, *see* chucks
Webster, Ambrose, 1, 2
Webster-Whitcomb lathe,
    origin, 2
    standards, 2
wheel cutting, 42, 75
Whitcombe, John E., 2
Wiskum lathes, 150–1
Wolf, Jahn lathes, 151–2